FRIENDSHIP THE MASTER-PASSION

FRIENDSHIP THE MASTER-PASSION

OR

THE NATURE AND HISTORY OF FRIENDSHIP, AND
ITS PLACE AS A FORCE IN THE WORLD

BY

H. CLAY TRUMBULL

SOLID GROUND CHRISTIAN BOOKS
BIRMINGHAM, ALABAMA USA

Solid Ground Christian Books
2090 Columbiana Rd, Suite 2000
Birmingham, AL 35216
205-443-0311
sgcb@charter.net
http://solid-ground-books.com

FRIENDSHIP: The Master-Passion
Henry Clay Trumball (1830-1903)

First published in 1891

Introductory Essay by Maurice Roberts

Solid Ground Classic Reprints

First printing of new edition December 2005

Cover work by Borgo Design, Tuscaloosa, AL
Contact them at nelbrown@comcast.net

Cover image is the painting *Departing of David and Jonathan*, by Rembrandt in 1642.

Special thanks to Maurice Roberts and Banner of Truth Trust, for allowing us to use the Essay "Christian Friendships," which appears in the book THE THOUGHT OF GOD by Maurice Roberts, and first published by Banner of Truth in 1993.

ISBN: 1-59925-030-6

TO THE MEMORY

OF

MY DEAR WIFE

WHO WAS THE BEST ILLUSTRATION I EVER KNEW

OF

A LIFE OF SELF-FORGETFUL FRIENDSHIP

AND WHO WATCHED WITH SYMPATHETIC INTEREST

THE PROGRESS OF THESE PAGES

TO THEIR VERY CLOSE

BEFORE CLOSING HER EYES TO EARTH

I DEDICATE THIS VOLUME

IN

GRATEFUL AFFECTION

Introductory Essay

Christian Friendships
BY MAURICE ROBERTS

The Christian discovers that, while he has fellowship with all his brothers and sisters in Christ, he has special friendships with only some of them. It is not always easy to say why such friendships between some Christians develop or why potential friendships with others come to nothing. But it is a fact of observation and experience which must ultimately have its explanation in the mystery of God's providence. Fellowship in a general sense exists among all who are born of God. But that special delight which friends find in each other's company is something which goes beyond this. Fellowship is there because of the grace which is enjoyed in common. But friendships occur almost mysteriously and yet not without explanation, as we shall see. No doubt in heaven, when grace becomes glory, this imperfect state of our relationships will improve so that all will be equally the friend of each. But it is not so now and no act of will can now make it so, it would seem.

The best of God's servants have had special friends and their names are wreathed together and intertwined in the pages of Scripture. Moses and Joshua, David and Jonathan, Daniel and his friends, Peter and John, Paul and Timothy—they belonged together on earth and their names come easily to our memory in pairs or groups. Even the Lord Jesus Christ had his special relationships with his own disciples. Out of the twelve, three were specially intimate: Peter, James and John. Out of these three, one was unique. Only John was 'the disciple whom Jesus loved', in the relationship of a friend *par excellence*. It appears clear therefore that we ought not, as Christians, to be surprised to find that we have closer relations with some of God's people than with others. This must not lead us to be dismissive of brothers who are not in our intimate circle of friends. But it reassures us that there is no sin in the Christian's having closer ties with some rather than with other believers.

Christian friendships are no doubt ordained to draw forth from us the highest powers of our soul and so to lead to our greatest usefulness and sanctification. It is not hard to see how this comes about. Most friendships, if not all, consist of a bond of affection between one who is more talented, or else more spiritually advanced, and another who is less so. Within this relationship there is a mutually felt, even if tacit, recognition of the need for grace and forbearance. The gifted brother must show his brotherliness by generous, but concealed, condescension, and the less-gifted brother must advance the friendship by mortifying his envy. Thus pride is weakened in the one and jealousy in the other. Both are strengthened in their graces and as a result 'iron sharpeneth iron'.

It belongs to the genius of our friendships that we must accept our brothers and sisters for what they are and extend affection to them accordingly. The gifted brother who cannot bear to be anything other than idolized will have admirers but not friends. There is a significant difference. An admirer loves us for the sake of our talents; a friend loves us for our own sake. Friendship is far more beneficial to us than admiration because it makes sanctifying demands upon our character. Those gifted brothers who want only our admiration seek only additional fuel for their own self-love. But genuine friendship leads to the destruction of self-love because it forgets itself in a sincere desire to do good to the other person.

To accept our brothers and sisters for what they are, within the bond of Christian friendship, is to leave them room to think and act as they wish, provided they keep within scriptural bounds. This is far from easy because we are all inclined to hold our opinions in lesser matters rather too strongly and, given opportunity, we tend to squeeze others into our own mould even in matters indifferent. It is notoriously easier to quote the dictum than to act according to it in our friendships: 'In things essential, unity; in non-essentials, liberty; in all things, charity.'

Friendship is good and necessary for us just as, in most cases, marriage is necessary. It corrects our angularity and rubs off our corners. The recluse is the first to fall into eccentricities.

The more we are with ourselves the more we become like ourselves. It is only when we come back into the circle of our godly friends once again we realize how awkward, or else opinionated, we have become as Christians. We all go astray 'like sheep', but we go astray less if we keep within the flock and refuse the temptation to wander off into solitary pastures where we are all on our own. This fact alone should have been enough to warn the early Christian ascetics against the monastic cell. But history shows that it was not. The monk's cell was the ideal situation for the development of quirks and crankish habits of spiritual character. Healthy Christian character, which is full-orbed, well-rounded and rich in good fruits, can best be formed within the circle of sanctified friendships.

It is a common proverb that 'a man is known by his friends'. This is not surprising because, as the Romans put it, 'a friend is a second self.' That is to say, our intimate friends are what they are to us because they are essentially like us in all that is morally important. We choose our friends, not by accident, but because their souls mirror ours and their minds vibrate in harmony with ours. Friendship begins as soon as this mutual harmony of hearts is felt, and it ends when the harmony ends. We can be respectful to believers with whom we feel we have little in common, but it is emotionally impossible for us to count them among our intimate friends.

Our best friends are those whose company most makes us afraid to sin. These friends are rare and to be valued like solid gold. It is clear that this was the effect which M'Cheyne had upon Andrew Bonar. Bonar could never be the same once he met M'Cheyne. All his life, and on anniversary occasions especially, he remembered that saintly friend whose presence made God more real and therefore sin more foul. Those who have seraphic friends will at last become angelic. It is one reason why we should aim more at godliness. An exemplary life may do as much good as a lifetime of sermons. There are some Christians who impress us by their talents. But there are also others whose awesome holiness makes us afraid. If we find one friend of this kind, we shall do well to cherish his friendship for life.

It is marvelous how different the effect of different men is on our spirit. Some men's company shuts our mouth and seals our lips as if we were imprisoned. Other believers unlock our tongue and draw forth the secrets of our hearts so that we can tell them all our thoughts and trust them with all our secrets. Some men cow and intimidate us so that we put up a wall of defense around our real thoughts till they are gone. Others win their way to our affections at once, and melt our reserve, so that we can share our choicest meditations with them. Some men bring out the best in us, and some bring out the worst. It is hard to say how all this works. But it is a fact of life. In this writer's opinion, we should take seriously our instinctive reactions to different men and not say more to anyone than we feel convinced would be wise and well-taken. When you meet a man who is not your friend, and who refuses to become your friend, you will not please him 'whether you rage or laugh' [Prov. 29: 9]. Therefore it is best to keep the secrets of your heart where they are, safely under lock and key.

A Christian ought to prize his friends and to preserve them. Much is owed to true friends. They impose duties and obligations on us which are not to be neglected, even when life is full of business. Church work can sometimes make us too dogmatic in minor things and the remedy for over-certainty is to listen at times to our friends' judgment of us. The wounds of a friend are 'faithful' [Prov. 27:6] in that they hurt us for our good. Therefore we should not resent them.

The temptation we all have is to keep the company of those who only admire us and never dare to stand up to us. Luther was a toweringly great man, but he would have been greater still if he had allowed Zwingli to correct his view of the Lord's Supper. It was Luther's weakness and the church's loss that he would not be moved by either the logic or the tears of his friends. Similarly, the Wesleys should have listened more to Whitefield. Edward Irving was a most brilliant speaker but he ought to have paid more attention to the frowns of Chalmers and other orthodox believers. Had he done so, or had he married differently, he would have given off more light and less smoke to the church. As it was, he felt too sure of his erratic opinions and so lost the chance of becoming a great leader of God's people.

One of the most painful parts of Christian friendship is to be honest with believers we love when we consider them to be wrong or misguided. We do not all have the moral courage to stand up to our brothers and sisters when they go off at a tangent. In this respect, we must remember how Paul faithfully 'withstood Peter to the face' [Gal. 2:11]. . We generally prefer keeping a criminal silence to giving a well-timed rebuke. But, when we do so, we do not act as friends should. We are not to 'suffer sin in our brother' [Lev. 19:17]. 'Open rebuke is better than secret love' [Prov. 27:5]. Our perfect Lord felt no inconsistency in altering his tone of voice to Peter from 'blessed art thou' to 'get thee behind me, Satan' [Malt. 16:23]. The two expressions appear to have come from Christ's lips in one and the same conversation. This shows how quickly we must sometimes change our voice from praise to blame when dealing with friends in Christ whom we love.

The price of real friendship is honesty therefore. A genuine friend must at times be ready to appear cruel. But we must be cruel to be kind. However much we have to wound those we love, we know that it is the part of hatred, not love, to see our brother wander from the path unchecked. However much we love our brother, we love Jesus Christ more. 'I love Plato, but I love truth still more,' said Aristotle. This sentiment is fully consistent with the gospel and, indeed, is the very essence of gospel friendships. But such friendships are rare because we either lack the courage to correct our brothers and sisters in their crankish quirks or else we take it badly when they put their finger on our own cherished eccentricities.

A good friend can be a sublime comfort to us in hours of loneliness. And the Christian will meet many occasions of loneliness in his pilgrimage. So we shall be both better in character and lighter in heart if we allow a due place to the forming and fostering of contacts with like-minded believers in the Lord. To start the day with a short phone call or with a brief letter from an esteemed saint can be the difference between a day of victory and triumph, and a day of depression and temptation.

Generally speaking, when we are depressed and dejected we should seek the remedy, not in prayer and fasting, but in fellowship and friendship. As Luther's *Letters* wisely say, we ought not to go to prayer when we are depressed, but into the company of good people. Satan is always more menacing when we meet him on our own. Depression dislocates all the parts of the soul and paralyses our creative powers. Every preacher knows that he has spent long hours preparing a sermon to no effect on one day only to complete it in no time at all the next morning, when joy has returned to his soul. Half an hour of fellowship, therefore, when the mind is dejected, will often release the springs of our creativity and cause the life-blood of Christian gladness to flow afresh in our veins. Whatever gives us a sense of well-being as Christians is good for us. High on the list of things which bring us a sense of well-being is friendship.

Perhaps we fail to notice, as we read the Bible, that the highest pattern of Christian friendship is in God himself. The manner in which the three divine persons relate to and refer to one another is the exalted out-flowing always of perfect mutual love. Let us apologize for the poverty of human language when we say so, but there is in each person of the Godhead a kind of self-effacing quality. The Father's attitude to the Son is expressed in the simple words: `This is my beloved Son, in whom I am well pleased' [Matt. 3:17]. The Son's love of the Father is reflected in the statement: `My Father is greater than I' [John 14:28]. Similarly, the Spirit does not speak of himself but bears witness to Christ [John 15:26]. Yet the Son declares that blasphemy against the Son will be forgiven but not blasphemy against the Spirit [Matt. 12:31].

Admittedly, many comments and qualifications to what is here said would need to be added if these texts were to be fully explained. But the important and instructive fact remains that the divine persons of the Holy Trinity never refer to one another except with perfect honour, respect and love. They each delight to give the other persons their high and honoured place. O how transcendentally perfect are these holy Three, whom we know as Father, Son and Spirit! How worthy of our imitation they are in the matter of our Christian friendships, as in all else! Sin makes men 'hateful and hating' [Titus 3:3]. Let us see to it that we have grace to be good friends one to another for life, or rather, for eternity.

PREFACE.

Although Friendship has been a theme of the ages, its nature and history have not been treated with any degree of fulness by any writer of the ages. Poets and philosophers and essayists have recognized the force and beauty of friendship as a human sentiment, from the days of Homer and Plato and Cicero to those of Bacon and Montaigne and Tennyson; but no one of them has attempted a careful analysis of its elements or a comprehensive record of its more important historic illustrations. Therefore it is that this volume is presented as a unique study of a subject that deserves greater prominence than has hitherto been accorded to it.

It is because of my own indebtedness to friendship that I have sought to uplift this sentiment before others, in its true worth as an ideal and in its practical value as an attainment. In my earlier life I was privileged to know the measureless gain of having a friend, and of being mentally and spiritually ministered to and inspired thereby. In my maturer years I came to experience the surpassing advantage of being drawn out of myself in a reverent and persistent purpose of being unselfishly true as a friend, without looking for any recognition or return of my devotedness. Finding thus how much I owed to the incitements and aspirations and self-conquests of friendship, I set myself to discover how much others also were indebted to the influence of this transcendent sentiment; and so it was that I was led to track along the passing centuries the glowing evidences of friendship as the master-passion of humanity.

This volume must speak for itself, of the measure of thoroughness with which its subject is treated, and with which the fields that it calls attention to have been searched; yet I may say that its pages represent the work of years, and that in its gradual preparation I have had the invaluable help of friends, who were illustrating its theme while gathering material for its enriching. My hope is that what is here said and shown will quicken the interest of others in the lofty ideal thus presented, and will inspire them to fresh endeavors toward its realizing.

H. CLAY TRUMBULL.

PHILADELPHIA,
September 15, 1891.

CONTENTS.

I. THE NATURE AND SCOPE OF FRIENDSHIP.

WHAT IS FRIENDSHIP? 13

LOVING, RATHER THAN BEING LOVED 19

WHOLLY UNSELFISH 27

WITHOUT ENVY OR DISTRUST 35

TRANSCENDING ALL LOVES 47

CHANGELESS IN CHANGES 59

OF WORLD-WIDE HONOR 69

GAINFULLY EXPENSIVE 87

LIMITATIONS AND IMITATIONS 93

WHO CAN BE FRIENDS? 105

II. FRIENDSHIP IN HISTORY.

OF SURPASSING POTENCY 117

INFLUENCING ROYALTY 121

PROMOTING HEROISM 155

IMPELLING RELIGIOUS MOVEMENTS	175
ADVANCING CIVIL LIBERTY	231
AFFECTING PHILOSOPHIC THOUGHT	251
INSPIRING POETRY	283
TRANSFIGURING ALL LIFE	381
EXCURSUS ON THE NEW TESTAMENT WORDS FOR "LOVE" AND "FRIENDSHIP-LOVE."	389
INDEX	395

I.

THE NATURE AND SCOPE OF FRIENDSHIP.

WHAT IS FRIENDSHIP?

"FRIENDSHIP," says Cicero, "is the only point in human affairs concerning the benefit of which all, with one voice, agree." Jeremy Taylor echoes the thought of the classic philosopher, in the asseveration, "Friendship is that by which the world is most blessed and receives most good." Yet Bacon declares: "There is little friendship in the world." According to Shakespeare's misanthropic Timon of Athens, "friendship's full of dregs." And Napoleon, with his close knowledge of the human heart, asserts that "friendship is but a name." What is this Friendship which is so much to the world, and which is so rare in the world; concerning which all agree yet disagree? What does the very term itself include and imply?

It is friendship as a personal sentiment, not friendship

as a mutual relation, that must be considered in order to an understanding of the term as a term. The primary question is not, What is the nature of that state or condition into which two friends are brought by the fact of their being mutual friends? but it is, What is that sentiment which actuates any person, who is truly a friend, toward the person to whom he is a friend? What is the distinguishing characteristic of the feeling or sentiment of friendship, on the part of him who is a friend, apart from the question of any response to, or recognition of, that feeling or sentiment, by him toward whom it goes out?

The more familiar a word, the greater its liability to vagueness of meaning in popular usage. And the deeper the underlying signification of a word, the rarer its recognition in any other than a superficial sense. The very fact that a word is the common possession of all, renders various conceptions of it inevitable in various minds; for no one idea, or its symbol, can be seen alike by all, and those who look only on the surface will gain no conception of a word's profounder sense. "Friendship" is a word that encounters these hindrances to its comprehending. It is too familiar to be well understood by all. It means too much to have its full sense easily perceived. Hence it means much or means little, in its varied use among men.

Our English word "friend," in its Anglo-Saxon form, is *freond*,—"one who loves." Etymologically the words "friend" and "lover" are synonymous, as are the words "love" and "friendship." But in common usage "love" and "friendship," as also "lover" and "friend," have very different measures of meaning, and are supposed to represent widely different grades of personal attachment. The question is, Wherein consists the true distinction between love that is friendship and love that is only love?

"Love," as we commonly employ that term when we speak of love as distinct from the love that is friendship, includes the idea of a reciprocal relation, existing or desired, between the one who loves and the one who is loved—the idea of possession, or of a possessory interest, secured or sought after. Thus, the love of parent and child, of brother and sister, of husband and wife, is supposed to proceed from and to rest on the intimate reciprocal relation existing between the two parties by the ties of nature or of conjugal compact; as, again, the love of "lovers" is recognized as growing out of, or as inevitably accompanied by, a desire for a reciprocal and possessory relation,—

> "The end of love is to have two made one,
> In will and in affection."

Self-interest is, in fact, a large element in ordinary human love.

"Friendship," on the other hand, does not of necessity include the idea of any mutual bond, or of any self-benefiting relation, either attained or reached after, between the one who is a friend and the one to whom he is a friend. One's friendship is certainly not limited to one's relatives and family connections; nor yet, beyond these, to one who is desired in marriage. In fact, the very suggestion of the attachment of friendship is commonly supposed to differentiate the affection which it represents from that affection which grows out of, or which tends toward, a possessory relation. "He is only a friend," is usually understood as signifying, "He has no thought of being a lover;" and to say of an attachment, "It is a mere friendship," is much like saying, "It is not in any sense real love." Yet few would venture to assert that one could not be a friend to a person with whom he was linked by family ties, or that real love excluded the possibility of real friendship.

Even when the affections go out toward objects that are other than personal, there is a similar distinction between the terms "love" and "friendship," as those terms are commonly employed. "Love" is supposed to involve some possessory relation with the object of attachment, while "friendship" does not necessarily imply any such relation. A *love* of country is a love of one's own country; a love which has its basis in what that country is to the patriot, or in that country's claim on him as its citizen, and in the recognition of benefits which that country confers upon him or upon those dear to him. But one can be the *friend* of a country which is not his country, which has conferred no benefit on him or on his directly, and which he would not even care to call his own country. So, again, when one is spoken of as "a lover of literature," or "a lover of art," or "a lover of science," as over against one who is "a friend of literature," or "a friend of art," or "a friend of science," the intimation is that the "lover" is in some special relation with the object of his affection, while the "friend" is not necessarily so related with that object. Self-interest is not an essential element of the sentiment of friendship; apart from any question of the supposed advantages of the state or

What is Friendship?

relation into which two persons might be brought by becoming mutually friends.

In languages older than our own, the distinction between the love that craves and the love that goes out uncravingly is indicated in equivalents of "love" and "friendship." Thus the Sanskrit—elder sister in our family of tongues—gives for "love," *lubh*, "covetousness" or "greed;" and for "friendship," *pri*, "unselfish love." The Greek has *philia* for that love which goes out "longingly" after its object, "an inclination prompted by sense and emotion;" while in the Septuagint and the New Testament it has *agapē*, a "love without desire." The Latin correspondingly has *amo* as representing the love that turns to another in a spirit of agreement and of longing; but, as an equivalent of *agapaō*, it has *diligo* for the act of "a distinguishing love—without desire," a love that selects and rests on the one selected without asking any return.

The common thought is, that "love" and "friendship" merely differentiate *degrees* of affection; and that intensity and devotedness are the distinguishing characteristics of "love" in comparison with "friendship." But the place given in both sacred and classic story to the illustrations of self-sacrificing friendship proves that no lack of depth and fervor limits the force and sway of this expression of personal attachment. Greater love hath no man than that love which is shown in friendship, at its best and truest manifestation. Not in its measure, but in its very nature, is an unselfish friendship distinguishable from a love which pivots on a reciprocal relation, secured or desired.

Friendship is love for another because of what that other is in himself, or for that other's own sake, and not because of what that other is to the loving one. Friendship is love with the selfish element eliminated. It is an out-going and an on-going affection, wholly and inherently disinterested, and in no sense contingent upon any reciprocal relation between its giver and its object, nor yet upon its return or recognition. Friendship, in short, is love apart from love's claim or love's craving. This is pure friendship, friendship without alloy. This is friendship at its truest and best; and this it is that makes the best and truest friendship so rare, so difficult of conception, so liable to misconception. This also it is that multiplies the specious resemblances of friendship—in hearts that are incapable of comprehending its full reality; and that gives to those imperfect substitutes for its reality such a disappointing power.

In all holiest and most unselfish love, friendship is the purest element of the affection. No love in any relation of life can be at its best if the element of friendship be lacking. And no love can transcend, in its possibilities of noble and ennobling exaltation, a love that is pure friendship.

LOVING, RATHER THAN BEING LOVED.

NASMUCH as friendship is loving another for that other's own sake, and not for what that other is to the one who loves, friendship by its very nature consists in loving, rather than in being loved. In other words, friendship consists in being a friend, not in having a friend; in giving one's affection unselfishly and unswervingly to another, not in being the object of another's affection, or in reciprocating such an affection.

Love, it is true, may beget love; and, again, love is likely to be a result, or an outgrowth, of qualities in both the loved and the loving one which make affection reciprocal: hence friendship is often a mutual affection. In every such case, however, each friend is a friend in his loving, rather than in his being loved; and he would be just as truly a friend, and his friendship would be just as hearty and just as abiding, if he were not loved in return, or if his love were unrecognized.

Herein it is that friendship has its distinction from, and its superiority over, all other loves. Other loves are based upon a love received or desired. Friendship is an out-going and unselfish love, without an essential thought of the affection's return. Friendship may exist conjointly with other loves. Again, the other loves may exist—they more commonly do—without the higher element of friendship. But only so far as a love finds its chiefest joy and its very life in loving, is it true friendship's love.

This distinction is the basis of Plato's teachings concerning the nature of the highest and purest love. Plato would distinguish between the love which is "friendship" and the love which is "desire;" between the love which goes out uncravingly, and the love which craves return. He even suggests that friendship, as the purest love, is dependent for its life on only one of the two parties involved; "that if only one of the two loves the other, they are both friends:" one being the friend who loves, and the other the friend who is loved; one the friend subjectively, the other the friend objectively. And in this sense only it is that it takes two to make a friendship.

Aristotle is yet more explicit on this point. His view is, that friendship "consists in loving, rather than being loved;" "that to love seems to be the excellence of friends; and that it is more the part of a friend to confer than to receive favors." "Those who wish good to their friends for their friends' sake," he says, "are friends in the highest degree,"—in contrast with those who have a selfish interest in desiring their friends' welfare. Even "the bad will be friends for the sake of the pleasant and useful; . . . but the good will be friends for the friends' sake; . . . the latter, therefore, are friends absolutely; the former accidentally, and from their resemblance to the former;" for "absolute" friendship is loving unselfishly, regardless of personal advantage, or of the love's return.

Cicero, discussing this question, concludes that the true prompting of every real friendship is a love for one's friend, unintermingled with any calculation of the benefits to be derived from the friendship; that, indeed, to be a true friend, "is nothing else than to be attached to the person whom you love, without any sense of need, without any advantage being sought; although advantage springs up of itself from friendship, even while you have not pursued it."

From the friendship of Lælius with Scipio, Cicero illustrates: " What did Africanus want from me? Nothing whatsoever; nor, indeed, did I want anything from him. But I loved him from admiration of his excellence; he, in turn, was perhaps attracted to me from some high opinion which he entertained of my character; and association fostered our affection. But, although many and great advantages ensued, yet it was not from any hope of these that the causes of our attachment sprang. . . . Thus I judge that friendship is to be sought not in the hope of the reward which comes with it, but because its whole gain is in the love itself. . . . Where, indeed, can there be a place for friendship; or who can be a friend to any one whom he does not love for that one's own sake? And what is *loving*,—from which the very name of friendship is derived,—but wishing a certain person to enjoy the greatest possible good fortune, even if none of it redounds to one's self?"

That the highest friendship never pivots on its reciprocal return, nor yet on its recognition and acceptance by the one loved, is characteristically illustrated by the Oriental Soofee poet, Jâmee; who has sometimes been called "the Persian Petrarch." Here is Alger's rendering of Jâmee's teaching:

> "Sheik Schublî, taken sick, was borne one day
> Unto the hospital. A host the way
> Behind him thronged. 'Who are you?' Schublî cried.
> 'We are your friends,' the multitude replied.
> Sheik Schublî threw a stone at them: they fled.
> 'Come back, ye false pretenders!' then he said;
> 'A friend is one who, ranked among his foes
> By him he loves, and stoned, and beat with blows,
> Will still remain as friendly as before,
> And to his friendship only add the more.'"

It is because this Oriental conception of the unfailing unselfishness of an out-going and an on-going affection, as the basis of every true friendship,—a conception which is primitive in the very idea of true friendship,—does not always prevail in the Western mind, that friendship is so often spoken of as dependent for its life on reciprocity. La Bruyère, for example, who writes admirably on some phases of friendship, falls sadly short of the true standard, in saying: "When we have done all that we can for certain people in order to secure their friendship, and we find that we have been unsuccessful, there is still one resource left to us, which is—not to do anything more." Ay!

and there is yet another and a better resource left to us, which is—to keep on doing. That is not real friendship which ceases its out-going and its on-flow when it finds that no return of its affection is a possibility or a hope.

Robert Browning has the higher conception, in his contrast of " Life in a Love " with " Love in a Life; " for friendship at its truest is simply life in a love—life in unfailing and unselfish love:

> " Escape me?
> Never—
> Beloved!
> While I am I, and you are you,
> So long as the world contains us both,
> Me the loving, and you the loth,—
> While the one eludes, must the other pursue."

Emerson grew to the fuller appreciation of this truth as he thought and felt more of the truest power of the truest friendship. " It has seemed to me lately," he wrote, " more possible than I knew to carry a friendship greatly on one side without due correspondence on the other. Why should I cumber myself with regrets that the receiver is not capacious? It never troubles the sun that some of his rays fall wide and vain into ungrateful space, and only a small part on the reflecting planet. . . . It is thought a disgrace to love unrequited; but the great will see that true love cannot be unrequited."

" Love without end hath no end " is a Spanish proverb, cited by George Herbert approvingly; and this is only another way of saying that a love which is not dependent on any attaining is a ceaseless love; it can never end in fruition. The proverb seems, indeed, to be a condensation of the Talmudic maxim (in Pirqe Aboth): "All love which depends on some thing, when the thing ceases the love ceases; but such love as does not depend on anything, ceases not forever." Francis Quarles seems to have had this maxim in mind when he wrote: "Convey thy love to thy friend, as an arrow to the mark, to stick there; not as a ball against the wall to rebound back to thee. That friendship will not continue to the end that is begun for an end." And so it is that true friendship is deathless, through being a love that is endless.

The very joy of friendship is found in loving, not in being loved. Epicurus is cited by Plutarch as saying, concerning this matter of friendship, "It is more pleasant to do good than to receive good;" and La Rochefoucauld, the French Epicurean, could see that in all the sphere of the affections the larger gain and the larger joy are from loving, rather than from being loved. "The pleasure of loving is to love," he says; "and we are much happier in the passion we feel, than in that we excite." It is in the light of this characteristic of friendship that La Rochefoucauld exclaims: "Rare as true love is, it is less rare than true friendship."

The gentle-spirited Whittier brings out this truth in its richer signifyings, in his words:

> "Love is sweet in any guise;
> But its best is sacrifice.

> "He who giving does not crave,
> Likest is to Him who gave
> Life itself the loved to save."

It is a woman's readier apprehension of the supremacy

of a self-abnegating love, that shows itself in the words
of Helen Hunt:

> "When love is strong,
> It never tarries to take heed,
> Or know if its return exceed
> Its gift; in its sweet haste no greed,
> No strifes belong.
>
> "It hardly asks
> If it be loved at all; to take
> So barren seems, when it can make
> Such bliss, for the belovèd's sake,
> Of bitter tasks."

In similar womanly perception of the spirit of true friendship it is that George Eliot affirms:

> "So if I live or die to serve my friend,
> 'Tis for my love,—'tis for my friend alone,
> And not for any rate that friendship bears
> In heaven or in earth."

This is the Bible view of friendship, both in the Old Testament and in the New. The Divine pattern of love is a love that loves without any condition of love returned, and that consists in loving, rather than in being loved. "The Lord did not set his love upon you, nor choose you, because ye were more in number than any people; for ye were the fewest of all people; but because the Lord loved you," says Moses to Israel. It was not because of your lovableness, but because of God's lovingness, that God loved you; and his love consists in loving. "And he *will* love thee," adds Moses. He will keep on loving you, because he is so loving toward you whom he does love.

"Ye did not choose me, but I chose you," says Jesus to those whom he calls his friends. " Herein is love,"—herein is Divine love, Divine friendship, says the disciple whom Jesus loved,—" not that we loved God, but that he loved us ;" *this* love consists in God's loving us, rather than in our loving God; for the truest, highest, purest, love which is friendship, or which friendship is—whether it be Divine love or friendship or human love or friendship—always consists in loving, rather than in being loved.

Only he who is unwilling to love without being loved, is likely to feel that there is no such thing as friendship in the world.

WHOLLY UNSELFISH.

RUE friendship being love without compact or condition, true friendship never pivots on an equivalent return of service or of affection. Its whole sweep is away from self and toward the loved one. Its desire is for the friend's welfare; its joy is in the friend's prosperity; its sorrows and trials are in the friend's misfortunes and griefs; its pride is in the friend's attainments and successes; its constant purpose is of doing and enduring for the friend; and even its unrest, if unrest there be, is because of its never-satisfied endeavor to advantage and benefit the friend. This is ideal friendship; this is true friendship in actual attainment.

Take, for example, that most beautiful of all illustrative friendships, the friendship of Jonathan for David, in the Bible narrative,—it was grandly, gloriously unselfish. Jonathan was a prince of the royal house, heir-apparent to the throne of a kingdom. He was himself a hero of high achievement, with a foremost place in the people's love and honor. His first glimpse of David was in the light of a successful rival. The stripling shepherd stood the new hero of the hour, brought into the presence of the king while the nation's praises were ringing in his ears because of the wonderful deliverance wrought by his faith-filled daring. Looking then upon him in his loveliness of person and of character, Jonathan saw with prophetic ken the sure future of David as the coming king of Israel, as the one in whose glowing light his own star of earthly hope must pale. But in the first flush of that discovery there was no shade of envy, nor yet the faintest trace of regret, in the more than royal heart of Jonathan. Joy in the recognition of so noble and lovable a character as David's, filled the whole being of the nobler and yet more lovable Jonathan. "And it came to pass, when he had made an end of speaking unto Saul, that the soul of Jonathan was knit with the soul of David, and Jonathan loved him as his own soul." And from that time onward every heart-throb of Jonathan's friendship for David was a heart-throb of unselfish devotedness to him to whom he was a friend. What wonder that David pronounced upon that friendship as "passing the love of women;" passing all craving love, all selfish desire!

Similarly, the unselfish devotedness of Ruth to Naomi gave her friendship a place in the sacred story, and marked the contrast of her love with Orpah's. The associations of a lifetime, the drawings of personal interest, of kindred, of patriotism, and of religion, combined for the attaching of the widowed daughters-in-law to Moab and its dwellers. Only a sacred friendship, a friendship which had its deepest roots in no obligations of blood or of marriage, could offer effectual resistance to these multiplied attractions, in such an hour as that when Naomi and Ruth and Orpah wept together in the thought of their final parting, on the boundary banks of the Jordan. Orpah loved her mother-in-law, and "kissed her" tenderly; but Ruth had friendship for her mother-in-law, and "clave unto her"—as friendship by its nature cleaves.

And the unselfish friendship of Ruth for Naomi spoke out then in that matchless asseveration of unswerving fidelity, which thrills through the ages, in its tremulous tenderness of womanly affection:

> "Intreat me not to leave thee,
> And to return from following after thee:
> For whither thou goest, I will go;
> And where thou lodgest, I will lodge:
> Thy people shall be my people,
> And thy God my God:
> Where thou diest, will I die,
> And there will I be buried:
> The Lord do so to me, and more also,
> If aught but death part thee and me."

The very name "Ruth" means, in the Hebrew, "A friend" (in its abstract form, "Friendship"); as if the sacred story would make this record of devotedness an illustration of true friendship. The name may, indeed, have been given to this faithful friend *after* her beautiful exhibit of its meaning, it being her new name in Israel. It was through her exhibit of friendship that Ruth won a place in the ancestral line of the Friend of friends, in his human descent from Abraham the friend of God.

Montaigne cites a story out of classic lore, in evidence

of this basal truth. "Endamidas, a Corinthian, had two friends, Charixenus a Sicyonian, and Aretheus a Corinthian. Endamidas coming to die, being poor and his two friends being rich, he made his will after this manner: 'I bequeath to Aretheus the maintenance of my mother, to support and provide for her in her old age; and to Charixenus I bequeath the care of providing for my daughter in marriage, and of giving her as good a marriage portion as he is able. And in case one of these executors chance to die I hereby substitute the survivor in his place.' They who first saw this will made themselves merry at the contents; but the executors, being made acquainted with it, accepted the legacies with great satisfaction; and one of them, Charixenus, dying within a few days thereafter, the survivor Aretheus, having by that means the charge of both devolved solely on himself, nourished that old woman with great care and tenderness; and of five talents he had in estate he gave two and a half in marriage with an only daughter of his own, and two and a half in marriage with the daughter of Endamidas; and in one and the same day he solemnized the nuptials of the two maidens."

In comment on this story, Montaigne adds that "Endamidas as a bounty and a favor here bequeaths to his friends a legacy of employing themselves in his necessity. He leaves them heirs to this liberality of his, which consists in giving them the opportunity of conferring a benefit upon him; and doubtless the force of friendship is more eminently apparent in this act of his than in that of Aretheus." In other words, Aretheus was here given the opportunity of evidencing as a friend that unselfishness which is the soul of friendship; and Endamidas simply acted on the conviction that because Aretheus and Charixenus were his friends, therefore their love for him was without selfishness, and they would rejoice in the privilege of showing it to be so.

Yet because friendship may thus be rested on as always essentially unselfish, it does not follow that a friend will be willing to put friendship to any test unnecessarily. The unselfishness of *his* friendship will forbid that. Therefore it is that a considerate friend is prompter to carry his friend's sorrow, than to carry his sorrows to his friend. "It would seem," says Aristotle, "that we ought to invite friends to share our prosperity with alacrity; . . . but to share our adversity, we should invite them with reluctance." And Sir Thomas Browne, who was ever ready to put his friend's welfare before his own, said, similarly: "Now with my friend I desire not to share or to participate, but to engross, his sorrows." His friend's joys he would share, and his joys he would share with his friend; but his sorrows he would carry by himself, and his friend's sorrows he would carry also, if he might. Whether, indeed, one confides his griefs to his friend or conceals his griefs from his friend, he is moved by the thought of what will please or advantage his friend, rather than of what will please or advantage himself.

Charles Kingsley tells the story, as a veritable fact, of two hermit-monks who had lived together in closest friendship for years in the same cave, with never a thought of envy or selfish rivalry in the mind of either. At last it occurred to them to try the experiment of a quarrel, after the common fashion of the outside world. "But how shall we quarrel?" asked one. "Oh!" said the other, "we can take this brick, and put it between us; and each can claim it. Then we'll quarrel over it." And that was agreed on as the plan. "This brick is mine," said the one. "I hope it is mine," said the other gently. "Well, if it is yours, take it," said the other, who could never hear his friend express a wish for a thing without having a desire to secure it to him accordingly. So that quarrel was a failure—because the friendship was not.

Even in the partial light which shone on immortality in the days of Cicero the question was discussed, whether it was consistent with the truest friendship for one to bewail the loss of his friend by death, since death was a gain to the friend taken away. "Now to be above measure distressed at one's own troubles, is characteristic of the man who loves not his friend but himself," said Cicero, in arguing against a selfish grief over the death of a friend. And this same view of a friend's duty of self-forgetfulness is in the mind of Goethe, when he says to his friend:

> " Death 'tis to part;
> 'Tis twofold death
> To part not hoping
> Ever to meet again.
>
> " Thou wouldst rejoice to leave
> This hated land behind,
> Wert thou not chained to me
> With friendship's flowery chains.
>
> " Burst them! I'll not repine.
> No noble friend
> Would stay his fellow-captive,
> If means of flight appear.

> "The remembrance
> Of his dear friend's freedom
> Gives him freedom—
> In his dungeon."

Shakespeare goes one step farther in illustration of the self-abnegation which is in the highest affection, in that series of Sonnets which breathes throughout the sentiment of an absorbing friendship. He would not even be remembered after his death, if memory would be a grief to his surviving friend:—

> "No longer mourn for me when I am dead
> Than you shall hear the surly sullen bell
> Give warning to the world that I am fled
> From this vile world, with vilest worms to dwell:
> Nay, if you read this line, remember not
> The hand that writ it; for I love you so
> That I in your sweet thoughts would be forgot
> If thinking on me then should cause you woe."

He who is capable of being a friend will, because he is a friend, find a joy in serving that he could never find in being served. Out-going is always preferable to in-coming, in friendship's thought. Thus it is with Browning's Jules the artist, in "Pippa Passes," when he considers whether or not he shall become the friend of the untutored Greek girl Phene. Because he can do for her, not because he can hope to receive from her, he decides to be her friend. Therefore it is that he hears God's voice summoning him to this grandly unselfish service of friendship:—

> "If whoever loves
> Must be, in some sort, god or worshiper,
> The blessing or the blest one, queen or page,

> Why should we always choose the page's part?
> Here is a woman with utter need of me,—
> I find myself queen here, it seems!
>   How strange!
> Look at the woman here with the new soul,
> Like my own Psyche,—fresh upon her lips
> Alit, the visionary butterfly,
> Waiting my word to enter and make bright,
> Or flutter off and leave all blank as first.
> This body had no soul before, but slept
> Or stirred, was beauteous or ungainly, free
> From taint or foul with stain, as outward things
> Fastened their image on its passiveness:
> Now it will wake, feel, live—or die again!
> Shall to produce form out of unshaped stuff,
> Be Art—and further, to evoke a soul
> From form, be nothing? This new soul is mine!"

Nor is this high standard of unselfish personal friendship one which is never practically attained in this matter-of-fact world of ours. Friends have lived for each other. Friends have died for each other. Friends have endured far more than death in each other's behalf. Friends have given up home, and kindred, and property, and hope of gain, and even good name, at the call of friendship. And wherever there is a real friendship to-day there is a readiness to do and to endure and to yield to the uttermost.

WITHOUT ENVY OR DISTRUST.

RIENDSHIP being in its very nature an unselfish love, all that savors of selfishness is necessarily excluded from its scope. It being an out-going and an on-going love for one who is prized for his own sake, every added proof that the one loved is all that the loving one has seen him to be, or more, gives joy of heart, and not disturbance of mind, to him who is his friend. Neither envy nor distrust—both of which have their center in self-interest—can have any play against one who is loved unselfishly.

He who is loved as a friend for his own sake, will continue to be thus loved while he is himself and his friend is his friend's self. Thus Montaigne accounts for his love for his friend by saying, "If a man should importune me to give a reason why I loved my friend, I find it could not otherwise be expressed than by the answer, 'Because he was he; because I was I.'" And this is in full accord with Aristotle's declaration that friendship is love for another "so far forth as the person loved exists," and not "so far forth as he is useful or pleasant."

Yet no man could be drawn away from himself in devoted love for another unless, for some reason and in some light, that other were looked up to as worthy of a reverent regard. Unselfishness looks upward as well as outward, and an unselfish love is sure to have a reverent upward look in the contemplation of its object. This is a recognized truth of the ages. When Wan Chang came to Mencius, a Chinese sage contemporary with Plato and Aristotle, asking the question, "What feeling of the mind is expressed in the gifts of friendship?" Mencius replied, "The feeling of reverence." Our Emerson, echoing many a thought of the Oriental philosophers, declares: "Friendship demands a religious treatment; . . . reverence is a great part of it." Austin Phelps, ever keen in his spiritual perceptions, points out the fact that "the purest and most lasting human friendships are permeated with an element of reverence." Sir John Taylor Coleridge, speaking of his love for his life-long friend, Keble, says that this "love was always sanctified as it were by reverence,—reverence that did not make the love less tender, and love that did but add intensity to the reverence." And so it is, in a measure, in every true friendship.

Various reasons may operate to give this feeling of reverence for one who is loved because he is what he is, as seen by him who loves him; but the effect of the reasons is practically the same in all cases. A man may be reverenced for the lofty ideal he holds before the one who loves him; or for the loftier ideal toward which he is manifestly striving; or for the undeveloped possibilities which are seen in him, or for him, by him who is his friend. He may be looked up to for what he is, or for what he desires to be, or for what he might become; whatever the cause may be, the effect is much the same in the mind of the up-looker.

And here is a reason why we can never be jealous of one to whom we are a friend, although we are prone to be jealous for him. We love him and we look up to him for his own sake, and not for our sake; for what there is in him, or for what there is for him, and not for what he is toward us or in our behalf. We are glad when he shows himself at his best; and we are never troubled that his best outshines our best, even though we should be troubled if he failed to shine as he might, while we surpassed him. Thus La Bruyère suggests, discriminatingly, that "in friendship we see only those faults which may be prejudicial to our friends; while in love we discern no faults but those by which we ourselves suffer."

This being so, it is evident that the faintest reluctance on our part to see the one to whom we claim to be a friend transcend or eclipse us in our sphere of influence or action, is so far a proof that our claim of friendship is a false one. "Friendship immediately banishes envy under all its disguises," says a fellow-worker of Addison in the Spectator. "A man who can once doubt whether he should rejoice in his friend's being happier than himself, may depend upon it that he is an utter stranger to this virtue."

If Jonathan had envied David when he saw that David was to have the throne which Jonathan was yielding without the credit of yielding, it would have evidenced a lack of surpassing friendship for David in the heart of Jonathan. But because Jonathan loved David as his own soul, loved him with a self-forgetful friendship, envy of David could find no place in the royal and loyal heart of Jonathan.

It was because John the Baptist was the friend of Jesus that John, at the very summit of his personal renown and of his commanding popular influence, could say, without a twinge of envious feeling, concerning him of whom he was the friend: "In the midst of you standeth one whom ye know not, even he that cometh after me, the latchet of whose shoe I am not worthy to unloose." And when, a little later, it was suggested to John that he was being transcended by Jesus, his glad answer was: "He that hath the bride is the bridegroom: but the friend of the bridegroom, which standeth and heareth him, rejoiceth greatly because of the bridegroom's voice. This my joy therefore is fulfilled. He must increase, but I must decrease."

Nor is this unenvious recognition of a friend's eclipsing power an attainment of characters in the Bible story only. It inheres in the very conception of the truest friendship everywhere. "I must feel pride in my friend's accomplishments as if they were mine, and a property in his virtues," says Emerson for us all. "I feel as warmly, when he is praised, as the lover when he hears applause of his engaged maiden."

Thus it is that Tennyson testifies of his unenvious pride in Arthur Hallam's recognized supremacy in the sphere of their common labors:

"On thee the loyal-hearted hung,
   The proud was half disarmed of pride,
   Nor cared the serpent at thy side
To flicker with his double tongue.

"The stern were mild when thou wert by,
   The flippant put himself to school
   And heard thee, and the brazen fool
Was softened, and he knew not why.

"While I, thy nearest, sat apart,
   And felt thy triumph was as mine;
   And loved them more that they were thine,
The graceful tact, the Christian art;

"Nor mine the sweetness or the skill,
   But mine the love that will not tire,
   And, born of love, the vague desire
That spurs an imitative will."

Because friendship always includes a reverent admiration of a friend's ideal,—the ideal seen in the friend, seen by the friend, or seen for the friend,—therefore it follows that every added indication of that ideal's realizing is added cause for rejoicing on the part of him who loves his friend as the embodiment of that ideal. Unless, indeed, the loved one had been looked up to for his own sake, as that ideal's embodiment, he could not have been loved as he is by him who claims to be his friend; hence envy is forestalled by the very friendship's existence; for envy is a selfish regret that another is in advance of us, while friendship is an unselfish affection for another because he is in advance of us—or ought to be, as we see it.

Nor, again, is distrust of a friend compatible with true

friendship, any more than is envy. Distrust of another is the result of a watchful interest in one's own welfare; it is, in fact, a fear that one is to be a loser from his relations to another; but friendship being in its very nature a forgetfulness of self in love for another, it carries with it supremacy of interest in the loved one and his welfare. How can a man be afraid for himself when he has forgotten himself? "There is no fear in love: but perfect love casteth out fear," says the loved and loving friend of Jesus. "He that feareth is not made perfect in love." He who distrusts is not yet a true friend.

In pagan wisdom, as well as in inspired Christianity, the duty of trusting a friend unfailingly has found full recognition. Among the maxims of Publius Syrus we read: "The one bond of friendship is confidence;" "So trust your friend that there be not place for enmity;" "He who fears his friend gives reason why his friend should fear *him;*" "He who fears his friend knows not the meaning of the name."

It is not that love for a friend will blind one to that friend's lack of attainments and capabilities, or to the possibility of his coming short of his ideal. But it is that friendship's love will make it impossible to question the fact that the friend is always himself, or to have any such fear of his action as comes from the selfish considering of possible consequences to the loving one through his being the other's friend unswervingly. "Though he slay me, yet will I trust in him," is ever the loving cry of a child of God whose love for his Father is for what that Father is in himself, rather than for what that Father is to his loving child. "Perfect love"—that unalloyed love that friendship is—is never less trustful than this.

In friendship, in real friendship, "we walk by faith, not by sight;" and faith is better than sight. A heart that trusts is a safer guide than eyes that see. In the highest and holiest friendship it is divinely declared: "Blessed are they that have not seen, and yet have believed." Conversely, in the best and truest human friendships there is a blessing to him who will not believe his own eyes against the one whom he loves.

Ebers, in his historical romances, has given illustrations of this unwavering trust, from the social life of the ancient Egyptians. In his "Uarda," when Nefert is told positively that Mena, her husband, has proved untrue to her, she repels indignantly the suggestion, and her answer is: "If . . . these eyes saw it,—ay, over and over again,— . . . not for one instant would I doubt his truth;" and the record shows that Nefert's trust in Mena never wavered, nor was ever misplaced.

Again, in his "Serapis," Ebers makes Constantine reproach Gorgo, who, having professed to love him, was ready to distrust him because of what she had heard from others. "Even if your own eyes had seen me, you ought not to have believed them," he said in honest indignation. And what is thus pictured in the ideal life of the old Egyptians is found as a reality wherever there is a true and consistent friendship to-day. Only by being disloyal as a friend can one have in question the loyalty of a friend to that ideal for which, in fact, he is loved and honored as a friend.

In the Icelandic sagas there is a story of one Hauskuld, who was a true friend to the sons of one Njal. When evil-minded men came to warn Hauskuld against his friends, his loyal rejoinder was: "Spare thy words: for I have no mind to hear slanders against Njal's sons. They are my friends, and I would rather die at their hands than doubt them. But thou art all the worse man, in my esteem, for speaking thus concerning them."

From Plutarch we learn that Alexander the Great was great enough, with all his faults, to know the scope and to feel the sway of true friendship. Alexander lay sick in Cilicia during one of his earlier campaigns for Asiatic conquest. The fate of the world seemed to pivot on his recovery, and because of the magnitude of the risk involved, and of the suspicions of intrigue on every side, the Macedonian physicians hesitated to assume the responsibility of his treatment. But Philip, an Acarnanian physician, loved Alexander, and was loved by him. "He was his true friend," says Plutarch, and Alexander trusted him accordingly. Philip would care for Alexander, at every risk to himself. He came to the king's bedside with his loving counsel. Meantime Parmenio, a jealous admirer of Alexander, had written from the camp, saying that the physician, Philip, had been bribed by Darius to poison Alexander, and warning Alexander to beware of him. Alexander, having read Parmenio's letter, showed it to no one, but put it under his pillow. When Philip proffered the medicine he had prepared, Alexander looked up into the face of his friend "with a cheerful expression of trust and kindly feeling," and drained the cup without a question. Then, taking the letter of warning from under his pillow, he handed it to Philip, that he might read it, and so learn how a friend could trust. Largeness of soul like Alexander's will show itself in such trust in a friend as Alexander showed.

It is in the very nature of friendship to fix its thought on that which is lovable in the one loved as a friend, and thereby to lose thought of that which is unlovable. Friendship makes so much of that in a friend which is worthy of confidence, that it will not have in mind those traits or actions of his which might tend to provoke distrust of him. One of the early disciples of Confucius, describing the characteristics of real friends, says: "They are ever ready to forget one's ill treatment of them; and, whether near or at a distance, they neither suspect nor doubt one." In one of the sacred books of the Hindoos it is declared: "He is not a friend who always eagerly suspects a breach, and looks out for faults."

It is Manuel, an old-time Castilian prince, who asserts indignantly:

> "He who would counsel your reserve to friends
> Has purpose of betraying you unseen."

Even the cynical La Rochefoucauld—whose chief thought, as Voltaire tells us, is that self-love is the spring of all our actions and determinations—insists that distrust has no part or place in friendship. "It is more dishonorable," he says, "to distrust a friend than to be deceived by him." It is contrary to the very nature of true friendship to be reckoning on the possibility of danger in trusting a friend absolutely. Thus Emerson, referring to the gain of loving on in a friendship where one's love is not reciprocated adds, as if self-reproachfully: "Yet these things may hardly be said without a sort of treachery to the relation. The essence of friendship is entireness, a total magnanimity and trust. It must not surmise or provide for infirmity."

Old Chaucer, in describing the various phases of love, emphasizes this unswerving trust in a friend as the joyous pre-eminence of the love which is friendship:

> " Love of freendshippe also ther is,
> Which makith no man done amys,
> Of wille knytt bitwixe two,
> That wole not breke for wele ne woo;
> Which long is likly to contune,[1]
> Whanne wille and goodis be in comune,
> Grounded by Goddis ordinaunce,
> Hoole withoute discordaunce;
> With hem holdyng comunte [2]
> Of alle her goode in charite,
> That ther be noon excepcioun,
> Thurgh chaungyng of entencioun,
> That eche helpe other at her neede,
> And wisely hele [3] bothe word and dede;
> Trewe of menyng, devoide of slouthe,
> For witt is nought withoute trouthe;
> So that the ton [4] dar alle his thought
> Seyn to his freend, and spare nought,
> As to hym-silf without dredyng
> To be discovered by wreying,[5]
> For glad is that conjunccioun,
> Whanne ther is noon susspecioun
> [That] they wolde [evere false] prove,
> That trewe and parfit weren in love."

And many a writer, earlier and later, has given point to the truth that the only time when a friend can prop-

---

[1] Continue. [2] Community. [3] Hide. [4] The one. [5] Betraying.

erly be distrusted is before he is a friend.   Thus Young counsels:

> " Deliberate on all things with thy friend.
> But, since friends grow not thick on every bough,
> Nor every friend unrotten at the core ;
> First, on thy friend, deliberate with thyself;
> Pause, ponder, sift ; not eager in the choice,
> Nor jealous of the chosen ; fixing, fix.
> *Judge before friendship, then confide till death.*"

And this would seem to be but a paraphrase of Quarles: " Deliberate long before thou consecrate a friend; and when thy impartial judgment concludes him worthy of thy bosom, receive him joyfully, and entertain him wisely; impart thy secrets boldly, and mingle thy thoughts with his ; he is thy very self, and use him so. If thou firmly thinkest him faithful, thou makest him so." Indeed, both of these statements are but elaborations of the words of Seneca the wise: "After friendship it is confidence; before friendship it is judgment." Shakespeare has the same idea in the advice of Polonius to Laertes, when that worldly-wise observer of sound maxims counsels his departing son :

> " The friends thou hast, and their adoption tried,
> Grapple them to thy soul with hoops of steel."

And practical Benjamin Franklin suggests again the thought in his maxim : " Be slow in choosing a friend, slower in changing."

Cicero protested against the suggestion out of a former generation—a suggestion ascribed to Bias, one of the wise men of Greece—that " a man ought so to love as if one day he would come to hate." Cicero was sure that "no speech could be found more hostile to friendship than this;" and his responding question was: "In what manner can any one be a friend to him to whom he thinks he may possibly become an enemy?"

How can friendship find a place for distrust? An out-going limitless love forbids and bars an incoming limiting doubt. The only unrest of a love that rests in the truth of one's truer other self, is the ceaseless craving to love more, and to be more true in loving.

> "The deepest hunger of a faithful heart
> Is faithfulness."

TRANSCENDING ALL LOVES.

NE need not go outside of the Bible record for proof that friendship's love has a place above all other loves; although the concurrent testimony of the ages, earlier and later than that record, is to the same effect. A truth like this could hardly fail of recognition in the Book of books.

When Moses is warning the children of Israel of the temptations to idolatry which will beset them in the land of Canaan, he names the possible tempters to evil in the order of their relative importance, and to a "friend" he assigns the place highest of all. "If thy brother, the son of thy mother, or thy son, or thy daughter, or the wife of thy bosom, or thy *friend, which is as thine own life,* entice thee secretly, saying, Let us go and serve other gods; . . . thou shalt not consent unto him, nor hearken unto him." And everything in the Old Testament history and teachings would go to show that this was the true climax of affections from the earliest ages of the world—friendship transcending all loves; which is only another way of saying that a love which is absolutely and devotedly unselfish is superior to a love which has in it any measure or taint of self-interest.

The loves competing with friendship are conjugal love and kinship love. David bore witness to a friend's love as "passing the love of women;" and Solomon affirmed unhesitatingly, "There is a friend that sticketh closer than a brother."

It is a pregnant fact that in all the Old Testament story only one human being is ever referred to as a "friend" of God. The Lord is referred to as "Father" of all, and as "Husband" of his entire people; but only Abraham is designated as the Lord's "friend." Once, indeed, in our English version, it is mentioned that "the Lord spake unto Moses face to face, as a man speaketh unto his friend;" but this is clearly an allusion to the *manner* of the intercourse on that occasion between Moses and the Lord; not a reference to the peculiar *relation* in which they two stood to each other. In fact, the Hebrew word here translated "friend" has no such suggestion of a loving intimacy as the word which is applied to Abraham's relation to God: it is a word more commonly rendered "neighbor." From first to last it is "Moses my servant," of whom the Lord speaks. It is "Abraham, my friend"—and only Abraham.

So clearly was the uniqueness of this relation of Abraham with the Lord recognized in the Oriental mind, that, after twenty centuries had gone by, the Apostle James pointed back to that uplifting of the Father of the Faithful, saying: "Abraham believed God, and it was reckoned

Transcending All Loves. 49

unto him for righteousness; and he was called the friend of God." And now, after wellnigh twenty centuries more, that one patriarch is still known in all the East—known by Jew, Muhammadan, and Christian—as "Ibraheem el-Khaleel," "Abraham *the* friend."

True it is that, under the new dispensation, when Jesus would honor above all precedent the disciples who had trusted him unswervingly, he said, as he was parting with them for a season: "No longer do I call you servants: . . . but I have called you *friends*." But this also was a recognition of the truth that no other relation can be nearer and dearer than friendship; hence the love which transcends all loves was fittingly given that name. Friendship is the love of loves, by the Bible standard.

It can hardly be supposed that it is of carelessness, or without intention, that in both the Old Testament and the New a distinction is repeatedly marked between the mere marriage tie and the highest attainment of friendship; whereby the former is counted of the flesh—the life here in the flesh; while the later is counted of the soul—the very life itself. It is Moses who records the institution of marriage, saying of the twain thereby made one, "Therefore shall a man leave his father and his mother, and shall cleave unto his wife: and they shall be one flesh." Moses again it is who describes "a friend" as in a relation to another closer and more vital than even that of "one flesh"—"thy friend which is as thine own life"—literally, "thine own self." It is Paul who points back to this original institution of marriage as a Divine declaration that "the twain shall become one flesh," and who counsels that "even so ought husbands to love their own wives as their own bodies." Paul also it is who, referring to his friend and his child in the faith, Onesimus, speaks of him as "my very heart," and again as "myself." Is there no meaning in these inspired distinctions?

It is not that the tie of marriage or the ties of blood ought, in any case, to exist without the sentiment of friendship; but it is that those ties do not in and of themselves secure such an interunion of very soul as is possible between those who are only friends. Friendship without conjugal or kinship love is a profounder and more sacred affection than conjugal or kinship love without friendship. He who has a duty of conjugal love or of kinship love has a duty also of friendship's love in the same direction. Without this love the other loves can never reach their highest and holiest possibilities, or be at their God-intended completion.

Jesus Christ and his church are, it is true, represented in the relation of a bridegroom to a bride; but he and his chosen disciples are also represented as united in the yet more intimate and enduring relation of "friends." The church, as a church, is his "body;" the personal believers in him are sharers of his very "life." "In the resurrection," says Jesus, "they neither marry nor are given in marriage." But in his farewell discourse to his disciples, as his "friends," Jesus says: "I come again, and will receive you unto myself; that where I am there ye may be also." The marriage tie by itself is of the life that is here, in the flesh. The tie of friendship, with marriage or apart from it, is of the life that is both here and hereafter. This is the distinction recognized by the keen-witted Frenchman, Joseph Roux, when he defines "love" as "two souls and one flesh," and "friendship" as "two bodies and one soul." Friendship has been called "the marriage of souls;" and that would seem to be the light in which the Bible presents it. Those who are united in marriage ought to be united also in friendship; but unless marriage includes this union of *souls*, marriage must end with the life that is.

Outside of the Bible text there is abundant evidence that the richest experiences of the human heart, the world over, have tended to give the first place, and the best, to a love without any admixture of possible self-interest, to a friendship closer than a tie of blood, and passing the love of women.

In the sacred books of the Hindoos the climax of crimes is declared to be a sin against one's friend. A declaration in the Mahâbhârata is:

> "To oppress a suppliant, to kill a wife, to rob a Brahman,
>   and to betray one's friend,
> These are the four great crimes."

A misuse of power is a sin; the murder of a wife is a greater sin; yet greater still is the robbing of a God-representing Brahman ; but the crowning sin of all is the betrayal of a friend,—for friendship transcends all loves, and crimes against friendship are chiefest of crimes.

Choo He, a follower of Confucius, makes a similar distinction to that which the Bible makes between marriage as a tie of the flesh, and friendship as a tie of the soul. "Marriage is the heaven-ordained relation on which depends succession," he says; "and friendship is the heaven-ordained relationship on which depends the correction of one's character; for by it the way of men is traced out, and men's highest principles are built up."

Classic literature is as rich as Oriental in its praises of the transcendency of friendship's love. Says Euripides:

> "A friend
> Welded into our life is more to us
> Than twice five thousand kinsmen, one in blood."

Sophocles characterizes a friend as a person

> "Dear as one's life which one loves most."

Aristotle reaffirms this idea of soul-union in true friendship, saying that a good man ought to feel "toward his friend as he does toward himself; for the good man has the same relation to his friend as he has to himself." And Cicero counsels unhesitatingly: "I can only urge you to prefer friendship to all human possessions; for there is nothing so suited to our nature, so well adapted to prosperity or adversity." And of the pre-eminence of friendship over any other human relation, Cicero says: "In this respect friendship is superior to relationship; because from relationship a loving regard can be withdrawn, while from friendship it cannot be. For with the withdrawal of affection the very name of friendship is done away, while that of relationship may remain."

Nor has later literature, philosophic or poetic, reversed the verdict of the classic writers as to the transcendency of friendship. Says Bacon: "It was a sparing speech of the ancients to say that a friend is another himself; for that a friend is far more than himself."

Sir Thomas Browne speaks out of his heart of hearts

when he testifies on this point: "I hope I do not break the fifth commandment, if I conceive I may love my friend before the dearest of my blood—even those to whom I owe the principle of life. I never yet cast a true affection on a woman [yet this was published, unchanged, by the author, two years after his happy marriage]; but I have loved my friend as I do virtue, my soul, and my God. From hence, methinks, I do conceive how God loves man; what happiness there is in the love of God."

"Nor yet," says Montaigne, "do the four time-honored kinds [of love],—natural, social, hospitable, and sexual,—either separately or conjointly, make up a true and perfect friendship;" since this has in it more than them all. Montaigne points out that the ties of blood are of necessity, and the ties of marriage are a covenant obligation, both ties being in their continuance compulsory, apart from the impulse of untrammeled affection; "whereas friendship has no manner of business or traffic with aught but itself," it being voluntary in its beginning, and its limitless on-going being unselfish and unswerving.

It is the German Engel who says: "Blood relationship is sweet, and is what nature brings about; but how much sweeter are alliances of the soul." And a German proverb runs: "We can live without a brother, but not without a friend." A corresponding English proverb is: "A father is a treasure, a brother is a comfort, but a friend is both." Or as Evelyn has it: "There is in friendship something of all relations, and something above them all." And our Emerson sums up the truth in his characterizing of friendship as "that select and sacred relation which is a kind of absolute, and which even leaves the language of love suspicious and common, so much is this purer; and nothing is so much divine."

Spenser leads off, among English-speaking poets, in explicit assigning of pre-eminence to friendship in comparison with all other loves:

> " Hard is the doubt, and difficult to deeme,[1]
> When all three kindes of love together meet,
> And doe dispart the hart with powre extreme,—
> Whether shall weigh the balance downe; to weet,
> The deare affection unto kindred sweet,
> Or raging fire of love to womankind,
> Or zeale of frends combynd with vertues meet.
> But of them all the band of vertuous mind,
> Me seemes, the gentle hart should most assured bind.
>
> "For naturall affection soone doth cesse,
> And quenched is with Cupid's greater flame;
> But faithfull frendship doth them both suppresse,
> And them with maystring[2] discipline doth tame,
> Through thoughts aspyring to eternall fame.
> For as the soule doth rule the earthly masse,
> And all the service of the bodie frame;
> So love of soule doth love of bodie passe,
> No lesse than perfect gold surmounts the meanest brasse."

Shirley is equally sure that there is no other love like friendship:

> "It is a name
> Virtue can only answer to: couldst thou
> Unite into one all goodness whatsoe'er
> Mortality can boast of, thou shalt find
> The circle narrow, bounded to contain
> This swelling treasure. Every good admits
> Degrees; but this, being so good, it cannot;
> For he's no friend who's not superlative.

---

[1] Decide.   [2] Mastering.

> Indulgent parent, brethren, kindred tied
> By the natural flow of blood, alliances,
> And what you can imagine, are too light
> To weigh with name of friend. They execute
> At best but what a nature prompts them to;—
> Are often less than friends when they remain
> Our kinsmen still: but friend is never lost.

Gay sees the inherent superiority of an out-going and on-going friendship in its contrast with aught there is in the intenser passion of love:

> "Love is a sudden blaze which soon decays,
> Friendship is like the sun's eternal rays;
> Not daily benefits exhaust the flame:
> It still is giving, and still burns the same."

Coleridge gives a more discriminating illustration of the true supremacy of friendship over love:

> "Love is flower-like;
> Friendship is a sheltering tree."

Charles Lamb cries out, in illustration of friendship's transcendent love:

> "Friend of my bosom; thou more than my brother!"

Tennyson echoes this estimate of the relative place of friendship among loves, when he sings of the one dearest to his heart:

> "My friend, the brother of my love;
>
> . . . . .
>
> Dear as the mother to her son,
> More than my brothers are to me.
>
> . . . . .
>
> The sweetest soul
> That ever looked with human eyes."

Longfellow shows his heroic John Alden as recognizing the superiority of self-abnegating friendship over the purest self-indulgent love. It was when Miles Standish appealed in the name of his friendship to the young lover of Priscilla, to win her for the sturdy chieftain, that the answer came back nobly and generously:

> "The name of friendship is sacred;
> What you demand in that name, I have not the power to deny you!"

So,

> "Friendship prevailed over love, and Alden went on his errand."

Browning, with his master power as a poet sets forth, in his "Saul," the truth that friendship's love is a revelation and an earnest of the transcendent love of God. David, finding himself helpless in his effort to restore the disordered spirit of the King, gains hope through the suggestion of his own never-failing affection as a friend.

> "And oh, all my heart how it loved him! but where was the sign?
> I yearned—'Could I help thee, my father, inventing a bliss,
> I would add, to that life of the past, both the future and this;
> I would give thee new life altogether, as good, ages hence,
> As this moment,—had love but the warrant, love's heart to dispense!'
>
> Then the truth came upon me. No harp more—no song more! out-broke—
>
> .   .   .   .   .
>
> 'Do I find love so full in my nature, God's ultimate gift,
> That I doubt his own love can compete with it? Here, the parts shift?
> Here, the creature surpass the Creator,—the end, what Began?
> Would I fain in my impotent yearning do all for this man,
> And dare doubt he alone shall not help him, who yet alone can?
>
> .   .   .   .   .   .

Transcending All Loves. 57

I believe it! 'Tis thou, God, that givest, 'tis I who receive:
In the first is the last, in thy will is my power to believe.

. . . . . .

See the King—I would help him but cannot, the wishes fall
 through.
Could I wrestle to raise him from sorrow, grow poor to enrich,
To fill up his life, starve my own out, I would—knowing which,
I know that my service is perfect. Oh, speak through me now!
Would I suffer for him that I love? So wouldst thou—so wilt thou!
So shall crown thee the topmost, ineffablest, uttermost crown—
And thy love fill infinitude wholly, nor leave up nor down
One spot for the creature to stand in!'"

And so it is that David, in the outreach of his unselfish love as a friend, comes to a realizing sense of the measureless scope of that Divine love of which friendship is the transcendent image and promise.

Thus always, from the earliest ages to the latest, in sacred writings and in secular, friendship finds its recognition as the pre-eminent and surpassing affection of the human heart. The distinction between the love that craves and seeks, and the friendship that would unfailingly serve, has been perceived, all along the centuries; as it was sententiously expressed by Publius Syrus (and afterwards by Seneca): "Friendship always benefits; but love also injures." Or, as Goethe expands the thought:

> "True *friendship* shows its worth in stern refusal
>   At the right moment; and strong *love* sometimes
>   Heaps the loved one with ruin, when it serves
>   The will more than the weal of who demands."

"A man who is a friend, such as the name imports,—except the gods nothing transcends him," says the pagan poet Plautus. The Christian illustrator of "holy living" and "holy dying" finds in friendship "the greatest love, and the greatest usefulness, and the most open communion, and the noblest sufferings, and the most exemplary faithfulness, and the severest truth, and the heartiest counsel, and the greatest union of minds, of which brave men and women are capable." As Katherine Philips, a poet of friendship, sees it,—

> "'Tis love refined and purged from all its dross;
> The next to angel's love, if not the same;
> As strong as passion is, though not so gross:
> It antedates a glad eternity,
> And is a heaven in epitome."

CHANGELESS IN CHANGES.

 LOVE that is not conditioned on reciprocity or recognition; a love that is unselfish, uncraving, ever out-going and ever on-going; a love that consists in loving rather than in being loved, and that is based on what the loved one is in himself, not on what he is to the one who loves,—cannot be brought to an end by any act, or by any lack, of another than the one whose best personality it represents and exhibits; nor by him while he is still himself. A true friendship is changeless in all changes. It is like the sun, shining just as truly toward the earth while clouds are between it and our planet, as when the atmosphere is clearest; not like the moon that shines only when it is shined upon.

"True friendship between man and man," says Plato, "is infinite and immortal." Aristotle argues that a friendship in order to be true must have a right basis, and that, having a right basis, a friendship "is, as we might expect, permanent;" that "with respect to time and everything else it is perfect; that a friendship, "because it is felt for its own sake, continues." Cicero similarly reasons: "If it were expediency that cemented friendships, expediency when changed would dissolve them; but because one's nature can never change, therefore true friendships are eternal." It is of friendship's love that Shakespeare says unqualifiedly:

> "Love is not love
> Which alters when it alteration finds,
> Or bends with the remover to remove:
> Oh, no! it is an ever-fixèd mark
> That looks on tempests, and is never shaken."

Mrs. Browning reiterates this truth in her denial that any true love ever knew a change:

> "Those never loved,
> Who dream that they loved once."

The intercourse of true friends is a joy of friendship that increases with its exercise, and that can never cloy the heart. But the intercourse of friends, while a joy of friendship, is not a necessity of friendship. What *may* be the intercourse of friends is a possibility without end. What *must* be the intercourse of friends is a possibility without beginning. A change in circumstances, that separates those who rejoiced in the joy of inspiring intercourse, does not change the character or the affection of him who is a true friend. "Friends, though absent, are still present," says Cicero. Dryden re-phrases this thought:

> "The souls of friends like kings in progress are;
> Still in their own, though from the palace far."

"It is sublime," says Emerson, "to feel and say of another, I need never meet, or speak, or write to him; we need not reinforce ourselves, or send tokens of remembrance: I rely on him as on myself; if he did thus or thus, I know it was right."

Wilhelm von Humboldt saw his friend Charlotte Diede for only three days, in his early manhood; but the friendship then awakened was maintained unswervingly during twenty-six years of absence, and of silence, which followed that meeting. Even after that, when the intercourse of these two friends was renewed, and was kept up by delightful correspondence for the twenty remaining years of his life,—both being married,—they saw each other only twice in all that time. Yet this is one of the friendships of history; and its record is consistent with all that is known of the high possibilities of changelessness in a friend, despite all changes in the intercourse of a friendship.

A true friendship cannot die; but a true friend can. Yet the absence of a friend through death need not change the love that goes out toward him. "Though dead they are alive," says Cicero, of friends who are real friends; "so entirely does the honor, the memory, the regret, of friends attend them." Similarly says Lavater:

> "True friends, nor death, nor separating fate,
>   can e'er divide."

And Whittier reminds us that our friends who are gone are as really friends as while they were with us here:

> "Not shadows in a shadowy band,
>   Not *others*, but *themselves* are they."

David's heart-cry of sorrow and of love for his dead friend was:

> "I am distressed for thee, my brother Jonathan:
> Very pleasant hast thou been unto me;
> Thy love to me was wonderful,
> Passing the love of women."

But David's friendship for Jonathan was not changed by the change that separated them thus sadly. It was long years after this that David, finally settled in his established kingdom, asked of those about him, "Is there yet any left of the house of Saul, that I may show him kindness for Jonathan's sake?" And when they told him of Mephibosheth, the crippled son of Jonathan, David brought that representative of his dead friend into his royal home, and gave him a place at the king's table, in proof of the changelessness of David's friendship for Jonathan. It is of the power over David of this changeless friendship, after Jonathan's death, that Cardinal Newman tells:

> "O heart of fire! misjudged by wilful man,
>   Thou flower of Jesse's race!
> What woe was thine, when thou and Jonathan
>   Last greeted face to face!
> He doomed to die, thou on us to impress
> The portent of a blood-stained holiness.
>
> "Yet it was well:—for so, 'mid cares of rule
>   And crime's encircling tide,
> A spell was o'er thee, zealous one, to cool
>   Earth-joy and kingly pride;
> With battle-scene and pageant, prompt to blend
> The pale, calm specter of a blameless friend."

No one need cry, with Dryden, to a surviving friend:

> "Be kind to my remains, and oh, defend,
> Against your judgment, your departed friend!"

He who is a friend is changeless in friendship:

> "Who heart-whole, pure in faith, once written friend,
> In life and death is true, unto the end;"

and the end of life is not a changeless friendship's end.

"Men have their time, and die many times in desire of some things which they principally take to heart," says Bacon; "the bestowing of a child, the finishing of a work, or the like. If a man have a true friend, he may rest almost secure that the care of these things will continue after him. So that a man hath, as it were, two lives in his desires. A man hath a body, and that body is confined to a place; but where friendship is, all offices of life are, as it were, granted to him and his deputy."

History, sacred and profane, is enriched with the record of the recognized and honored legacies of friendship. Hiram, king of Tyre, the friend of David, proffered his loving service to Solomon, when Hiram was the survivor, and Solomon was the successor, of David; "for Hiram was ever a lover of David,"—after David's death, as truly as before. Homer tells us that Menelaus, when he discovers that a stranger guest in his house is Telemachus, the son of Odysseus, his friend and former fellow-soldier before the walls of Troy, exclaims: "Zeus forfend it and all the other deathless gods, that ye should depart from my house to the swift ship. . . . Never shall the dear son of this man, even of Odysseus, lay him down upon the ship's deck, while as yet I am alive and my children after me are left in my hall." It was the hereditary, or the transmitted, friendship of the elder Laelius for the elder Scipio Africanus, as manifested in the loving friendship of the younger Laelius and the younger Scipio, which was made the basis of Cicero's immortal *De Amicitia*.

So, always, he who can be trusted as a friend to a living loved one, can be trusted as a friend to those whom death bequeaths to him as a legacy from that loved one. Nor absence nor death can change any friendship that is worthy of its name.

But there are changes more trying than those of absence or of death. He who won a friend's love and seemed to return it may cease to be loving, or may cease to be true. Can a friendship be changeless in such changes as these? This is an old-time question, that is as important to-day as ever. "There is a difficulty," says Aristotle, "in the question whether or not we should dissolve friendship with those who do not continue the same as they originally were. . . . If one admits another to his friendship as being a good man, and then that loved one becomes wicked, or is thought to be so, must he still love him? Or is this impossible? . . . If again the loved one continues the same, while the other becomes better, and widely different in virtue, must the latter still consider the former as his friend? Or is that not possible? The case is plainest when the difference becomes very great, as in friendships contracted in childhood; for if one continues a child in intellect, and the other becomes a man of the highest character, how can they be friends, since they no longer take pleasure in the same things, nor sympathize in joy and grief together?"

It is in view of such changes on the part of the one loved,—changes that seem to make him another man, or to put him outside of the pale of the old friendship,—that Aristotle asks, as to the friend who has been sincere and true in his affection for him: "Must he, thenceforward, feel no otherwise toward him than if he had never been his friend? Or, ought he to remember their past intimacy; and just as we think that a man should confer favors on friends rather than on strangers, ought he, in like manner, to bestow some consideration on those who were his friends, for the sake of past friendship?" And these questions of the great Greek philosopher have been puzzled over and reiterated from his day to ours.

The intimacies of a friendship are one thing; but the friendship itself is quite another thing. The intimacies depend on the reciprocal relations of the two friends; but the friendship of either is independent of the course or the attitude of the other. A friendship may be changeless, while the intimacies of that friendship change greatly. A loved one's ways may change, and in consequence there may be a change in the intercourse and the seeming relations between him and the one who has loved him; but that does not in itself involve, or justify, a change in the love of him who has claimed to be his whole-hearted, unselfish friend.

If, indeed, a friendship were based on a process of reasoning concerning the characteristics and consequent conduct of the one loved, it might change with a disclosed change in that basis of estimate. But because a friendship is based on the fact that the one who loves is himself, and that the one who is loved is himself, a true friendship cannot change while the one who loved remains himself, and the one whom he loves is, with all his changes, still himself. Failure on the part of the one loved may sadden a friend's heart, or treachery may break it, but no such change as this can change that heart's fidelity.

It was while Jesus was troubled in spirit over his already planned betrayal by one whom he had loved as a friend, that he made exhibit of his still-continuing unselfish love for him by giving to him the morsel, or sop, of affection, out of the dish from which they were partaking together in friendship. In all the changes of that night of gloom, the friendship of Jesus was changeless. The nearer one's friendship approaches to the standard of Jesus, the surer it will be to remain unfailingly true, despite every failure of its object of love.

When Josephus was defending the Jews against the attack on them by the pagan Greek Apion, he laid emphasis on their habit of unchanging fidelity in all the changes of a chosen friendship. "Secrecy among friends is prohibited," he said; "for friendship implies an entire confidence without any reserve." "Nay, where friendship is dissolved," he added, "we must not be false to a former trust." It would hardly be admitted that the Christian standard at this point is lower, on this verge of the twentieth century, than was that of the Jews at the beginning of our era.

One's self, rather than one's friend, is on trial when the question is mooted whether a love given in a friendship is to continue changelessly, or is to change. If a man was wise and true in giving his love, let him be wise and true in its continuing. If, however, it would seem that he was not wise, let it not also appear that he is not true. Even if it be too late to choose a true friend wisely, it is not too late to be wisely true as a friend.

This thought it is that Cicero emphasizes when he says: "We should employ such carefulness in forming our friendships that we could not at any time begin to love the man whom we could possibly ever hate. Moreover, if we have been but unfortunate in our selection, . . . this should be submitted to, rather than that a time of alienation should ever be contemplated. . . . For nothing can be more disgraceful than to be at enmity with him with whom you have lived on terms of friendship."

Coleridge, in the greatness of his mind, perceived the truth that no change in the intimacies of a friendship should change the friendship itself:

> "Unchanged within to see all changed without
> Is a blank lot and hard to bear, no doubt.
> Yet why at others' wanings shouldst thou fret?
> Then only mightst thou feel a just regret,
> Hadst thou withheld thy love or hid thy light
> In selfish forethought of neglect and slight.
> O wiselier then, from feeble yearnings freed,
> While, and on whom, thou mayst—shine on! nor heed
> Whether the object by reflected light
> Return thy radiance or absorb it quite:
> And though thou notest from thy safe recess
> Old friends burn dim, like lamps in noisome air,
> Love them for what they are; nor love them less,
> Because to thee they are not what they were."

At the best, a change in the intimacies of a friendship is a loss to both him who loves and him who is loved. It is with all estranged friends as it was with Lord Roland

and Sir Leoline, in Coleridge's "Christabel," in their estrangement:

> "Each spoke words of high disdain
>   And insult to his heart's best brother:
> They parted—ne'er to meet again!
>   But never either found another
> To free the hollow heart from paining—
> They stood aloof, the scars remaining,
>   Like cliffs which had been rent asunder;
> A dreary sea now flows between;—
>   But neither heat, nor frost, nor thunder,
> Shall wholly do away, I ween,
>   The marks of that which once hath been."

A changeless personality, that must unceasingly suffer from the changed relations of a once joyous friendship, cannot be so untrue to itself as to be untrue to the memories, the inspirations, and the obligations, of that friendship. At the worst, in recognition of that which is called a hopeless change in the friendship itself, its reverent cry will be:

> "We that were friends, yet are not now,
>   We that must daily meet
> With ready words and courteous bow,
>   Acquaintance of the street;
> We must not scorn the holy past,
>   We must remember still
> To honor feelings that outlast
>   The reason of the will."

OF WORLD-WIDE HONOR.

EVERY heart is human, and every human heart has its possibilities in the direction of best and truest outreachings of affection. In all lands and in all ages the reciprocal ties of blood and of marriage have found their comparative measure of binding force; and with like universality there has been recognized the binding force of the tie in a noble and an ennobling friendship— above the dearest of these reciprocal ties.

Marriage has had its varying degrees of obligation and sacredness among different peoples of the world. Polygamy, polyandry, and promiscuity, have in turn tended to destroy or diminish the beauty and sanctity of the primal institution of dual union in conjugal love. Parental and filial and fraternal affections have had greater or lesser sway according to the circumstances and characteristics and religious beliefs of diverse nationalities and communities. Savage customs, or selfish cravings, or ecclesiastical requirements, have had their part in crushing out the divinely implanted love for offspring. Perverted reasoning, or the hard struggle for personal existence, has at times so far obliterated from the mind all loyal regard for the authors of one's being, as to cause the desertion or destruction of helpless or infirm parents to be deemed justifiable, or even praiseworthy. All these causes have again, in their turn, operated to neutralize the love which would bind in unity the several children of a common parentage. Yet no people has fallen so low in the social scale, nor has any risen so high, as to be without the clear conception of a union, real, sacred, and abiding, between two persons made one in the love of an unselfish and inviolable friendship.

An absolute merging of two personalities into one, in this union of friendship, has been sought, among primitive peoples everywhere, by the intermingling of the blood of the two, through its mutual drinking, or its inter-transfusion; with the thought that blended blood is blended life. Traces of this custom are found in the traditions and practices of the aborigines of different portions of Asia, Africa, Europe, North and South America, and the Islands of the Sea. Nor is there any quarter of the globe where traces of this rite, in one form or another, are not to be found to-day.

Almost invariably this formal seeking of a friendship union by intermingled blood has been accompanied by an appeal to God, or to the gods, in witness of its sacredness, and in pledge of unswerving fidelity to its obligations. A sundering of this tie—unlike that of marriage—has ever been deemed an impossibility; and no claims of personal interest, of family, of caste, of country, or of religion, have been recognized as justifying a denial, by either party, of the pre-eminent hold on him by his other very self; and fidelity to this tie has been always held to be the duty of each friend, apart from the fact of the fidelity of the other. It may, indeed, be affirmed unqualifiedly, that no other human tie or bond has had the sacredness and inviolability which attaches to this soul intermerging in friendship—in every age and everywhere.

Even where the intermingling of very blood no longer prevails as a method of seeking or symbolizing soul union in friendship, that union is often pledged by solemn vows in the presence of protecting and avenging divinities, in evidence that it is put beyond recall by the parties who assume its sacred responsibilities and obligations. Thus, in China, two friends will covenant with each other by burning incense together before some popular idol, or they will together worship Heaven and Earth, invoking a blessing on their friendship, and imprecating a curse on its violation. In Syria, in Arabia, in Egypt, and in Turkey, it is customary to solemnize the ratifying of a friendship by the two parties visiting together some holy shrine where their formal promises of mutual fidelity shall be made doubly binding. Similarly, for centuries it was the habit of Christian friends to hallow their vow of friendship by partaking together of the Holy Communion at the church altar. And to the present time, in Russia, there exists the practice of an interchange of blood-symbolizing crosses in a sacred friendship, as an apparent survival of the primitive custom of reverently intercommingling the blood itself in God's sight. Among some tribes of North American Indians the "Friendship Dance" is a rude religious ceremony by which a formal recognition is made of the union in friendship of two warriors, in the presence of their tribe and of unseen spirits above. Again, it will be by the dividing of a bloody scalp between two Indians who are drawn to one another, that a common life in friendship is sought; as if by the help of him who is the Author of all life. In some such solemn way, "two young men agree to be perpetual friends to each other, or more than brothers. Each [thenceforward] reveals to the other the secrets of his life, and counsels with him on matters of importance, and defends him from wrong and violence, and at his death is chief mourner."

In incidental proof of the primitive idea that in friendship's highest attainment there is an absolute intermingling and merging of two natures into one, there is the world-wide custom of ratifying a covenant of friendship by the exchanging of garments, or armor, or weapons, or of personal names. This exchanging of names in friendship, which prevails widely among primitive peoples, is peculiarly significant of this idea. It is not, as in the case of marriage, the acceptance of one name for both parties, as a matter of convenience, or as a seeming surrender of one personality to another; but it is rather a mutual transference of personal identity. It is as if the friendship which originated "because he was he, and because I was I," had issued in the conclusion, " Now he is I, and now I am he." Nor is the idea here suggested one which marks a lower degree of intelligence, cultivation, or spiritual perception and attainment. It is found in the sacred writings of the East; and it shows itself in the choicest classic lore and Christian literature. It enters into the shaping of human language concerning human affection. It is, in fact, of the very being of friendship at its truest and best.

It is said of the loving union of two divine friends, Rā and Osiris, in the theogony of ancient Egypt, that "each embraced the other, and [they] became as one soul in two souls"—as one life in two lives. Hence, "Rā is the soul of Osiris, and Osiris is the soul of Rā." Similarly it is declared of two divine friends, Vishnoo and Sivâ, in the theogony of India: "The heart of Vishnoo is Sivâ, and the heart of Sivâ is Vishnoo." The one is the other, and the two are one.

Aristotle cites among the time-honored proverbs of Greece in his day, in illustration of the union wrought by a sincere friendship: "One soul [in common];" "Friendship is equality;" "The property of friends is common." And for his own definition Aristotle gives: "A friend is another self." Not partnership, but union, is found in friendship.

Says Cicero: "He who looks on a true friend looks as it were upon a kind of himself;" for "a true friend . . . is as it were a second self;" and so either is the other. Horace again apostrophizes Virgil as "the half of my soul;" and the two halves of a soul are equal, and are equally incomplete.

This idea of an intermerged identity in true friendship is found in a common root-term which enters into words meaning "friendship" or "unselfish love," in many of the Indo-European languages. The Latin *amo*, "to love," from which comes *amicitia*, "friendship," as also the

Sanskrit *kam*, "to love," is cognate with the Greek *hama*, "together with," "at one with," "the same as;" and this term again has its correspondents in the Sanskrit *sama*, the Zend *hama*, the Latin *simul* and *similis*, the Gothic *sama*, the German *sammt*, the Anglo-Saxon *same;* the radical thought throughout being that of "likeness" even to "sameness." In the aboriginal languages of both North and South America there are many illustrations of this idea, especially among those people who distinguish closely between different kinds of affection. It is in recognition of this idea that we speak of "liking" one whom we love, or of being like him, as a cause, or as a result, of our love for him. And herein is the justification of the saying of Publius Syrus: "Friendship either finds men equal, or makes them so."

Friendship is a theme of themes in the world's esteeming. The sacred books of the ages give it a foremost place among the holiest of human relations; and neither the works of cold philosophy nor those of fervid imagination, nor yet the writings of hard unbelief, ignore it, or deem it unworthy of high extolling.

The wisest of the Old Testament writers, who had exhausted the treasures and the pleasures of the world in their power to minister to his advantage, testifies to the pre-eminence of friendship in its enduring gain:

> "A friend loveth at all times,
>   And is born as a brother for adversity."

> "Ointment and perfume rejoice the heart:
>   So doth the sweetness of a man's friend that cometh
>   of hearty counsel.
>   Thine own friend and thy father's friend, forsake not."

> "Iron sharpeneth iron;
>   So a man sharpeneth the countenance
>   of his friend."

And, in the New Testament, One wiser than Solomon declares: "Greater love hath no man than this, that a man lay down his life for his friends"—as friendship has many a time prompted a friend to do gladly.

Says the Son of Sirach, in the Apocrypha:

> "A faithful friend is a strong defence:
> And he that hath found him hath found a treasure.
> There is nothing to be exchanged for a faithful friend,
> And his excellence is invaluable.
> A faithful friend is the medicine of one's life;
> And they that fear the Lord shall find him."

Rabbi Eleazer, in the Talmud, says: "Let the honor of thy friend be dear unto thee as thine own." And a Talmudic proverb summarizes the gains of friendship in the exclamation: "Friends, though they be as the friends of Job; or else death!"

Every Muhammadan is designated in the literature of Arabic theologians as *el-Habeeb*,—"the friend;" since in their opinion there can be no more sacred bond of unity than that which is thus indicated. Even the author of the Qurân, himself, who had forbidden mourning over the death of a believer, wept sorely when Zayd, his loved personal friend, was taken from him; and his answer to the question why he should thus transgress his own commandment was: "*This* is not forbidden; for this is but the yearning in the heart of friend for friend." Other relations may be sundered tearlessly, but the parting of friends cannot be borne without sorrow.

In the most ancient Chinese classics,—the Shoo King and the Shi King, which were venerable sources of wisdom to Confucius,—the relation of "friend and friend" is pointed out as a Heaven-ordained and a Heaven-honored relation. Of him who has found a true friend, it is there affirmed:

> "Spiritual beings will then hearken to him.
> He shall have harmony and peace."

The teachings of those works tend to show that the cultivation of friendship is a sure means of promoting one's spiritual welfare. Confucius laid emphasis on the importance of friendship; and he admitted that he had not attained to the highest demands of its standard of pure and unselfish affection. A successor of Confucius said sweepingly: "From the emperor downwards all must have friends. Friendship is the first of the social relationships, and may not be abandoned for a single day."

The Institutes of Mănu are a basis of Hindoo teaching concerning truth and duty. These Institutes picture the relation of "friend" as surviving all relations of blood or marriage in the world to come; and they point to a "betrayer of a friend" as one who should be excluded from the sacred funeral feasts. In the Mahâbhârata, the epic-thesaurus of Hindoo wisdom, a like prominence is given to friendship and to the sin of its betrayal. In the Sanatsugâtîya, an episode of the Mahâbhârata, "six characteristics" are specified as pertaining to friendship: That one should rejoice with his friend at anything pleasing; that one should grieve with his friend at anything disagreeable; that, with a pure heart, one, when solicited by his friend, should give to him whatever he seeks, even though it be something that ought not to be asked for—as one's wealth, one's sons, or even one's own wife; that when one has given thus freely to his friend, he should not continue to dwell near him through a desire to secure some return for his gifts; that one should live by his own toil, rather than by the toil of a friend; and that one should freely forgo his own profit for a friend's sake.

At the very basis of the Zend-Avesta—the inspired guide of the Parsee—is the conception of friendship at its holiest and best. Mithra, or Mitra, "the god of the heavenly light," is in himself a personification of friendship. "Mitra means, literally, 'a friend,'" says the scholiast. Max Müller gives the term as "derived from the word *mid*, 'to be fat,' 'to make fat,' 'to make shining,' 'to love,'" the root idea being that of shining out and shining on enrichingly toward a loved one. Hence the Parsee conception of the nature and mission of a true friend is that of the free shining of a heavenly light, regardless of its reception or reflection by the object shined on. Rashnoo, again, is "the genius of truth," in the Parsee theogony. The Zend-Avesta says that Rashnoo gave all his soul for long friendship to Mitra. This makes the interunion of light and truth an illustration of holy friendship, in the Parsee religion. "I will sacrifice unto friendship, the best of all friendships, that reigns between the moon and the sun," says a devout believer, as cited in the Zend-Avesta. The sun here represents the friend, who sends out the light of his love unfailingly toward the moon. The moon receives and reflects that brilliant light; but even if it were not to do so, the sun would keep on shining in that direction.

Perhaps the one form of religion in all the world which is by its very nature inimical to that which is holiest and noblest in a pure friendship is Booddhism; for Booddhism, as a religion, is the incarnation and deification of Self; while friendship is in its very soul and essence the abnegation of self. Yet even Booddhism testifies to the admirableness and worth of the highest conception of friendship, while giving warning against the outlay of that love which is the life of such a friendship. "From love comes grief, from love comes fear," says the Dhammapada; "he who is free from love knows neither grief nor fear." "So long as the love of man towards women, even the smallest [measure of it], is not destroyed, so long is his mind in bondage." "Sons are no help, nor a father, nor relations; there is no help from kinship, for one whom death has seized."

This is the starting-point of Booddhism with reference to the ties of marriage and of kinship; and the whole trend of that self-seeking religion is in the direction of hostility to these ties. The counsel of the Booddhist Suttas is: "In him who has intercourse (with others) affections arise, (and then) the pain which follows affection; considering the misery that originates in affection, let one wander alone like a rhinoceros." "He who has compassion on his friends and confidential (companions) loses (his own) advantage, having a fettered mind; seeing this danger in friendship, let one wander alone like a rhinoceros." "Having left son and wife, father and mother, wealth and corn and relatives, the objects of desire, let one wander alone like a rhinoceros."

But while it is inconsistent with the self-seeking spirit

of Booddhism to *be* a friend, it is not inconsistent with that spirit to *have* a friend, if true friendship proffers its disinterested and unswerving love to the self-seeker. Therefore the Booddhist Suttas go on to say, complacently: " Surely we ought to praise the good luck of having companions; the best (and such as are our) equals ought to be sought for; *not* having acquired such friends let one, enjoying (only) allowable things, wander about like a rhinoceros." But, again, " If one acquires a clever companion, an associate righteous and wise, let him, overcoming all dangers, wander about with him glad and thoughtful." Then, in recognition of the fact that it is not easy, for one who is unwilling to be a friend, to command a pure and disinterested friendship, the Suttas moan out: " Friends without an object are now difficult to get!" Thus the selfishest religion in the universe pays its tribute to unselfish friendship, by affirming that friendship is better worth having than any other human affection—if only it can be had without cost to its receiver.

The Icelandic sagas and the Norseland Eddas are as explicit in their recognition of the beauty of the unselfish fidelity of friend to friend, as are the Vedas and Suttas of India. Thus, in the renderings of Taylor and of Howitt, from the Hava-mal:

> " He is the faithful friend who spares
> Out of his pair of loaves the one."

> " Love your own friends, and also theirs;
> But favor not your foeman's friend."

> " If thou hast a friend
> Whom thou canst confide in,
> And wouldst have the joy of his friendship,

> Then mingle thy thoughts with his,
> Give gifts freely,
> And often be with him."

> "The tree withereth
> Which stands in the courtyard
> Without shelter of bark or of leaf.
> So is a man
> Destitute of friends.
> Why should he live on?"

In every record of man's thought or feeling, in all the ages, wherein is any gleam of heavenly wisdom or of heavenward aspiring, there are sure to be found the recognition and praise of friendship as God's good gift to man, and as a human reflection of Divine love. Prophet, evangelist, sage, philosopher, poet, and truth-seeker,—all have their eyes on this lofty ideal.

A versified citation from the Greek Menander runs:

> "Not on the store of sprightly wine,
>   Nor plenty of delicious meats
> Though generous Nature did design
>   To court us with perpetual treats;—
> 'Tis not on these we for content depend,
> So much as on the shadow of a friend."

From the ancient Sanskrit the reminder comes:

> "The words which from a stranger's lips offend,
> Are honey-sweet if spoken by a friend:
> As when the smoke of common wood we spurn,
> But call it perfume sweet when fragrant aloes burn."

It is Ennius, who has been called the Chaucer of the Romans, who asks,

> "How can life be true life without friends?"

And the Russian poet Dimitriev re-echoes this thought when he says for himself, despondently:

> "I've been seeking a friend!—there's none below;
> The world must soon to ruin go."

Hafiz, the Persian, sings:

> "Every one the friend solicits,
> Be he sober, quaff he wine."

Germany's Schiller reiterates this asseveration, as he sings of the surpassing light that is seen

> "In friendship's eloquent and beaming eye."

> "Lo! arm in arm, through every upward grade,
>   From the rude Mongol to the starry Greek
> (Who the fine link between the mortal made
>   And heaven's lost seraph),—everywhere
> Union and bond we seek—till in one sea sublime
> Of love, be merged all measure and all time."

The Swiss Lavater says in his "Words of the Heart:"

> "Noble friends are a pledge, to the noble, of God and the future;
> True friends, nor death nor separating fate can divide."

It is that intensest of Frenchmen, Voltaire, who extols this sentiment, as

> "Friendship divine, true happiness of heaven,
> Sole motion of the soul wherein excess
> Is righteous."

The Spanish poet Calderon bears witness:

> "There is no better book
>   In life, than a wise friend;
> For with his teaching-look
>   His teaching-voice shall blend."

And the English Matt Prior links the old and the new, in the thought that everywhere is both new and old:

> "Of all the gifts the gods afford,
> (If we may trust old Tully's word,)
> The greatest is a friend, whose love
> Knows how to praise, and when reprove."

Finally our own Emerson, both philosopher and poet, rounds out the sphere of friendship's praise, in his declaration, " A friend may well be reckoned the master-piece of nature."

The world's folk-lore, which is the world's preferred traditions of primitive beliefs, gives a foremost place, in its exhibit of noblest purpose and endeavor, to unswerving fidelity in the sphere of purely disinterested friendship. The earliest traditions preserved to us out of the records of Babylonia and Egypt and China and India, as also those of the Norseland, of Southern Africa, and of North and South America, include multiplied illustrations of such faithfulness of friendship in its heroic aspects.

An Arabic classic on friendship is the Book of 'Enoch, which has appeared also in Hebrew and in French. Its main feature is the story of two friends, the one of Bagdad and the other of Cairo. He of Cairo, finding that he of Bagdad was enamored of a slave-girl, just purchased by the Cairene, and counted by him as a peculiar treasure, insisted on making a gift of her to his friend in token of his friendship. When the girl had been taken to Bagdad the Cairene found his own love for her not yet vanquished, and he visited Bagdad in the hope of seeing her again. Ashamed to show himself to his friend—as one who might seem regretful of his act of self-denial—he, while wandering a stranger in the great city, was suspected of a murder which had been committed, and in his heart-sickness he would not deny the charge. As he was led through the streets to be executed, his friend, in passing, recognized him, and, on learning the facts of the case, insisted that he himself was the murderer, in the hope of saving his friend. Then came the conflict of friendship,—each friend seeking to die in the other's stead, until the real murderer, moved by this scene, came forward to confess the deed, and so to save them both.

Down in Southern Africa, one of the folk-lore tales of the negroes is not unlike this story in its purport. A rich man finding that one of his wives is in love with his own dearest friend, who is a poor man, makes a pretense of quarreling with that wife, in order to drive her from his home so that his friend may marry her—without any conflict in his feelings of friendship. Then her first husband makes generous gifts to his friend, in evidence of his unbroken friendship with him, and as a help to his and her happiness. When a son is born of this new marriage, the father is told that nothing short of the sacrifice of this son will avail to save his self-denying friend. This sacrifice is willingly assented to, and for seven years the father supposes that his loved son is dead. Never once, meanwhile, does he mention his loss, nor yet does his love for his friend ever fail or waver. But his friendship, also, having thus been tested, his son is finally restored to him, to his great rejoicing. "This is the old widely spread saga," says Grimm, "told, in so many different forms, of the two faithful friends who reciprocally sacrifice what they hold dearest." Another phase of this same story appears in Arabia, another in Scandinavia, and yet another in the old English legends. In every instance a husband and a father is ready to give up his own and only son in order to save the life of an imperiled friend.

There is another folk-lore story in Africa, of a Muhammadan imâm and his heathen friend, who journeyed together toward Mekka. The imâm broke friendship with his friend, the heathen was faithful in his friendship. On reaching Mekka, the heathen was admitted to the Holy House, and the imâm, because of his unfaithfulness in friendship, was excluded. These two men died on the same day. The earth refused a grave to the imâm, and Paradise was shut against him. The heathen who had been true as a friend found a grave for his body and a heaven for his soul.

Out of the collection of European folk-lore tales known as the *Gesta Romanorum*, there is the legend of a king's son who thought he had three friends, the first of whom he loved better than himself, the second as well as himself, and the third little or none. At his father's suggestion he put their friendship to the test by assuming to be in danger of crucifixion because of having killed a man by accident; and he asked them, one by one, for their assistance in his dilemma. The first coolly proffered him the needful cloth for wrapping his dead body in. The second more tenderly expressed a willingness to be near him as a comforter until his death. The third was prompt and earnest to say he would gladly die for him if he could, or else he would die with him.

An Icelandic folk-lore tale tells of Gunnar and Njal,

two loyal friends, who were so true to each other that, when their wives quarreled, the husbands would not consent to be separated on account of them, but "their friendship only grew the closer for the contentions of their women." When one of Njal's kinsmen was killed by a member of Gunnar's household, Njal would not have the deed avenged on Gunnar's people, but settled the matter by "blood money." When Gunnar was in want, in time of famine, Njal sent him food in abundance, as "a friend's gift to a friend." Gunnar's response to Njal was: "Good are thy gifts, but better than all gifts is thy friendship." Because those two friends would be true to each other in spite of the quarrels of their wives and their kinsfolk, first Gunnar lost his life, and then Njal was burned to death in defense of his sons and their friend, in a quarrel that had its origin in the quarrel of the wives of Gunnar and Njal. The friendship was proof against all trials, even unto death.

In the folk-lore stories of the poor Eskimo, hardly any phase of personal fidelity is more prominent than that shown in a persistent and affectionate confiding in a friend who is untrustworthy and false. Again and again the story is there told of a man who was betrayed by his friend, yet who would love that friend unswervingly, in spite of every experience of his faithlessness, and in defiance of all the dangers of such a misapplied confiding. There, as everywhere, it is not the *gain* of being true and of trusting, but it is the instinctive impulse to be true and trustful, that sways the friend in his friendship.

Even with the world's imperfect standard as it is, there is an ideal conception of the beauty of self-abnegating fidelity. "All praise the faithful friend," is the testimony of an eminent folk-lore gatherer. "All praise to the faithful friend!" responds the world.

And thus along the centuries and out of every clime! From the torrid wastes of Sahara to the frozen peaks of Iceland, from the ancient seat of empire in the far East to the unsettled prairies of the still receding West, there sounds one voice of sense and sentiment, instinctive or inspired. Egyptian seer, and Hebrew lawgiver, and Greek philosopher, and Roman scholar, and Christian apostle, and Chinese sage, and Persian mystic, and Hindoo devotee, and Arab enthusiast, and Russian doubter, and German schoolman, and French skeptic, and Italian dreamer, and Spanish romancist, and Swiss theologian, and Norseland bard, and English and American essayist and poet, and every primitive teller of folk-lore tales from pole to pole,—all are at one in their emphatic testimony to the surpassing preciousness of the unselfish love and the unswerving fidelity of a human friend.

"What a thing friendship is, world without end!"

GAINFULLY EXPENSIVE.

HILE friendship is by its very nature unselfish and out-going, friendship is also by its very nature a constant gainer through its loving expenditure of self. It receives by its outlay.

"Friendship renders prosperity more brilliant, while it lightens adversity by sharing it and making its burden common." It was Cicero who popularized this thought; although he re-phrased it from Euripides, and again it is cited in substance among the sayings of Confucius. Whoever may have first given currency to this idea, it has come down through the ages as the accepted epitome of the advantages of the expensive and remunerative relation of friendship.

"This communicating of a man's self to his friend," says Bacon, "works two contrary effects; for it redoubleth joys, and cutteth griefs in halves. For there is no man that imparteth his joys to his friend, but he joyeth the more; and no man that imparteth his griefs to his friend, but he grieveth the less." Jeremy Taylor gives, as usual, an added finish to this figure, when he says: "A friend shares my sorrow and makes it but a moiety; but he swells my joy and makes it double. For so two channels divide the river and lessen it into rivulets, and make it fordable and apt to be drunk up at the first revels of the Sirian star; but two torches do not divide, but increase, the flame: and though my tears are the sooner dried up when they run upon my friend's cheeks in the furrows of compassion, yet when my flame hath kindled his lamp we unite the glories, and make them radiant like the golden candlesticks that burn before the throne of God, because they shine by numbers, by unions and confederations of light and joy."

So often and so earnestly has this truth of the incidental gain of a mutual friendship been urged in poetry and in prose, that many have recognized in its affirmations an inducement to friendship. But just so soon as a friendship is sought for its reward, that friendship falls short of being the friendship which has this reward. In all holiest service of love the truth remains, that "whosoever shall seek to gain his life shall lose it: but whosoever shall lose his life shall preserve it." Friendship brings its largest returns to him who asks no return, but who lavishes love without a thought of gain.

Friendship is indeed profitable to him who exercises it, but its profit is in proportion to its expensiveness; and the expensiveness of friendship is cumulative and ceaseless. He, therefore, who would fain have the gains of friendship, may well ask himself if he is willing to make the necessary outlay of friendship. "Grant unto

Gainfully Expensive.   89

us," asked two of the friends of Jesus, "that we may sit, one on thy right hand, and one on thy left hand, in thy glory. But Jesus said unto them, Ye know not what ye ask. Are ye able to drink the cup that I drink? or to be baptized with the baptism that I am baptized with?" Many a longing one since the days of John and James has wished for the returns of a loving devotedness without counting the countless cost of such devotion.

> "All like the purchase; few the price will pay:
> And this makes friends such miracles below."

"Ye canna' be a guid freen' ohne peyin' for't," is a Scotch proverb with a truth for all peoples. The outlay in a real friendship's cost is threefold: an outlay in self-surrender; an outlay in suffering for one's friend; an outlay in suffering from one's friend; and these three items of outlay are expensive and remunerating in the order of their naming.

Only through an unfailing forgetfulness of self is friendship a possibility; and self-forgetfulness is an expensive virtue. Publius Syrus said: "Enmity costs less than affection;" that is, there is no such outlay involved in the disregarding of others as in giving to others loving service. This is unmistakably true; but it is also true that affection gains more than enmity, and that there is no such personal advantage in loving only one's self as in loving another above one's self.

He who is a friend suffers with his friend because he is his friend. No suffering on one's own account can, indeed, be such a grievous trial to a friend as the suffering he endures when the one whom he loves best is a sufferer. He inevitably shares the burden of that suffering, and he would be glad if he could bear it wholly. Now the sharing, or, what is more, the bearing and engrossing, another's griefs and trials, demands a larger outlay of sympathy and of strength in endurance than is called for in carrying only one's personal sorrows; yet this very outlay is its own return accordingly, enlarging and strengthening the heart which it taxes.

This certainty of an increased outlay of heart's blood through the demands of an unselfish affection it is that prompted the selfish maxim of the icy-hearted Booddha: "Let, therefore, no man love anything; loss of the beloved is evil. Those who love nothing and hate nothing have no fetters." And it is in answer to this disloyal cry of the self-insulating soul, that our Christian laureate rings back the rejoinder:

> "I hold it true, whate'er befall;
> I feel it when I sorrow most;
> 'Tis better to have loved and lost
> Than never to have loved at all."

In no realm is it truer than in the realm of the affections that "it is more blessed to give than to receive;" and it is in illustration and in proof of this primal principle that in that outlay of self which makes one a friend there is gained that income of added capability of friendship, which, after all, is the chiefest reward of being a friend.

The uttermost outlay of an unselfish friendship is, however, liable to be in the loving endurance of suffering from a friend. And nothing better proves, or more surely advantages, a true friendship, than this willing outlay of self, when the need exists, under the inflictions of pain,—

unkind, thoughtless, or all unconscious, as they may be, —on the part of the one loved. The very capacity for an absolutely unselfish affection includes a keen sensitiveness in the direction of that affection; and no love is more liable to misconception—through its very absence of apparent motive—than a love that is without limit or claim or craving. Hence no one can so deeply wound a true friend as the one to whom a person is a true friend.

"The Autocrat of the Breakfast Table" tells of the side door of the heart which enters at once into the secret chambers of one's being, and of the peril of trusting a key to that door to any loved one. "Be very careful to whom you trust one of these keys of the side door," he says. "The fact of possessing one renders those even who are dear to you very terrible at times. . . . Some of them have a scale of your whole nervous system, and can play all the gamut of your sensibilities in semitones,—touching the naked nerve-pulps as a pianist strikes his instrument. . . . No stranger can get a great many notes of torture out of a human soul; it takes one that knows it well." Susan Coolidge phrases this same thought more seriously:

> "Roses have thorns; and love is thorny too;
> And this is love's sharp thorn which guards its flower,—
> That our belovèd have the cruel power
> To hurt us deeper than all others do.
>
> "The heart attuned to our heart like a charm,
> Beat answering beat, as echo answers song,—
> If the throb falter, or the pulse beat wrong,
> How shall it fail to grieve us or to harm?"

That there is in the truest friendship a possible call to

this outlay of suffering from a friend's fault or a friend's failure, or from some mutual misunderstanding, is obvious because of the human imperfectness of both the loving and the loved; yet it is also evident that, because a true friendship is in its essence unselfish and unswerving love, therefore the larger the outlay of necessary unselfish performance, or of necessary unselfish endurance, in a friendship, the larger the subjective results of that friendship in the enlarged and ever-enlarging heart that thus loves and does and endures unselfishly.

What if one must generously give himself in love for a friend, in suffering with a friend, and in endurance from a friend:

> "A friend is worth all hazards we can run.
> Poor is the friendless master of a world:
> A world in purchase of a friend is gain."

LIMITATIONS AND IMITATIONS.

N affection that transcends all loves, and that has ever commanded the highest honor among men, must, inevitably, have its limitations and its imitations. Its limitations will be found in the restricted possibilities of the individual whom it sways, while its imitations are a result of the widespread desire for its supposed advantages.

He who is capable of friendship at its best, cannot be a true friend alike to all. The very intensity of this sentiment demands a positive limit to the extension of its scope. And, on the other hand, many a person who tells of his "host of friends," or of her

"Dear five hundred friends,"

never had, nor ever could be, a friend in the truest sense. The most unselfish and expensive of human affections cannot be for all, or from all, alike. Its exacting demands fix its limitations, its recognized attractiveness multiplies its imitations.

The highest conceivable attainment of a personal friendship is a union of two souls through a mutuality of affection. Such a union is, indeed, an incidental result of the conjunction of two friendships, rather than the primitive aim of either of the two; but it is obvious that a union of this sort is inevitably limited to one person on either side. More than two cannot be one, as two can be.

The suggestion of this truth is found in the words of Moses concerning "thy friend who is as thine own self." It is recognized as a truth of the ages by Aristotle, when he cites as a proverbial symbol of friendship the term, "one soul in two bodies." St. Augustine has it in mind as he tells of a friend who has been taken from him: "I thought that my soul and his were but one soul in two bodies: and therefore [at his death] I loathed life because I was unwilling to live by halves."

Montaigne seems to have been reading both Aristotle and St. Augustine, when he writes of the soul-union illustrated in his relation with his friend: "In the friendship I speak of, the souls mix and work themselves into one piece with so perfect a mixture that there is no more sign of a seam by which they were first conjoined. . . . The union of such friends, being really perfect, deprives them of all acknowledgment of mutual duties [love being the fulfilling of the law], and makes them loathe and banish from their conversation words of separation, distinction, benefit, obligation, acknowledgment, entreaty, thanks, and the like; all things—wills, thoughts, opinions, goods, wives, children, honors, and lives—being in effect common between them; and that absolute concurrence of affections being no other than one soul in two bodies

Limitations and Imitations. 95

(according to that very proper definition of Aristotle), they can neither lend nor give anything to one another."

Dryden had evidently been reading Montaigne, and so gaining lessons from St. Augustine and Aristotle at second hand, when, in his "All for Love," he made Mark Antony tell of his union with his then missing and sorely lamented friend, Dolabella:

> "I was his soul; he lived not but in me:
> We were so closed within each other's breasts,
> The rivets were not found that joined us first,
> That did not reach as yet. We were so mixed
> As meeting streams, both to ourselves were lost.
> We were one mass; we could not give or take
> But from the same; for he was I, I he."

It is in joyous appreciation of the interunion of his soul and the soul of his "dear friend," that Shakespeare confesses his inability to divide that united self, even for the purpose of sounding his friend's just praises:

> "Oh! how thy worth with manners may I sing
> When thou art all the better part of me?
> What can mine own praise to mine own self bring?
> And what is't but mine own, when I praise thee?"

Even the devout Jeremy Taylor, while insisting that the New Testament idea of friendship is that "charity," or "love," which in its fullest exercise would take in all mankind, recognizes the truth that in its practical application, within the sphere of our being, "this universal friendship . . . must be limited, because we are so;" and that while we should be "friendly" toward all, "all cannot be admitted to a special actual friendship" in our affections. And his conclusion is, that Christianity justifies the Christian in choosing as a friend "the bravest, the worthiest, and the most excellent person" to be found.

In the very nature of things a true man cannot give the homage of his truest self except to one who commands his love and confidence in a unique degree; and this fact marks both the limitation and the grace of the supremest friendship. The gradations and limitations of friendship's power are forcefully outlined in this illustration of John Foster's: "One is not one's 'genuine self'—one does not disclose all one's self—to those with whom one has no intimate sympathy. One is, therefore, several successive and apparently different characters, according to the gradation of the faculties and the qualities of those one associates with. I am like one of those boxes I have seen enclosing several boxes of similar form though lessening size. The person with whom I have least congeniality sees only the outermost. Another person has something more interesting in his character: he sees the next box. Another sees still an inner one. But the friend of my heart, with whom I have full sympathy, sees the innermost of all."

It is in this very limitation of the truest friendship that the truest friendship finds its transcendent and unique power. "There can never be deep peace between two spirits," says Emerson, "never mutual respect, until in their dialogue each stands for the whole world." So it is that Tennyson, mourning his one friend, finds himself wholly friend-bereft:

"And unto me no second friend."

Limitations and Imitations. 97

Browning's Abbe seems to have this thought also, when he exclaims concerning the varying grades of human affection:

> "The love which to one and one only has reference
> Seems terribly like what perhaps gains God's preference."

There is a popular tendency to confound "friendship" with "friendliness;" to think of that quality of friendliness which makes its possessor prompt to show a kindly, tender, and sympathetic interest in his fellows generally, as in some way akin to, or a phase of, that unselfish outgoing of the whole soul to another, in a ceaseless and unswerving affection, which alone is worthy of the name of friendship. But friendliness and friendship are separate and distinct attitudes of being. Friendliness may be exercised by one person toward a hundred, or a thousand, others alike. Friendship is in its very nature exceptional, and can find its exercise only toward those personalities to which for some reason it gives a pre-eminence. Cicero goes so far as to say that "scarcely in the history of the world are three or four pairs of friends mentioned by name;" and, even before the days of Cicero, the Chinese had it for a maxim: "There are plenty of acquaintances in the world, but very few real friends."

Aristotle recognizes the limitations and imitations of true friendship in his discrimination between friendship and friendliness or good-will. "Friendliness resembles friendship," he says, "and yet it is not friendship." Friendliness may, indeed, "be the beginning of friendship, in the same manner that the pleasure derived from sight is the beginning of love: for no one feels love unless he is first pleased with personal appearance; but he who takes pleasure in the personal appearance is not necessarily in love. . . . Similarly, also, it is impossible to be friends without friendliness; but those who have friendliness are not necessarily friends. . . . Hence, one might call friendliness, metaphorically speaking, friendship in a state of inactivity." That friendliness is, at the best, only an imitation of friendship, is suggested by Aristotle when he says: "Those who have many friends and are friendly with everybody, are by none thought to be their friend, except in a social sense; and they are reckoned mere men-pleasers." And as to the limitations of friendship, Aristotle says: "It is not possible to be a friend to many men, on the footing of the perfect kind of friendship."

It is true that Aristotle has been quoted as saying, "O my friends! there are no friends." But this is a misquotation, which seems to have grown out of the error of a copyist in an early edition of "The Lives of the Philosophers," by Diogenes Laertius, continued in a series of editions, but corrected in the later ones. This error has come down to us in the literature of friendship, through Montaigne and others. The saying of Aristotle thus misquoted, is in the seventh book of his Ethics: "He who has many friends has no friend,"—a very different suggestion from that in the words "There are no friends."

Inspired wisdom is at one with speculative philosophy and poetic sentiment, in recognition of the contrast between friendship in its limitations, and friendliness with its imitations of friendship. Yet even here the popular English mind has manifested its confusion over this line

Limitations and Imitations. 99

of distinction, in the translations of the Hebrew words distinguishing the two relations.

For example, at Proverbs 18 : 24 our common English version has long read :

> "A man that hath friends must show himself friendly :
> And there is a friend that sticketh closer than a brother."

The ordinary understanding of this has been, that a man who would have the benefits of friendship must exhibit the quality of friendliness; and that out of many friends won in this way he may find one or more of rare lovableness and fidelity. In the Revised Version, however, this passage is rendered :

> "He that maketh many friends doeth it to his own destruction :
> But there is a friend that sticketh closer than a brother."

The meaning here clearly is, that friendship with no limitations cannot have the gain of true friendship, while a true friendship within due limitations is the safest of all relations.

Even this new translation fails to bring out the distinction between friendliness and friendship as it is indicated in the original Hebrew. In the one case the word translated "friend" is *rē'a*, meaning "neighbor,"—our adjacent fellow-being, whom we must love as ourselves, against whom we must never bear false witness, and whose possessions we must not covet. In the other case, the word translated "friend" is *ōhēbh*, "one who loves." The one term suggests a nearness of body; the other, a nearness of soul. The passage might, indeed, be rendered :

> "He that seeketh many companions, doeth it to his own destruction:
> But there is a friend that sticketh closer than a brother."

It is a pity that the distinction between these two Hebrew terms is not brought out more clearly, in our English Bible, in such a way as to show that friendliness is quite another thing from friendship; for the Bible itself is too true to nature to ignore this fact. In one instance, at least, the translators have felt compelled to recognize this distinction, which shows itself in the Hebrew all through the Old Testament. David says (Psa. 38 : 11):

> "My friends [*ŏhabheem*] and my neighbors [*rē'eem*] stand aloof from my plague."

Here our common English version reads:

> "My *lovers* and my *friends* stand aloof from my sore."

A similar distinction is made at Psalm 88 : 18 :

> "*Lover* and *friend* hast thou put far from me."

And so it might be all along the Bible text; for a real friend is always a lover, whereas a neighbor may be friendly to-day and unfriendly to-morrow. Job's three "friends," by the way, were "neighbors," not "lovers."

The Apocrypha sounds its warnings against the self-interested imitations of friendship:

> "Those living at peace with thee, let them be many;
> But thy counselors, one of a thousand.
> If thou wouldst get a friend, get him through testing,
> And be not hasty to trust in him.
> For many a one is friend in a time opportune for him,
> And will not abide in the day of thy affliction.
> And there is many a friend who is transformed into
>   an enemy,

> And will reveal thy disgraceful strife.
> And many a one is friend as companion at table,
> And will not abide in the day of thy affliction.
> Yea, in thy prosperity he will be as thyself,
> And will speak roughly to thy servants.
> If thou be brought low he will be against thee,
> And will hide himself from thy face.
> Separate thyself from thine enemies,
> And be wary of thy friends."

It is this teaching of the Son of Sirach that gives the suggestion of Claude Mermet's epigram:

> "Friends are like melons. Shall I tell you why?
> To find one good you must a hundred try."

And the world's experiences bear witness to its central truth that the imitations of friendship are as numerous as its highest attainment is rare.

Let it not be supposed, however, that the essential limitations of the loftiest friendship restrict the possibilities of the most sincere and attractive friendliness, toward others near or remote, on the part of him who is a true friend at the highest and best toward one above all. A real friendship is uplifting and expanding, taking him who is the friend away from himself, and opening his heart in a generous love beyond the possibility of its closing or cramping. He, indeed, who is capable of the loftiest friendship, can easiest attain to the loftiest standard of affection in every relation in life,—as husband, father, son, brother, or neighbor. The love that reaches to the highest is not likely to come short of any mark below the highest; and a love that is intensest at its focal center will glow with exceptional warmth from that center toward the extremest circumference. "Oh! love one heart purely and warmly," says Jean Paul Richter; "then thou lovest all hearts after it; and thy heart in its heaven sees, like the journeying sun, in all that it looks upon—from the dew-drop even to the ocean—nothing but mirrors which it warms and fills."

The limitations of friendship are in the possibilities of our nature to center our profoundest affections on an object that is capable of calling them forth at their best. The imitations of friendship are in those affiliations and alliances that depend upon personal interest, or personal convenience, or personal fancy, and that change with changes in the parties to them, as a true friendship does not.

But between the poorer imitations of a friendship, and a friendship at its highest and best, with its essential limitations in that sphere, there are gradations of genuine and joy-giving friendship. Even he who knows the fullest joy of soul-union with a true and congenial friend is sure to have that spirit of sympathetic friendliness which will cause him to be rightly counted as a friend by many; and some of his minor friendships are likely to be so hearty and so generous that only he and one other will ever know that the difference between his one realest friendship and all his other friendships is a difference in kind instead of a difference in degree.

He, moreover, who has never realized the measure of the highest friendship, and to whom, by his very nature, such a measure of friendship is unattainable, may find a delight and an inspiration in the measure of friendship he does exercise, such as he gains by no other means of

Limitations and Imitations. 103

enjoyment and uplifting. And if such a man be unable to apprehend the absolute ideal of a transcendent friendship, he can at least be advantaged by his partial conceptions of an unselfish affection, toward which he strives in all his friendships and his friendlinesses.

While, as Solomon suggests, there is danger in an indiscriminate seeking of personal intimacies, there is a correspondent safeguard in the affection of hearts won through an unfailing friendliness of spirit. As the Oriental proverb has it:

> "He who has a thousand friends has not a friend to spare,
> And he who has one enemy will meet him everywhere."

"The more we love, the better we are," says Jeremy Taylor; "and the greater our friendships are, the dearer we are to God." And Wordsworth's counsel to a child is:

> "Of humblest friends, bright Creature! scorn not one."

There are hearts, however, which, while never realizing the highest friendship in its limitations, would never be satisfied with the imitations of friendship. We live in a world where not every precious seed comes to full fruition. Some falls where there is not much earth, and its up-starting blades wither away from lack of soil-nourishment; some springs up only to have its new life choked out by the crowding thorns of the exacting world; yet other is trodden under foot by the careless passer along the way. And so it is that all the possibilities of a high and ennobling friendship are sometimes missed through lack of opportunity of their fostering, through the crushing force of misunderstandings, or through the misrepresentations of outside parties; causing those who might have been the best and truest of friends to live without even the advantages of unbroken friendliness.

> "A word unspoken, a hand unpressed,
> A look unseen, or a thought unguessed;
> And souls that were kindred may live apart,
> Never to meet or to know the truth;
> Never to know how heart beat with heart,
> In the dim past days of a wasted youth."

Yet no love is ever wasted; least of all can there be waste or loss in the love of an unselfish friendship. He whose heart swells or thrills with such a love, even while it aches with a sense of its misconception or its non-recognition, is himself the sure and permanent gainer from his loving; whether his friendship be known as a friendship at its best with its essential limitations, or be looked upon by all as only one of the imitations of friendship.

WHO CAN BE FRIENDS?

BY whom are the privileges and possibilities of this highest and purest of human relations, this unselfish, ever-outgoing, reverent and transcendent affection, attainable? Who can be real friends, knowing the joy and sharing the gains of the best and truest friendship with all its limitations, and in contrast with its imitations? Must friends be only of the one sex, or only of the other? or can they be of either or both? Is friendship at its highest necessarily limited to those who are not united by the ties of blood or marriage? or can it co-exist in its fulness with any and every sacred relation? These are questions which press themselves on the heart and thought, and in the answer of which there would hardly be an instant agreement among all.

Since the truest friendship is the purest and most unselfish love, it follows that whoever is capable of such a love is capable of friendship. And those who love each other with such a love are friends, whatever be the barriers between them, or whatever human relation be a bond of their union.

Between man and man, all admit the possibility of the highest friendship. It is there that friendship has found its most notable historic and traditional illustrations. It is David and Jonathan, Orestes and Pylades, Damon and Pythias, Epaminondas and Pelopidas, Alexander and Hephæstion, Horace and Virgil, Pamphilus and Eusebius, Muhammad and Aboo Bekr, Roland and Oliver, Godfrey and Tancred, St. Thomas Aquinas and St. Bonaventura, Erasmus and Colet, Luther and Melancthon, Sir Philip Sidney and Lord Brooke, Hampden and Pym, William of Orange and William Bentinck, Goethe and Schiller, Alfred Tennyson and Arthur Hallam. Few, again, would now question the reality of exalted and abiding friendship between woman and woman; although classic writers were not always willing to admit its possibility, and many modern writers have adhered to the classic skepticism on this point. There is no more beautiful example of a self-forgetful and devoted friendship than that of Ruth and Naomi; and in many an instance since their day, two women have been to each other dearer far than sisters. In the very nature of things the closest friendships of women are less prominent to the world's eye than the friendships of men; but history has noted such illustrious examples as Queen Philippa and Philippa Picard, Mary Queen of Scots and Mary Seton, Queen Anne and the Duchess of Marlborough, Mme. de Staël and Mme. Récamier, Lady Dorothea Sydney and Lady Sophy Murray, Catharine Talbot and Elizabeth Carter, Lady Eleanor Butler and Miss Sarah Ponsonby,—known as "the Ladies of Llangollen,"—Katherine Philips and Annie Owen, and others also:

> "For men have known
> No firmer friendships than the fair have shown."

But because true friendship is love with the element of selfishness eliminated, because it is love apart from any relation which involves possession or the craving of possession, for that very reason friendship has found some of its choicest, its most refined, and its most unmistakable, illustrations between two persons of opposite sexes. And just here the truth in its purity has had most difficulty of securing acceptance, in consequence of the weakness and folly and wickedness of the world. Yet everywhere and always at this point the truth has had its recognition and its inspiring power in the hearts of the noblest and the most nobly aspiring of the children of men.

In the far East, where woman has so generally occupied a lower plane in the opinions and estimates of man, and where the very marriage-bond has failed to give her equality by the side of him who has chosen her as his companion,—even there the most sacred, tender, and inviolable friendships between man and woman have been attained, and have commanded honor and admiration, in all the ages.

In India such friendships are often sealed by the gift from the woman of a bracelet, which the man acknowledges by some appropriate gift in return. Life itself is of small account in comparison with this tie, in India, when once it is recognized; and even religion is not more reverently guarded there. Yet in this relation either party or both parties may be married or be single, as circumstances shall ordain, and years perhaps will pass without either seeing the other.

In Arabia, with all the jealous separation of the sexes, men and women have become one in the bond of holy friendship by sharing each other's blood; and in such a case marriage would be deemed incest,—hence the relation is of the purest and most unselfish nature. A similar state of facts is found in some portions of Africa; and there, as elsewhere, the tie of friendship thus formed between persons of the two sexes transcends all other ties in its abiding and hallowed nobleness.

The pre-eminent beauty and purity of such a friendship as this between man and woman underlay the philosophy of the truth-loving Plato, in his treatment of a possible affection uniting them without the weaknesses, or the self-seeking element, of ordinary loves. It would be a pity indeed if Christianity—in which "there is neither male nor female" as such—gave no instance of as pure and refined a love between men and women whose interests were not made identical in holy marriage, as was pointed out in pagan philosophy, and as is still realized among the primitive peoples of Africa and Asia. Nor has there been any lack of proof that Christianity represents the highest and holiest standard in this realm also of practical ethics.

Prominent in the records of the early Christian Church stand out the hearty and devoted personal friendships of St. Jerome and Paula, St. Chrysostom and Olympias, of St. Ambrose and Monica, and of others hardly less illustrious. So all the way down along the later centuries, even the cynic and the scoffer have had words of admiring approval for such friendships of this nature as those of St. Francis of Assisi and St. Clare, Michael Angelo and Vittoria Colonna, John Locke and Lady Masham, Dr. Johnson and Mrs. Thrale, William Cowper and Mary Unwin, Fenelon and Mme. Guion, Wilhelm von Humboldt and Charlotte Diede, Lacordaire and Mme. Swetchine, and many like these in every land, which have furnished illustration of the truth that no love is truer, and none more tender, more abiding, or more admirable, than a sacred sexless friendship.

While friendship is not the love which is an immediate outgrowth of, or which necessarily pivots on, a relation by kinship or by marriage, such a relation is certainly no barrier to the existence of that unselfish and sexless love which is the essence of the truest and purest friendship. Brothers and sisters are not friends merely by loving each other as brothers and sisters; but they can be friends over and above, if not on account of, their fraternal relationship. So with parents and children, with husbands and wives, with lovers and loved ones,—friendship is possible between them; but that friendship must ever be a measure of love over and above that love which is of the relation that formally binds them to each other. No love can fairly be counted the love which is friendship, unless it could exist at its fullest and best either with or without the binding force of any other relation than simple friendship.

History abounds with illustrations, actual and mythical, of close friendships within the various relations formed by family alliance. Castor and Pollux are not only brothers by birth; they are more than brothers in friendship. If

Castor must die, immortality is no joy to Pollux. So essential is each friend to the other, that the gods permit them to share each other's destiny, dying and reviving day by day, in turn; and their prominence in the heavenly constellations is as the twins by friendship, not as the twins by birth. The two Scipios and the two Gracchi are friends as well as brothers, and the loving friendship of Publius Rutilius and his brother is given special prominence in the writings of Pliny.

In a noteworthy monograph on "Friendships of Women," W. R. Alger has brought together many examples of memorable friendships between mothers and sons, between daughters and fathers, between sisters and brothers, between mothers and daughters, between sisters, and between wives and husbands; as well as between women and men, and women and women, whose bond of closest friendship was their only common bond. St. Augustine and his mother, St. Monica; Cicero and his daughter Tullia; George Herbert and his mother, Lady Magdalen; Mme. de Sévigné and her daughter, Mme. de Grignan; Mme. de Staël and her father, M. Necker; Mme. Guizot and her illustrious son, Francois Pierre Guillaume; Mrs. Hemans and her mother, Mrs. Browne; Richard Edgeworth and his daughter Maria; Sara Coleridge and her daughter Sara; Aaron Burr and his daughter Theodosia, —are instances of friendship between parents and children whose "kinship becomes friendship," and in whom "the relative is hidden in the friend."

Apollo and Diana, like Castor and Pollux, are twins in friendship as well as twins by birth; and Orestes and Electra stand out in their companionship as loving friends rather than in their dutifulness as brother and sister. The joint canonization of St. Benedict and St. Scholastica bears even more emphatic witness to the love which united them in a sacred friendship than to the tie which had bound them through their birth from the same mother. And how many brothers and sisters have gained a higher plane and a nobler place through their becoming friends! Bishop Burnet said of Catherine, Countess of Ranelagh, and her brother Robert Boyle, the eminent experimental philosopher: "Such a sister became such a brother; and it was but suitable to both their characters, that they should have improved the relation under which they were born, to the more exalted and endearing one of *friend*." And a similar record of progress from mere fraternal affection to the truest and most devoted friendship might be made of Philip and Mary Sidney, of William and Caroline Herschel, of Ernest and Charlotte Schleiermacher, of Felix and Fanny Mendelssohn, of Charles and Mary Lamb, of William and Dorothy Wordsworth, and of many another well-known and affectionate brother and sister; or again of devoted sisters, such as Hannah and Martha More, or Charlotte, Anne, and Emily Brontë.

If a husband be truly the friend of his wife,—as he ought to be,—his love for her as a friend could be just as strong, just as tender, just as permanent and unswerving, if she were not his wife nor ever might be. It is such a friendship as this which gives a superadded joy—in its then abounding opportunities and unhindered privileges of freest expression—to the rarest blessings attainable in the closest and holiest of all human companionships.

A gleam of such wedded friendship would seem to

show itself in the records of Mausolus and Artemisia, of Shah Jehan and Nour Jehan, of Seneca and Paulina, of Giambattista Zappi and Faustina Maratti, of M. and Mme. Roland, of Julius Mohl and Mary Clarke, of Herder and his Caroline, of John and Lucy Hutchinson, of John Flaxman and Ann Denman, of Sir William and Lady Hamilton, of Baron Bunsen and Frances Waddington, of Earl and Lady Beaconsfield, of John Stuart Mill and Mrs. Taylor, of Charles Kingsley and Fanny Grenfell, of Robert Browning and Elizabeth Barrett, of William Ewart Gladstone and Catherine Glynne, and of many another "happy couple . . . making one life double, because they made a double life one."

Wilhelm von Humboldt was a model friend as a friend, in his constancy and unswerving attachment. And this spirit of friendship showed itself in his married life as well as in his other spheres of affection. "When he had attained the certainty that Caroline von Dacheröden was to be his wife," says his biographer, "he immediately made the vow to make her happy under any circumstances;" not to seek his own happiness, nor yet to seek the mutual happiness of the two, but to live for her happiness, as her true friend. "He never forgot this vow during his whole life, and fulfilled it faithfully to the best of his ability." When, soon after his marriage, his wife's life was in imminent peril, he deliberately purposed suicide, and "gave as a reason for his suicidal purpose, that he could not tell whether the beloved one might not stand in need of him in the future life." Not that he must seek her society for his own sake, in another world, but that he must be at hand in the hope of yet serving her there.

She recovered, however, and "during the long years that his wife lived with him on earth, and constituted his greatest happiness, this zeal continued in every circumstance of life, to the complete negation and forgetfulness of self, sacrificing even privileges which would seem inseparable from such an excess of love." He was all the more a friend to his wife through being meanwhile so truly and purely a friend to a woman whom he knew before he was a lover or a husband.

A true friendship between a husband and a wife may precede the love which led to their marriage union, or, again, it may follow that love as the choicest of its incidental results; but whether it come earlier or later than mere wedded love as such, there, as everywhere, the love which is friendship transcends all other loves. Of the friendship which follows wedded love as the richest blessing of a marriage union, Chateaubriand, writing of the danger of a diminution of the power of love by "the fever of time, which produces lassitude, dissipates illusion, undermines our passions, withers our loves, and changes our hearts even as it changes our locks and years," says earnestly: "There is but one exception to this human infirmity. There sometimes occurs in a strong soul a love firm enough to transform itself into impassioned friendship, so as to become a duty, and appropriate the qualities of virtue. Then, neutralizing the weakness of nature, it acquires the immortality of a principle."

Of the friendship which precedes wedded love, and which shines transcendent through and above it, no better description is needed than that supplied in the graceful dedication to her husband, of a volume of her poems, by one who has written with a woman's tenderness and a woman's truth:

> "A year ago to-day, love, for the space
>   Of a brief, sudden moment, richly fraught
>   With deeper meaning than our light hearts thought,
> You held my hand and looked into the face
> Which, poor in gifts, has since by God's good grace
>   Grown dear to you; and the full year has brought
>   Friendship, and love, and marriage; yet has taught
> My heart to call you in its sacred place
> Still by the earliest name;—for you who are
>   My lover and my husband, and who bring
>   Heaven close around me, will not let me cling
> To that near heaven; but tempt my soul afar
>   By your ideals for me;—till life end,
>   My calm, dispassionate, sincerest *friend*." [1]

Wherever there is a pure and unselfish love for another for that other's own sake, a love contingent neither on its return nor on its recognition, *there* is a true friendship, whether there be any other relation than this between the loving and the loved, or not. Friendship is, in fact, distinct from even the choicest other relationship with which it may coexist.

[1] Alice Wellington Rollins.

II.

FRIENDSHIP IN HISTORY.

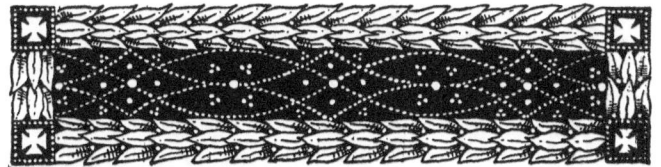

OF SURPASSING POTENCY.

HE world's history is the history of individuals whom God has used in the helping forward of the world's progress. Every epoch of history has its center in some man who, for the time being, is the embodiment of the mental and moral forces that are making and marking that epoch. And, back of the man who is the leader of men, there is always the special force of that sentiment which influences and impels him in the direction of his providential leading. Hence it follows that the sentiment which is most potent as a factor in man's best being and doing is most potent as a factor in the world's highest achieving and truest progress.

Ambition and avarice and love are known to have power over men in every field of human endeavor, and patriotism and religion are recognized as supreme incitements to self-denying efforts on the part of the children of men. But friendship is a sentiment that transcends all loves, and that represents the purest, the most self-abnegating, and the noblest affection, in a man's relations to his fellows, to his country, and to his God; and therefore the sentiment of friendship is, in its nature, of surpassing potency in swaying those persons who, in their generation, are enabled to sway the forces of the living world. It is the master-passion of humanity.

This is not a matter of unprovable theory; on the contrary, it is one capable of illustration and proof out of all the pages of human history. In the councils of state, in the clash of arms, in the molding of social customs, in the aspirations of religious endeavor, in the movements of civil reform, in the researches of philosophic thought, in the creations of literature and art, and in every other realm of thinking or doing, friendship has evidenced itself as an element of character-shaping and character-swaying, beyond any other sentiment or passion that shows itself as a factor in controlling and directing the human mind and heart.

Friendship has, in all ages, shown its power to restrain ambition, to hold avarice in check, to triumph over selfish love, to render more wisely effective the best instincts of patriotism, and to give increased purity and sacredness to religious thought and feeling and action. Friendship has had its strongest hold on those who were strongest, and has done its best work in the best natures. Not the base but the nobler, not the low but the lofty, not the dependent but the self-contained, in all spheres of life, seem to value most, and to be best fitted for, the gains and privileges and responsibilities of friendship. And therefore it is that friendship is most potent with those whose potency with others is greatest.

No new suggestion is this; it is a truth of the ages. "To the rich, and to those who possess office and authority," says Aristotle, "there seems to be an especial need of friends." Similarly Cicero affirms: "Just in proportion as a man has most confidence in himself, and as he is most completely fortified by worth and wisdom, so that he needs no one's assistance, and feels that all his resources reside in himself,—in the same proportion is he most highly distinguished for seeking out and forming friendships." Of the upward outlook that promotes the exercise of this sentiment, Jean Paul Richter says earnestly: "When man stands before the sea, and on mountains, and before pyramids and ruins, and in the presence of misfortune, and feels himself exalted, then does he stretch out his arms after the great friendship."

And of the spirit and character that incline one to friendship, Sir Thomas Browne, acute observer of his fellows, says positively: "This noble affection falls not on vulgar and common constitutions, but on such as are marked for virtue;" similarly, the keen-witted La Bruyère declares: "Pure friendship is something which men of an inferior nature can never taste;" while great-hearted Charles Kingsley asseverates: "It is only the great-hearted who can be true friends: the mean and cowardly can never know what true friendship means." The possibilities and the needs of friendship are largest in the nature of those whose position and personal characters make them more influential over their fellows and over their surroundings.

In an effort to test the correctness of this estimate of

the lessons of history, it will obviously suffice to pass rapidly from mountain-peak to mountain-peak of the world's historic panorama, and to note in passing the personal friendships which had their share in uprearing or in capping those lofty summits. Such a survey is now to be attempted; and the claim is confidently made that it will disclose unmistakably the surpassing potency of human friendship in the world's essential forces.

INFLUENCING ROYALTY.

KINGS are raised above their fellow-men, but they cannot be raised above their own manhood. And while a king is a man, a king cannot but find a joy and a gain in loving and being loved. Having so many under him, a king must crave the privilege of having at least one alongside of him, or one to whom he may in some sense look up. Accustomed to expect everything that he longs for, a king will seek some means of gratifying his instinctive desire for disinterested fellowship and sympathy.

Bacon, dwelling upon the help and comfort of freely opening one's heart to a friend, points out the fact that royalty is peculiarly ready to avail itself of this privilege. "It is a strange thing to observe," he says, "how high a rate great kings and monarchs do set upon this fruit of friendship: . . . so great as they purchase it, many times, at the hazard of their own safety and greatness. For princes, in regard of the distance of their fortune from that of their subjects and servants, cannot gather this fruit except (to make themselves capable thereof) they raise some persons to be, as it were, companions and almost equals to themselves; which, many times, sorteth to inconvenience." And the world's history abounds in illustrations of the truth thus hinted at by Bacon.

Earliest among the kings mentioned in the Bible record is Nimrod, ruler of a kingdom in the "Land of Shinar." Prominent among the recovered traditions of ancient Babylonia is the story of King Izdubar, identified by many with the Nimrod of Bible history. And the story of this primeval king is the story of a king seeking, finding, rejoicing in, and afterwards mourning over, a loved and loving friend. Izdubar was in need of counsel. He had heard of Eabani, famed for his wisdom and worth. Izdubar sought Eabani, who was living a hermit life in the wilderness. After repeated trials, and through heroic struggles, Izdubar secured Eabani as a friend; and the two entered into a covenant of eternal brotherhood, under the third sign of the Zodiac,—thenceforward known as the *Gemini*, the brother-friends. In the bonds of a sacred friendship, Izdubar and Eabani wrought deeds of valor and prowess that lifted their names high above their fellows; and together they were in conflict with enemies celestial and terrestrial. But death came to Eabani, and his mourning friend Izdubar could not be comforted, until, in pity for his grief, the god Ea brought back to him Eabani, in order that the friendship which had been so much to the king might be the king's forever. And thus, in the very earliest records of a kingly life among men, there is

Influencing Royalty.   123

the story, ever old and ever new, of the inspiring and pervasive power of a sacred friendship as a main factor in the aspirations and achievements of royalty. It is only, however, because we have no specific records of history prior to the days of Nimrod, that Nimrod, as Izdubar, is the earliest known sovereign-friend.

Ancient Egypt furnishes completer records of the remote past than are found outside of the Bible text. The most ancient of these records show us that the highest title known in the court of the Pharaohs was that of " The One Friend,"—a designation applied to the intimate and loved companion of the king, who was the sharer of his affection and confidence to an extent unknown in any other relation. The term "friend" was applied to quite a number of persons who held high position in the king's favor; but this term, "The One Friend," was confined to *one* who stood all by himself in loving union with the king. And "The One Friend" was nearer and dearer to the king than wife or parent, than prince or priest.

An inscription in a tomb at Abydos tells the story of Una, who was The One Friend of Pharaoh Merira Pepi, a king of the sixth dynasty, before the days of Abraham. This inscription is "one of the oldest historical texts known" and, like the earliest texts from Babylonia, it is the record of friendship's potency in the realm of royalty. Telling of his uplifting by the king's choice above all the servants and ministers and friends of the king, Una says, in this inscription : " It happened that my wisdom pleased his Majesty, and that also my zeal pleased his Majesty, and that also *the heart of his Majesty was satisfied with me.*" Una was even dearer to the king than the king's "great royal wife Amitsi," and when the latter came under suspicion, Una was commissioned by the king to go alone into the royal hareem, and ascertain the truth in the case, "because," again says Una, "*the heart of his Majesty was satisfied with me.*" In peace and in war, the king Merira leaned on and loved his one friend Una; and the glory of the king's reign corresponded with the fidelity of the king's friendship. Una was sure that there had never been anything like this before; although, as a matter of fact, it was just what had been, and what would be, simply because a king's heart is human, and, with sovereign as with subject, friendship transcends all loves.

There is, indeed, reason for believing that Joseph, the son of Jacob, was chosen as The One Friend of Pharaoh, when he was taken from the prison to the palace, long centuries after the days of Merira and Una. When Joseph had made clear to the king the interpretation of his dream, and had disclosed to him the secrets of the future, the heart of Pharaoh seemed to go out toward Joseph in trustful affection. "And Pharaoh said unto Joseph, Forasmuch as God hath shewed thee all this, there is none so discreet and wise as thou: thou shalt be over my house, and according unto thy word shall my house be ruled: only in the throne will I be greater than thou. ... And Pharaoh said unto Joseph, I am Pharaoh, and without thee shall no man lift up his hand or his foot in all the land of Egypt." When Joseph told his brethren of God's dealings with him, he said, as our English version has it: "He hath made me a *father* to Pharaoh, and lord of all his house, and ruler over all the land of Egypt." The word here translated "father" is, by some scholars, thought to refer, in this place, to this relation of intimate or confidential friend,—a relation which had pre-eminence in the court of the kings of Egypt from the earliest days of Egypt's history.

This relation of intimate friend to the king was continued, among the Hebrews, to the days of David and Solomon, when Ahithophel, as afterwards Hushai, was the "own familiar friend" of David, and "Zabud the son of Nathan was chief minister, the king's friend," in the court of Solomon. And who can estimate the importance to the world of those royal friendships in Egypt and Palestine, from the days of Merira to Solomon?

China would claim a rivalry with Egypt in its antiquity; and its sovereigns have held themselves more proudly above their people than the most exalted of the Pharaohs. But friendship has shown itself in its peerless supremacy in China as in Egypt and Assyria. Mencius, a Chinese philosopher of more than twenty centuries ago, illustrates his claim of the duty and beauty of friendship by a reference to the power of this sentiment in the heart of royalty in China's golden age. Long before the days of Joseph in Egypt, a Chinese emperor named Yâo loved as a friend an untitled but wise and worthy citizen named Shun. Yâo so loved his friend Shun that he heaped honors upon him, gave him one of his daughters in marriage, invited him to the royal court, put at his disposal the second palace of royalty, and then visited him in that palace. "Alternately," says Mencius of the Emperor, "he was host and guest.

Here was the Emperor maintaining friendship with a private man." Because of Yâo's friendship with Shun, Shun became Yâo's associate and then his successor on the throne of the Middle Kingdom. Shun is supposed to have been a contemporary of Abraham; and, in the veneration of countless millions in China, in all the generations from that day until now, Shun, the loved friend of the Son of Heaven, has had hardly a lower place than that accorded by the descendants of Abraham to him whose highest honor was that he was called the Friend of God.

Coming down along the ages, we find a new era of government inaugurated in the reign of Alexander of Macedon, when first a great sovereign and conqueror gave distinct recognition to moral and social influences in the sway of empire. And we see that he who conquered the world was himself held captive in the bonds of a devoted friendship. Alexander the Great was a pupil of Aristotle, who gave such prominence to the privilege and responsibilities of friendship; and the principles emphasized in the teachings of the great philosopher found expression in the better nature of the great ruler. No one thing in the story of Alexander's life shows him at such an advantage, personally, as the exhibit of his unwavering trust in his physician-friend Philip, when he had been told that that friend was conspiring to poison him. And he who could thus trust a friend could be a friend.

Obviously, no personal influence had such power over Alexander's feelings and conduct as his friendship with Craterus and Hephæstion. He declared that these "were the two men that he loved best in the world;"

and of the distinction which he made between the two Plutarch says: " He loved Hephæstion and respected Craterus above all the rest of his friends, and was wont to say that Hephæstion loved [the man] Alexander, but that Craterus loved [Alexander] the king." Quintius Curtius says of Hephæstion, that " he was by far the dearest of all the king's friends, meeting the king himself on equal terms, and being master of all his secrets. He had also a like liberty of admonishing the king." Alexander's friendship with Hephæstion became more and more a controlling force in the life of Alexander. It is said that "when he went forth to the East, to make Hellenic civilization the common possession of the world, Alexander desired to renew in his own friendship with Hephæstion the pattern that heroic times had bequeathed in Achilles and Patroclus." In his case, as many times before and since, the sentiment of friendship was a swaying force in the power that swayed the world.

When Hephæstion was dead, the joy of Alexander was at an end, and the waning of his power had begun. "Alexander's grief for him," says Plutarch, "exceeded all reasonable measure. He ordered the manes of all the horses and mules to be cut off in sign of mourning; he struck off the battlements of all the neighboring cities; he crucified the unhappy physician [who had been unable to save the sick man]; and he would not permit the flute or any other musical instrument to be played throughout his camp, until a response came from the oracle of Ammon, bidding him honor Hephæstion, and offer sacrifice to him as to a hero." The entire male population of a conquered tribe was offered by Alexander in sacrifice to the spirit of Hephæstion. Then Alexander determined to outdo all the works of man in a costly monument to his lamented friend. He summoned architects and engineers to aid him in this undertaking; and among the plans considered by him was the carving of Mt. Athos itself into a mighty statue of him whom he loved. But the moving force of Alexander's mind was no longer kept in equilibrium by the controlling influence of a living friend; he grew restless and suspicious and timid, and it was not long before he lay down to die.

As with the older empires of the East, so with the empire of ancient Rome; its highest summit of sovereignty was capped by the aid of friendship, in the person of one who felt the inspiring force of a friend's unselfish devotion. Rome's greatest glory was attained in the reign of him who is known as Augustus Cæsar, but whose earliest name was Caius Octavius; and the story of his elevation to supreme authority is a story of friendship's potency. Octavius was a grand-nephew of Julius Cæsar. In his early youth he won the friendship of a fellow-youth, Marcus Vipsanius Agrippa, of his own age, but much his inferior in family and social status. This friendship was the making of Octavius. The two friends were at school together in Apollonia when they heard of the assassination of Julius Cæsar. They were barely nineteen years of age. Away from the capital, with no advantage of position or experience, assured only that the enemies of his family were for the time triumphant, young Octavius might well have thought first of his own safety and of the hopelessness of any move for the retrieving of his family fortunes; nor were cautious counselors lacking to warn him against the folly of turning his face Rome-ward. Then it was that his young friend showed himself a friend indeed. Agrippa urged Octavius to hasten to the capital and assert his rights, promising to accompany him and stand by him. His action, in accordance with this counsel of friendship, was the beginning of Octavius's progress to power. Hearing, near Brundisium, that he had been named in the will of his grand-uncle as his heir, young Octavius, cheered and strengthened by his friend's presence and counsel, boldly assumed the name of Octavianus Cæsar, and pushed on to Rome to assert his claim to the succession. He found Mark Antony in possession of power, with no thought of surrendering it to the young heir of the dead Cæsar, while senators and nobles were little inclined to follow his lead for his name's sake.

The struggle for the mastery began, and the strength of Agrippa's friendship for Octavianus proved the strength of Octavianus in his claim of a right to be the world's ruler. "We know that Agrippa's courage never wavered," says a historian, "though Octavianus seemed at times ready to falter and draw back. To the many-sided activity of Agrippa, and to his unfailing resolution, the success of that enterprise seems mainly due. He was the great general of the cause that triumphed, the hero of every forlorn hope, and the knight-errant for every hazardous adventure in distant regions." Agrippa had an important share in defeating the land forces of Luke Antony at Perusia, of Mark Antony at Sipontum, and of the Aquitani in Gaul. He pushed on victoriously into Germany. Recalled to Italy by the peril of his friend from the fleets of Pompey, Agrippa made a harbor for a navy by connecting Lake Avernus and the Lucrine Lake with the sea, and then organized, equipped, and trained a navy there, for competition with the naval forces of the world. He won victories on the sea at Mylæ and at Naulochus, thus securing protection to the Mediterranean borders of the Roman Empire. After this he won the final victory over the fleets of Mark Antony at Actium, which "fixed the empire of the world on Octavianus."

Three times Agrippa was chosen consul. Again he was chosen ædile, with the responsibility for the public works of the city; and in that position he built and repaired aqueducts and other public works, and did much to justify the subsequent claim of Octavianus that he found Rome a city of bricks and left it a city of marble. In commemoration of his victory at Actium, whereby he had secured the world's throne to his friend, Agrippa erected the Pantheon, which stands to-day as a memorial of the power of a sacred friendship. It was in recognition of the glory won so largely by the ability and faithfulness of Agrippa, that the Roman Senate accorded to Octavianus Cæsar the unique title of "Augustus," and named after him the sixth month of the Roman year. Agrippa was no less successful as a civil ruler than as a military commander. His administrative skill was displayed all the way along from Gaul to Syria, and he was left by the emperor in charge of Rome during his temporary absence. He is said, indeed, to have been "the greatest military commander of Rome since the days of Julius Cæsar, and the most honest Roman governor in any province." From first to last, Agrippa was unswervingly loyal as a friend, and Augustus was royal enough to realize this. Agrippa married the daughter of Augustus. Had he outlived the emperor, he would probably have succeeded him on the throne. After his death, two of his sons were named by Augustus as his heirs; but they also died before the emperor, and the succession was secured to Tiberius. The world's history centers in the reign of Augustus Cæsar. It was in that reign that the Friend of friends was born among the sons of men. And, next to that supreme event in the Augustan Age, there stands out in its beauty and power the friendship of the royal Augustus with the loyal Agrippa.

Even sovereigns who were themselves incapable of inspiring or enjoying a noble and self-abnegating friendship have been impressed, and hence influenced, by the unselfish devotedness of friends. Thus Dionysius, the tyrant of Syracuse, is said to have realized the emptiness of all his possessions of honor and power in comparison with the mutual love of Damon and Pythias, and to have been moved, as he gave them their lives anew, to entreat from them the privilege of being a sharer in the bond of their friendship. Similar, and yet better, is the story of Nooman III., a king in Arabia in the fifth century of our era, who, from being a tyrant and an idolater, was made a convert to Christianity through "witnessing the devoted friendship of a Christian Arab, who had pledged himself to undergo the punishment intended to be inflicted on his friend, should the latter fail to return at the time appointed,"—as in the case of Damon and Pythias, long centuries before.

A sovereign of sovereigns in Europe, at the close of the eighth and the beginning of the ninth century, was the Emperor Charles the Great, or Charlemagne. His reign was the beginning of a new order of things in Europe. He gave to religion and learning a new place and power in the world's governing, as over against the blind force of military despotisms. And the best work of this sovereign was largely influenced and shaped by his friendship with Alcuin, an English Christian scholar. Alcuin was one of the best informed men of his age, and one of the most remarkable. It was while on a journey from England to Rome, in 781, that he met King Charles at Parma, and won his friendship. At the royal invitation, Alcuin made his home at the court, and was brought into pleasant relations with the king's wife and children as well as with the king himself. During this period a good beginning of schools in the growing empire was made, and plans for yet better things were in discussion. Moved by a spirit of patriotism, Alcuin desired to return to England, in order to promote the educational interests receiving new attention there. But, as a biographer of Alcuin says: "Charlemagne knew too well how to value a man like Alcuin to be willing to lose him, and prized too dearly the rare happiness of possessing a true and sincere friend not to desire his longer and, if possible, permanent residence, and to offer everything that might induce him to remain." Hence, after a brief absence in England, Alcuin returned to the court of his royal friend, and passed the remainder of his useful life there.

As showing the bearing of this friendship of Alcuin and Charles the Great on the king's life-work, one of the latest biographers of the latter says, concerning the former: "His relations to Charles were intimate, cordial, and confidential. One can hardly err in ascribing to him all the theological documents and writings interblended with the political growth and development of the Frankish Empire in that reign; the theology of Charles; the theology, and probably much of the jurisprudence, of the Capitularies. To his influence must be traced some of the enlightened views of Charles; the mercy, the lofty aims, and the ethical apothegms, so remarkable in the life and speech of that remarkable monarch.... Alcuin ... influenced his age by his writings, his teaching, and the force of his virtuous example, and conferred a lasting benefit on mankind at a time when darkness covered the mind of the world and thick darkness the liberal arts." In fact, the face of history was changed, and the welfare of mankind for future generations was promoted by the friendship of Alcuin and Charles the Great.

Next after Charles the Great, in the extent of his empire and in the importance of his reign as a European sovereign, down along the centuries, was Charles the Fifth, the foremost soldier of his age, and a ruler of world-wide influence in the stormy days of the sixteenth century. Despotic and self-willed though he was, he did not lack a measure of responsiveness to the thoughts and feelings of one whom he selected as a close personal friend, and to whom he opened his heart in an exceptional confidence. It was a young page in his court whom the emperor chose as his friend; and the choice was a deliberate one, he priding himself, not without reason, " on his power of reading and of using men." While yet but fifteen years old, this page, as Motley tells us, "was the intimate, almost confidential, friend of the emperor;" and, as the years went on, the intimacy and friendship were closer and closer. "The youth was so constant an attendant upon his imperial chief, that, even when interviews with the highest personages, and upon the gravest affairs, were taking place, Charles would never suffer him to be considered superfluous or intrusive. There seemed to be no secrets which the emperor held too high for the comprehension of his page." Nor was it merely as a confidant that this friend was valued by the emperor. Before he was twenty-one, he was appointed general-in-chief of the army on the French frontier, to be over against such soldiers as Admiral Coligny and the Duc de Nevers; and the issue seemed to justify this appointment. When, finally, the emperor decided to abdicate his throne, he must have that loved friend by his side; and the young soldier was recalled from the frontier to stand in the presence of the august assemblage at Brussels, while the crippled emperor leaned affectionately upon his shoulder as he read his message of imperial farewell.

That such a friendship had its influence on the rule of the emperor who rejoiced in it so greatly would scarcely be questioned; but that the influence of that friendship was potent in the life and rule of him whom it distinguished, when he himself became a ruler of men, —as "William the Silent," the founder of the Dutch Republic,—is quite as evident. It was while Prince William was the young page and friend of the Emperor Charles that he gained his first lessons in statecraft, while observing the interviews of others with the emperor, and in his personal conferences with his imperial friend. "His perceptive and reflective faculties, naturally of remarkable keenness and depth, thus acquired," says Motley, a "precocious and extraordinary development. He was brought up behind the curtain of that great stage where the world's dramas were daily enacted. The machinery and the masks which produced the grand delusions of history had no deceptions for him." And Motley adds, that, "carefully to observe men's actions, and silently to ponder upon their motives, was the favorite occupation of the prince during his apprenticeship at court." Moving on in the direction of impulses given to him in the atmosphere of the emperor's friendship, and in the exercise of powers developed through the partialities of that friendship, Prince William was instrumental in liberating the Netherlands from Spanish tyranny and in laying the foundations of a great republic. He stood for a time as the bulwark of Protestant Christianity, and he was first among the royal rulers of men to administer civil government on the principle of religious toleration. Loved royally by his ruler in his early life, he was royally loved by those whom he ruled in his maturer years. "As long as he lived he was the guiding star of a whole brave nation, and when he died the little children cried in the streets."

A century after William the Silent, one of his descendants came into prominence as a ruler of men under the name of William Henry, Prince of Orange and Count of Nassau, and afterwards as King of England—first as co-sovereign with Mary, and then by himself. That he was a power in the world—through having "a greater part in shaping the destinies of modern England than any of her native sovereigns"—is as evident in history as that a close personal friendship was a potent factor in his life as a ruler. It was while he was still in his early manhood, in Holland, that Prince William Henry was taken ill with malignant small-pox. In that time of his peril, young William Bentinck, who loved him for his own sake, devoted himself to his nursing, and was the means of saving a royal life. "Whether Bentinck slept or not, while I was ill, I know not," said the Prince, in referring to this experience. "But this I know, that, through sixteen days and nights, I never once called for anything but that Bentinck was instantly by my side." Bentinck gave the sick prince his food and medicine, and helped him to rise or lie down, watching him, meanwhile, with unfailing tenderness. Only when the prince was finally convalescent did Bentinck turn to his home to lie down with the same disease, and to battle it through in a determination to be again at the service of his royal friend in whatever perils beset him.

From that time onward the intercourse of the two friends was close and confidential to the last degree. The prince counseled with Bentinck in affairs of state, and shared with him his personal joys and sorrows. He showed the warmest interest in the family affairs of his friend. When a son was born to Bentinck, the prince wrote: "He will live, I hope, to be as good a fellow as you are; and, if I should have a son, our children will love each other, I hope, as we have done." When Bentinck's wife was sick, in her husband's absence, the prince snatched time from pressing cares of state to despatch special messengers, several times a day, with messages concerning her condition; and it was "with tears of joy" that he finally reported her as in the way of recovery. Bentinck proved himself, in the main, worthy of such a friendship. He was wise in counsel and brave in action. He was the prince's trusted supporter on the field of battle, and representative in negotiations of highest moment. When the prince went to England to lead a revolution there, Bentinck was still nearest and dearest as friend, helper, and counselor. When the Prince of Orange had become King of England, Bentinck was created Earl, and then Duke, of Portland. He was made the chief officer of the royal household. On journeys of state he had a seat in the king's carriage. He was largely instrumental in securing the treaty at Ryswick, that gave peace to three kingdoms. For twenty-five years William and Bentinck were rarely separated, save for a very brief period at a time, and then their thoughts were constantly on each other, and they were impatient to be together again.

Of the two friends, William seemed truer and tenderer in this affectionate relation than Bentinck. He who was deemed by many "the most cold-blooded of mankind," and even as "destitute of human feelings," was ever full of warmth and affection as a generous and unswerving friend, in accordance with the true royalty of his great nature. There came a time when Bentinck grew unreasonably sensitive to the king's interest in a new attendant and courtier, and showed his dissatisfaction so rudely that the king permitted him to leave England as ambassador to France, because Bentinck was no longer contented in the companionship of his royal friend. But even then the king's friendship knew no change. Writing to Bentinck a few days after the latter had left for France, the King said touchingly: "The loss of your society has affected me more than you can imagine. I should be very glad if I could believe that you felt as much pain at quitting me as I felt at seeing you depart; for then I might hope that you had ceased to doubt the truth of what I so solemnly declared to you on my oath. Assure yourself that I was never more sincere. My feeling toward you is one which nothing but death can alter." In fidelity of conduct Bentinck never failed his friend the king. He was true to his interests to the last, in any service that he undertook for him; but in his tenderness of feeling as a friend he showed no such royalty of nature as the king. Finally, Bentinck, as the Duke of Portland, insisted on retiring from the court to the immense estates which the king's favor had secured to him as his own. The king sought in vain to retain him near him, but the irritated friend was obstinately unreasonable. Then again the king showed himself a friend unswervingly. "I hope that you will oblige me in one thing," he wrote. "Keep your key of office. I shall not consider you as bound to any attendance. But I beg you to let me see you as often as possible. That will be a great mitigation of the distress which you have caused me. For, after all that has passed, I cannot help loving you tenderly." Great-hearted king! Royal in friendship!

At last the deliverer of England lay on his death-bed.

Macaulay describes the scene. His breathing grew more and more difficult. "'Can this,' he said to the physicians, 'last long?'" He was told that the end was approaching. He swallowed a cordial, and asked for Bentinck. These were his last articulate words. Bentinck [who had already been summoned] instantly came to the bedside, bent down, and placed his ear close to the king's mouth. The lips of the dying man moved, but nothing could be heard. The king took the hand of his earliest friend, and pressed it to his heart. In that moment, no doubt, all that had cast a slight passing cloud over their long and pure friendship was forgotten. It was now between seven and eight in the morning. He closed his eyes and gasped for breath. The bishops knelt down, and read the commendatory prayer. When it ended, William was no more." The work of another royal friend was finished.

While William the Third was on the throne of England, there came to his realm a royal visitor from a distant land, whose very visit was an illustration of the power of friendship, and who was himself a power in the world largely because of his friendships. Peter the Great came from Russia to England at the close of the seventeenth century. He traveled incognito, as a member of a party at the head of which was General Franz Lefort, an Italian-Swiss by birth, to whom the Tsar of the Russias was attached in a warm personal friendship, —a friendship that did much to shape the career of this royal ruler of men. Peter was a man of great strength and of great weakness. His violent outbursts of temper would have neutralized in large measure the power of his tireless energy, if there had been no one whom he loved and trusted sufficiently to accept as a check on his intense nature. Peter had the elements of greatness, but those elements required the unifying factor of a friendship to make them wisely effective for good. Referring to these warring elements of his nature, a recent biographer says of him: " The character of Peter exhibits a strange congeries of opposed qualities." But "in spite of his errors no one will deny that he was a man of great genius. . . . All Russia seems but the monument of this strange colossal man. . . . The title of 'great' cannot justly be refused to such a man."

Peter was only eighteen years old when he became acquainted with Franz Lefort, who was some seventeen years his senior, and was at that time an officer in the Russian army. Lefort was capable, upright, warm-hearted, unselfish, sympathetic, and winsome; and the tsar quickly saw in him the friend he needed. " From this time on," says Schuyler, " Peter became daily more intimate with Lefort. He dined with him two or three times a week, and demanded his presence daily." When the two friends were separated, they corresponded familiarly. " No one, except Catharine [first mistress, then wife, of Peter], was able to give Peter so much sympathy, and so thoroughly to enter into his plans. Lefort alone had enough influence over him to soothe his passions, and to prevent the consequences of his sudden outbursts of anger." But for that friendship, that great nature might have gone a-wreck! Lefort was fittingly cared for by his royal friend. He was advanced in rank, "first to lieutenant-general, then to full general, commander of the first regiment, admiral, and ambassador." Lefort's home became the center of social interest to the tsar, "a sort of club-house for Peter's company;" and the expense of its extensive entertainments was met by Peter himself. The intimacy of the two friends extended to all the thinking and doing of the tsar. After seven years of this intimacy, the journey to Western Europe was undertaken, with Lefort, as has been said, at the head of the embassy, and the tsar as professedly an humble member of the party. This journey of Peter's, says Macaulay, speaking from an English standpoint, "is an epoch in the history, not only of his own country, but of ours, and of the world." Schuyler, while not willing to concede to it all this importance, says explicitly: "Peter's journey marks the division between the old Russia, an exclusive, little-known country, and the new Russia, an important factor in European politics. It was also one of the turning-points in the development of his character, and was the continuation of the education begun in the German suburb" of Moscow, where Peter first visited Lefort and became his friend. But for Lefort's influence, this journey of Peter's might never have been made, or have proved of such importance in its results. It was after the return of the tsar to his dominions that his friendship with Lefort was interrupted by the death of the latter. ".At the news of the death," says Schuyler, " he burst into thick sobs, and, with a flood of tears, broke out in these words: 'Now I am left without one trusty man. He alone was faithful to me; in whom can I confide henceforward?'"

The impulse of Lefort's friendship had given Peter his start, and its steadying power had given him his balance in his work of wise reforms for his vast empire. Its influence was with him as a memory and an incentive to the close of his busy life. Missing its help and stimulus, and longing for the sympathy that it had secured to him, Peter turned, after the death of Lefort, to one of his companions who had been with him from boyhood; and gradually he drew him closer to himself as a friend, in the vain hope of finding Lefort's place supplied. "It was after the siege of Noteberg [three years after the death of Lefort]," says Schuyler, "that Menshikof was admitted to the full friendship of his master, became the confidant of his plans and feelings, and his trusted adviser, and in every way occupied the place in Peter's friendship which had been vacant since the death of Lefort." Menshikof had large ability, good-humor, and attractiveness; and his influence with Peter was very great during the remainder of the latter's lifetime. But Menshikof had no such integrity and unselfishness as were the charm of Lefort, nor could he be so true a friend. "He was ambitious and avaricious." He "misused his powers and position, as well as the confidence which the tsar so freely gave him." Again and again the tsar was compelled to put away Menshikof, because of his misdoing; and as often his longing for a true friend, and his love for this treacherous one, induced him to recall him to a new opportunity of betrayal. It was after one of these many recalls that Peter said to Catharine, in heaviness of heart: "Menshikof was conceived in iniquity, born in sin, and will end his life as a rascal and a cheat; and, if he do not reform, he will lose his head." Although estranged from Peter during the latter years of the tsar's life, it was not until Peter's grandson was on the throne that Menshikof finally died, in exile and disgrace. Up to that time he swayed vast power in the councils of Russia; and that power he would never have won, but for the tsar's sincere friendship for the true-hearted Lefort, and his vain hope of a substitute for it in the friendship of Menshikof.

In noting the world's great sovereigns, it would never do to pass unmentioned Napoleon Bonaparte; for he was in his day a king of kings, and, in spite of all drawbacks, he must be reckoned great among the world's greatest. On the one hand, Napoleon seems to us so self-enclosed and so self-reliant, if not actually so absorbed in self, that we can hardly think of him as having any special need of a personal friend, or as likely to be held or swayed by the power of a personal friendship. On the other hand, because friendship is what it is in the world's history, it would seem impossible that a man so great as Napoleon could be what he was without the aid of this force of forces. It is not to be wondered at, therefore, that the denial and the recognition of friendship's potency are both to be found in the story of Napoleon. " Friendship is but a name," said Napoleon. " I love no one.... I know well that I have not one true friend. As long as I continue what I am, I may have as many pretended friends as I please." Yet Napoleon had friends whom he loved and trusted, and who loved and trusted him; and Napoleon honored the sentiment of friendship. When, in 1804, Pichegru and Cadoudal were leaders in a conspiracy against the life of Napoleon, the Legislative Assembly of France passed an ordinance making it a crime punishable with death to shelter one of these conspirators. M. Marbois, one of Napoleon's ministers, was an old friend of Pichegru, and when the latter, in desperation, came to him for temporary shelter, he gave it to him for friendship's sake. Subsequently Marbois reported this fact to Napoleon, and Napoleon wrote him a letter expressive of his admiration of that spirit which prompted him to give shelter to one who, though an outlaw, had been his friend. Again, a few years later, when Napoleon was speaking in severe censure of one of his generals, at a meeting of the Privy Council, a member of the Council spoke earnestly in defense of his absent friend. At first, Napoleon was angered. Then, recovering himself, he said warmly: "But he is your friend, sir. I had forgotten it. You do right to defend him."

While yet but a boy in the military school at Brienne, Napoleon won the friendship of a school-fellow named Démasis, who loved him for his own sake, and who was glad afterwards to be his comrade in their earliest artillery service. There came a time, after his first military exploits at Paris and Toulon, when Napoleon was deprived of his command, and seemed destined to a life of hopeless inaction. Without money and without position, knowing that his mother was in want and that he could not help her, he gave way to temporary despair, and was actually on his way to the river-bank to commit suicide by drowning, when he came face to face with a man dressed as a mechanic, whom he did not recognize, but who warmly embraced him, crying out: "Is it you, Napoleon? How glad I am to see you again!" It was his friend Démasis, who had recently come back to

France in disguise, in order to visit his aged mother. Seeing the evident depression of Napoleon, Démasis lovingly pressed him to disclose its cause, and, when he had learned the whole story, he said cheerily, "Is that all?" and, unclasping a belt from underneath his coarse waistcoat, he thrust it into Napoleon's hands, with the words : " Here are six thousand dollars in gold, which I can spare without any inconvenience. Take them, and relieve your mother." Long years after, Napoleon related this incident in his St. Helena prison-home, adding: "I cannot to this day explain to myself how I could have been willing to receive the money; but I seized the gold as by a convulsive movement, and, almost frantic with excitement, ran to send it to my distressed mother."

As showing that this act of Démasis was wholly the prompting of an unselfish friendship, Napoleon said that, for fifteen years after that meeting with Démasis, he hunted in vain for some trace of his friend ; and when at last he found him, he learned that he had purposely kept himself out of sight, lest Napoleon should endeavor to reward him for his affectionate service. Napoleon, referring tenderly and with reverence to this incident in his career, recognized it explicitly as the resultant outcome of an "early friendship," which, by "one of those mysteries of Providence that we so often witness," had an "immense influence" upon his personal destiny. If this occurrence were all by itself as a proof of the potency of friendship in the life-course of Napoleon, it would be enough to show that he was no exception to the world's great sovereigns in his dependence on this all-prevailing sentiment. But it does not stand alone in his life-story.

Even before this fortunate meeting with his old friend Démasis, Napoleon had made the acquaintance of a young soldier named Duroc, to whom he became warmly attached in the bonds of a personal friendship. Duroc was three years younger than Napoleon. In 1796, while only twenty-four years old, he was appointed on the staff of the great commander as a personal aide; and from that time on, with all his varied promotions, Duroc was kept close to his master and friend, until he was killed in his service, in 1813. That such a friendship had its influence on both parties to it, is as patent as its existence. Sir Archibald Alison, referring to this friendship, says: "Duroc loved Napoleon for his own sake, and possessed perhaps a larger share of his confidence than any of his other generals." Duroc was the close companion of Napoleon in Egypt; and, returning with him, in advance of the main army, to Paris, he had an active part in the Revolution of Brumaire, which placed Napoleon on the throne of France. When Napoleon was emperor, he made Duroc marshal of the palace, and created him Duke of Friuli. He sent him on special missions of importance to the courts of Berlin, Vienna, Dresden, Stockholm, and St. Petersburg, and he was affectionately intimate with him in his home life in Paris. He even wished Duroc to marry Hortense, the daughter of Josephine; but Josephine was unwilling to sanction this match. Duroc was with Napoleon in Russia, and he was one of the little party that accompanied the emperor in his hurried return to Paris at the close of that disastrous campaign. It was a few months after this return that Duroc was killed, in the battle of

Influencing Royalty. 147

Merkersdorf, in Saxony, May 21, 1813; and the record of Napoleon's grief over the death of this friend is a touching page in the history of human friendship.

Napoleon seemed to have a presentiment of evil to himself or to his friend that day. "Duroc," he said in the early morning, when one of his aides was hit, "fortune is determined to have one of us to-day." In the afternoon, as the emperor, with members of his staff and of his guard, was riding through a ravine in the smoke of the battle, a cannon-ball, glancing from a tree, struck Duroc, and mortally wounded him. When told of this, Napoleon seemed for a moment completely paralyzed with grief. Then he cried out in agony: "Duroc! Duroc! Gracious Heaven, my presentiments never deceive me! This is indeed a sad day—a fatal day." It mattered not to Napoleon that the battle needed his attention, now that his one friend was dying. Dismounting from his horse, he said earnestly, "I must see him. Poor, poor Duroc!" Duroc had been taken into a cottage, and he lay there in terrible suffering. Coming to him, Napoleon threw his arms around his neck, and embraced him affectionately. Duroc took the hand of the emperor, and pressed it to his lips with words of devotion. "All my life," he said to his imperial friend, "has been devoted to you; and now my only regret is that I can be useful to you no longer." "Duroc!" sobbed out Napoleon, as if in recognition of the imperishableness of a real friendship, "Duroc! There is another life. There you will await me. We shall one day meet again." Napoleon, deeply moved, sat with his head resting on the left hand of Duroc, while their two right hands were clasped tenderly. It was not until Duroc insisted that Napoleon should leave him that the latter finally arose from his friend's side, and found his way, in tears, to his own tent, where he shut himself up to his great grief for the night, absolutely refusing to see any one of his generals, even on the most pressing business, until the morning.

The next day Napoleon summoned to his presence the proprietor of the cottage in which Duroc died, together with the rector of the parish and the magistrate of the village, and arranged, with the payment of four thousand dollars, for the purchase of the property and for the erection there of a monument to his friend, bearing this inscription: "Here General Duroc, Duke of Friuli, grand marshal of the palace of the Emperor Napoleon, gloriously fell, struck by a cannon-ball, and died in the arms of the emperor, his friend." "The emperor was cut to the heart by the loss of his dear friend Duroc," wrote Napoleon's trusted minister, Caulaincourt, years afterward; and it was evident to all that Napoleon never forgot that "dear friend." When Napoleon was in the hands of his enemies, after the battle of Waterloo, he asked permission to live as a private citizen in England under the name of "Colonel Duroc," bearing the name of his one "other self." Even on his dying-bed, in St. Helena, he made provision in his will for the daughter of Duroc. Although the overthrow of Napoleon prevented the erection of the monument he had planned to Duroc's memory, the remains of that faithful friend were, in 1847, brought to Paris, to find their fitting resting-place, together with those of General

Bertrand, his immediate successor in office, alongside of the remains of the emperor in the Church of the Invalides. Napoleon owed much to the loyal friendship of Duroc, and he realized it. Such a friendship became such a man; and it is well that its record is so unmistakably plain.

But Napoleon's truest friend was Josephine. It has been already said that a wife, or a husband, who is a true friend in the conjugal relation, might be just as truly a friend apart from that relation; for friendship is the love of another for that other's sake, and not for what that other is to the loving one. And this truth finds its fullest illustration in the love of Josephine for Napoleon. Josephine came to love Napoleon for his own sake after their marriage, if not before; and she continued to bear for him an unselfish love, even through their differences, to the close of her life. Her thought was of what she could do for his truest welfare and to advance his highest interests. To this end she was ever ready to make any personal sacrifice, and even to risk the loss of his favor. "Josephine seemed his good angel," says Saint-Amand. "We may say that throughout his career, so long as he was with her he always enjoyed the most brilliant success." Her eyes saw dangers that he had not perceived. Her tact averted perils against which he, if alone, would have been powerless. "All the brusqueness and violence of Bonaparte's manners were tempered by the soothing and insinuating gentleness of his amiable and kindly wife. She was to exercise direct influence on the victims and accomplices of the *coup d'état* [which gave him supreme power],—on Barras, Gohier, Sieyès, Fouchè, Moreau, and Talleyrand. Who knows? Without

Josephine's skill and tact, Bonaparte might, perhaps, have made a failure." "Without her, he would hardly have attained such wonderful results." And Napoleon ultimately realized that he had a true friend and a real helper in Josephine.

So, long as this friendship was exercised co-ordinately with the marriage relation it might have been looked at as nothing more than wifely love; but the time came when its power beyond that was tested, and it stood the test. When Napoleon decided to put away Josephine as a wife, although it was the breaking of her heart to leave him, she assured him that she should still be his "best friend;" and she made good her word. "I have the pleasure of giving him the greatest proof of attachment and devotedness that was ever given on earth," she said, in her formal request, at his desire, for the sundering of the marriage tie that had bound them. "But the dissolution of my marriage will in no respect change the sentiments of my heart," she added. "The emperor will ever find in me his best friend." And she spoke truly, as the emperor subsequently realized. Napoleon was never himself after that act. Josephine was herself to the last. When the longed-for son of Napoleon was born, not even that child's imperial father or mother had greater or more grateful joy than filled the heart of Josephine, as the cannon of the garrison near her sounded the intelligence that he to whom she was a friend had now received the chief desire of his heart. Writing at once in congratulation to the glad father, she had words of tenderness also for the favored mother. "She cannot be more tenderly devoted to you than I am," she said; "but she has been enabled to contribute more to your happiness by securing that of France. . . . Not till you have ceased to watch by her bed, not till you are weary of embracing your son, will you take your pen to converse with your best friend. . . . Meanwhile, it is not possible for me to delay telling you that, more than any one in the world, do I rejoice in your joy." And in abounding evidence of the sincerity of her delight, she presented to the page of the emperor, who was already bringing her the glad intelligence while her congratulatory note was on the way, a diamond breast-pin and a thousand dollars in gold, in token of her joy in his message.

Thus always in this friendship; Josephine never wavered, never changed. When the overthrow of Napoleon by the allies caused his banishment to Elba, with his separation from his wife and child, Josephine realized that her mission as his friend was at last at an end. She wrote to Napoleon in hearty assurance of unswerving fidelity, and in profoundest regret, that she was unable, through his act, to follow him into his solitude. "Now only can I calculate the whole extent of the misfortune of having beheld my union with you dissolved by law," she said. And then she lay down and died, with a prayer for him on her lips. Napoleon could see, in looking back upon his stormy career, that the richest blessing of his life had been the friendship of Josephine, and that the greatest error of his life had been the practical rejection of her friendship. "She was the best woman in France," he said at St. Helena; and he had before said, that to her love he was indebted for the only few moments of happiness he ever enjoyed on earth. And he spoke sadly, in those later years, of his divorce from Josephine, as the time when he set his "foot on an abyss covered with a bed of flowers." The record shows that that friendship of Josephine was very much to Napoleon while it was cherished, and that its rejection was one of the causes of his ruin.

In the East and in the West, earlier and later, the story is much the same. History and fiction combine to celebrate the praises of friendship in royalty, as of royalty in friendship.

The most widely known of all the Muhammadan khaleefs, and the one whose sway was most extensive in the East, was Haroon-ar-Rasheed of Bagdad; or Haroun Alraschid, as he is called in our English versions of the Arabian Nights. He was a contemporary of Charles the Great, at the close of the eighth and the beginning of the ninth century, and is said to have been in friendly correspondence with that great emperor of the Franks. It is not easy to separate the true from the fanciful in the story of this khaleef; but all writers agree in declaring that the rise and glory of his wonderful reign were linked with his friendship for Jaafer, a son of his grand vizier, Yahya. In the stories of the Arabian Nights, Jaafer is the favorite companion of Haroon in his many marvelous adventures. Careful biographers also agree in saying that Jaafer was the constant sharer of Haroon's enjoyments, and would often be found with him in his pleasure-seeking when the hour of early morning prayer closed the night they had had together. "Haroon's attachment to Jaafer was of so extravagant a character that he could never bear him to be absent from his

Influencing Royalty. 153

side," says Professor Palmer ; "and he even went to the absurd length of having a cloak made with two collars, so that he and Jaafer could wear it at one and the same time." Jaafer was advanced in wealth and dignity by his royal friend. He came to have almost limitless influence, and he made use of it according to his own ideas of expediency. In order to open the way to the hareem for his friend, that they might not be separated even there, the khaleef arranged a nominal marriage between Jaafer and the sister of Haroon, with the distinct agreement that the relations between the two should be purely Platonic. Because this agreement was not adhered to by Jaafer, Haroon turned against his friend, and destroyed him and his family. The friendship, while it lasted, was a swaying force in the khaleefate; and its rupture was a beginning of the end to the dynasty represented by Haroon.

Greatest and best of the Mogul emperors was Akbar Muhammad, or Jelal-ed-Deen, who reigned in the latter half of the sixteenth century. He was great as a soldier and a statesman. He was practically the founder of the empire of India. He bore the title of Joogat Gooroo, " Protector of Mankind," and he is said to have been the only Oriental sovereign who ever deserved such a designation. Such a ruler must have appreciated friendship, and have known how to be a friend. Among the many stories that are told of the greatness and goodness of Akbar (and "Akbar" means "greatest") are stories of his friendship for Shaykh Solayman, whom he trusted with a royal confidence. It is even said that, while Akbar was away from his capital on his important campaigns, he practically gave over his palace and his kingdom to his friend Solayman, putting into his charge the care of his wives and children, his treasury, and his affairs of state. Tradition whispers that Solayman was not always true to his trust as the emperor's friend; but no one ever questioned the emperor's royal and unswerving love for his friend, as his other self. At Sicandra, near Agra, there rest the remains of Akbar in a magnificent mausoleum. At Futtipoor Sicri, not far from the same capital, is the tomb that contains all that was mortal of Solayman. Both burial-places are revered as sacred shrines; and pilgrims who go from the one to the other tell, to this day, of the friendship whereby the Shaykh Solayman was honored by the Emperor Akbar.

So it is always and everywhere; royalty shows itself royal in its appreciation of friendship, and friendship finds its fitting sway in the heart of him who is royal. Friendship is not dependent on royalty; but true royalty realizes its dependence on friendship.

PROMOTING HEROISM.

 EROISM is more than royalty, but heroism is not more than friendship. Friendship can make men's spirit heroic, as friendship can make men's characters royal. In heroism and in royalty friendship proves an incitement and an inspiration.

In Plato's Banquet, Phædrus says that if an army could be made up of men who loved one another as friends, "such persons, fighting side by side, although few in number, would conquer, so to say, the whole world; for a lover-friend would less endure to be seen by his beloved deserting his post or throwing away his arms than by all others; and rather than to leave his friend when fallen, or not to assist him when in danger, he would prefer to die many deaths." And Phædrus adds: "There is not a man so much of a coward that love would not divinely inspire him to deeds of valor, and make him equal to the very best of birth." Aristotle, likewise, lays emphasis on friendship as peculiarly a necessity "to those in the vigor of life, in order to further their noble deeds;" and, in enforcement of this thought, he cites from Homer: "If two go together, one before another perceiveth a matter, how there may be gain therein; but if one alone perceive aught, even so his wit is shorter, and weak his device." Or, as the inspired Preacher expresses it, as rendered by Tayler Lewis:

> "Better are two than one, for then there is to them
>   A good reward for all their toil.
> For if they fall, the one shall raise his friend.
> But wo to him who falls alone, with none to lift him up!"

Budgel, a friend of Addison, suggests, in the Spectator, that "there is something in friendship so very great and noble that in those fictitious stories which are invented to the honor of any particular person, the authors have thought it as necessary to make their hero a friend as a lover. Achilles has his Patroclus, and Æneas his Achates."

Fable and history thrill with illustrations of friendship's heroism. The legendary Hercules (now thought to be a Greek adaptation of the Babylonian Izdubar) had the companionship and cheer of his friend Iolaüs in daring and brilliant exploits. Iolaüs was the charioteer of Hercules, and he won a victory for his friend in the Olympic races. The two were together in slaying the Lernean Hydra, and Eurystheus denied to Hercules the honor of this triumph on the ground that he could not have wrought it without the assistance of his friend. Iolaüs outliving Hercules was first in offering sacrifices to his hero-friend as a demigod; and after the death of Iolaüs he obtained permission to return to earth in order to give assistance to the children of Hercules. Having slain Eurystheus, the oppressor of the children of Hercules, Iolaüs returned again to the lower regions. Because of the recognized beauty and power of this friendship of Iolaüs for Hercules, the tomb of Iolaüs was made a sacred shrine for friends; whither, as Plutarch tells us, they went to register their vows of unswerving affection.

Theseus was an Attic hero second only to Hercules in ancient story. Linked with him in his deeds of courage was his friend Pirithoüs, whom he first came to love when they met as enemies. Together these friends gave battle to the centaurs. It was with the help of Pirithoüs that Theseus carried off Helen of Sparta—who became the cause of the Trojan war. When Pirithoüs would invade Hades to abduct Proserpine, his friend Theseus would not desert him in his mad enterprise. Both heroes were held captive by Pluto, until Hercules visited the lower world in order to release the one who had gone thither as an act of friendship.

The highest achievements of heroism at the siege of Troy pivoted on the friendship of Achilles and Patroclus. It was from friendship for Achilles that Patroclus first took part in that conflict; and when the aggrieved Achilles had withdrawn from the field, Patroclus clad himself in the armor of his friend and renewed the fight for both. The death of Patroclus brought Achilles once more to the front; as no entreaty of his countrymen, and no proffered reward, could compass it. Not patriotism, but friendship, incited the heroic deeds of Achilles, by which the doom of Troy was sealed.

Next after Achilles in heroic prominence at that siege came Ulysses; and as Patroclus was an inspirer to Achilles through his friendship, Diomedes was the inspiring friend of Ulysses. Affectionate and covenanted brothers-in-arms, Ulysses and Diomedes were doubly heroic because they were friends. Together they ventured by night into the very camp of the Trojans; and it was while planning for that perilous exploit that Diomedes told of his trust in Ulysses as one "whose heart is passing eager, and his spirit so manful in all manner of toils;" saying of the inspiration of his presence: "While he cometh with me, even out of burning fire might we both return, for he excelleth in understanding." Together Ulysses and Diomedes brought away from within the walls of Troy the sacred palladium, on the presence of which the city's safety had depended. Together the two hero-friends passed into immortality, because of achievements they never could have wrought without their friendship.

The heroic daring and doing of the two friends Orestes and Pylades were a delight in Grecian song and story, and have been rejoiced or wept over in all the ages since. It was from his unselfish love for Orestes that Pylades went with his friend on his perilous expedition to Taurus, to bring thence to Athens the image of Diana that had fallen from heaven. These heroes gloried in their friendship, and were ready to die for it.

"Are ye twin-brothers from one mother born?"

was the question asked of them, when they stood unrecognized before the priestess of Diana, having been seized and brought thither for immolation. Their answer, by Orestes, came:

"By friendship are we, not by kinship, lady."

When it was declared that one of them must die, while the other might return to Greece, a kindly strife arose between them in the effort of each to die in the other's stead. Being urged by Pylades to yield this privilege of sacrifice to his friend, Orestes insisted that it were basely inconsistent with the spirit of true friendship for one to secure his own safety at the cost of his friend's life; and that he must insist on dying, rather than live at such a cost. This answer it was that called from Iphigenia the admiring acclaim:

"O lofty spirit! from some generous root
  Hast thou uprisen, a true friend to thy friend."

And because these hero-friends were such heroes as friends, both were permitted to live, and their fame has never died.

Epaminondas and Pelopidas were Theban hero-friends, whose friendship made them heroic, and whose heroism made and showed them friends. Pelopidas refused to use his great wealth for his own comfort, when his friend declined to be enriched by it and lacked the means to rival it. Side by side the two friends fought heroically. When Pelopidas fell in battle, and was supposed to be dead, Epaminondas protected his body at the peril of his own life. Recovering from his wounds, Pelopidas aided Epaminondas in expelling the Spartans from Thebes. When Pelopidas was held captive by Alexander of Pheræ, Epaminondas fought heroically for his rescue. Their whole lives were an exhibit of the power of friendship in inciting to heroism; and Thebans and Thessalonians united in honoring their memory as hero-friends.

The famous "Sacred Band of Thebans" was, according to Diodorus, a band of one hundred and fifty pairs of friends, every man of whom was distinguished for strength and discipline and bravery and friendship, and was expected to be always with his chosen friend. Two by two in a bond of sacred friendship those soldiers enlisted for a life-and-death struggle together; and such heroes they were, through being such friends, that their band was never overborne in conflict until the great battle of Chæronea; and then they all stood and fell together, "faithful unto death." When Philip of Macedon looked down upon those three hundred hero-friends, "dead in their armor, heaped one upon another, having met the spears of the phalanx face to face, he marveled at the sight; and, learning that it was the Band of Friends, he burst into tears, and said, ' Perish those who would suspect these men of doing or abetting anything base!'"

In confirmation of the truth, as thus illustrated, that there is no incitement to heroism like friendship, Plutarch refers to a current "saying of Pammenes, that Homer's Nestor is not a good general when he bids the Greeks assemble by their tribes and clans:

'That tribe to tribe, and clan to clan, give aid;'

whereas he ought to have placed side by side men who loved each other; for men care little in time of danger for men of the same tribe or clan, whereas the bond of affection is one that cannot be broken."

Friendship as a spur to heroism is as prominent in the song and story of ancient Rome, as of Greece. Æneas was the ancestral hero of the Romans; coming, as it is said, from Mount Ida to Latium, with the sacred palladium of Troy after the fall of that city. Side by side with Æneas in his heroic exploits by land and sea was his devoted friend Achates. In sympathy, in inspiration, and in stalwart aid, this hero-friend was so much to Æneas that to the Romans in their best day the term "*fidus Achates*" was a synonym of unswerving fidelity in friendship; and the force of that proverbial term has remained unbroken even to our day.

In the same poem in which Virgil tells, in undying verse, of the heroic deeds of Æneas and Achates, he tells of the daring and doing, in their affectionate emulation, of Euryalus and Nisus in the siege of Pallanteum. When Euryalus had proposed to go alone, in the darkness of the night, into the Rutulian camp, his friend Nisus pleaded for the privilege of sharing with him the perils of the undertaking. For very love's sake Euryalus protested against this needless exposure of his friend; but Nisus would not be dissuaded, and the two went out together. After brilliant deeds of valor, the friends were intercepted, on their way back, by a troop of three hundred horsemen. Nisus, who could have made good his own escape, seeing that his friend's life was endangered, sprang before him for his vicarious rescue.

> "'Me, me; 'tis I,' he cried, 'who did the deed!
> On me direct your steel, O Rutuli!
> The offense is mine alone. He did no harm;
> He could not! Yonder sky and conscious stars

> Bear witness that the words I speak are true.
> He only loved too much his hapless friend!'"

Seeing, however, that he could not save his friend, he was determined to die with and for him:

> "And dying dealt a death-blow to his foe.
> Then, on the lifeless body of his friend
> He threw himself, pierced through with many a wound,
> And there, at last, in placid death he slept."

Cæsar, in his "Commentaries on the Gallic War," tells of the heroic deeds, in Aquitania, of a band of six hundred friends known as "Soldurii," under the leadership of Adiatunnus—to whom they were solemnly pledged in a vow of friendship. These Soldurii of Aquitania seem to have been somewhat like the Sacred Band of Theban friends; for Cæsar says that their vow of friendship bound them to be true in life and death to him who called them friends; and if they were unable to save him in an extremity, they were to die with and for him. "Nor hitherto in the memory of man," adds Cæsar, "has there been found one of these who refused to give up his life, when he to whose friendship he had devoted himself was slain."

In the legends of the far North, heroism went always hand in hand with a loyal friendship known as "foster-brotherhood;" a brotherhood of choice, and of blended blood, that was more binding between brave men than any tie of family or clanship. Viking, the first great hero of the Northern Seas, is told of in the Icelandic sagas as the foster-brother of Halfdan, a son of Ulf; and the heroic exploits of these two friends were famous from Sweden to India. Afterwards Viking became the friend and foster-brother of Njorfe, ruler of the Norwegian Uplands; and the new deeds of the new friends were more heroic than any that either of them had known before. Always, moreover, it was the friendship that incited to the highest reach of heroism.

Again, Thorstein, a son of Viking, became the friend and foster-brother of Bele, son and successor of King Skate, after the two had met as opponents in battle. For a time the power of these brother-friends was wellnigh resistless in all the North. When, at length, they met their match, one by one, in Angantyr, they proposed to him to become their brother-friend, and he gladly accepted their proffer. Thenceforward the three friends were the three great heroes of their day. It is the friendship of the heroes, quite as much as the heroism of the friends, that receives honor in the Icelandic sagas; as when King Bele and Thorstein are represented in their cordial intimacy in the king's palace, when their days of war are over:

> "Thereafter talked the heroes both,
>   In many a heartfelt tone,
> Of their long friendship's troth,
>   Through all the Northland known;
> And how their true-fast union,
>   In weal and wo the same,
> (Like two hands firmly grasped in one,)
>   More tight-knit shall become."

The epic songs of Russia pivot the heroism of their heroes on the sworn friendship, or "cross-brotherhood," of the mighty men, two by two, whose exploits they commemorate. Svyatogór, latest of the older cycle of Russian heroes, "exchanged crosses" with Ilyá of Múrom, and "Svyatogór taught Ilyá all heroic customs and traditions." After the death of Svyatogór, Ilyá opened a new era of heroism in the strength and wisdom that he had gained through this friendship. Dúnaï Ivánovich and Dobrýnya Nikítich were cross-brother friends; and it was in their mutual trust in one another as friends that they went out fearlessly on their perilous mission, for the winning of the Princess Apráxia of Lithuania as a bride for their liege lord Prince Vladímir. And the heroism of Dúnaï was inspired by the friendship of Dobrýnya. So, again, with the two mighty heroes of Rostóf, Alyósha Popovich and Akím Ivánovich, brother-friends as they were; they were fearless in danger because they were faithful in friendship. "Shoulder to shoulder rode the warriors, heroic stirrup pressed stirrup," as they rode, says the Russian epic. And it was when his friend Akím was by his side that Alyósha slew Tugárin, the Dragon's son.

In India, there are not lacking stories of heroism incited by friendship. Homâyoon, one of the Great Moguls, son of Bâber, and father of the yet greater Akbar, was poet, astronomer, and soldier, as well as ruler. Ten generations have sung his praises as a hero-friend. While yet a youth, Homâyoon became the sworn friend of Koornivati, a princess of Rajasthan; in accordance with a primitive custom of India, whereby persons of the opposite sex might enter into a pure and sacred friendship, by the giving of a golden bracelet on the one hand, and of an embroidered outer garment on the other. In maturer life these friends were widely separated; but their friendship never wavered. At a time when Homâyoon was engaged in active warfare in Bengal, there came to him a call from Koornivati for help against her enemies, by whom she was besieged in her royal residence at Cheetore. Instantly he yielded all thought of his personal interests, and of his very kingdom, and turned his army with forced marches to the rescue of his friend at Cheetore. With all his haste, however, he was too late to save her. The city had fallen before he reached it, and she had destroyed herself rather than fall into her conqueror's hands. Then Homâyoon gave battle to the victory-flushed enemy; and to this day they tell of his deeds of valor and heroism as he avenged the death of his friend Koornivati by the destruction of the forces of her enemy.

It is the same in the far West as in the far East; among all primitive peoples, no tenderer or nobler sentiment is known than that of an unselfish personal friendship, nor can any incitement to heroic action transcend its play. An officer of the United States army, who has given much study to the customs of the North American Indians, tells of the warm friendship sometimes existing between men of the same tribe, or even between two men of hostile tribes, under the name of "brothers by adoption." Speaking of the Arapahoe warriors in this connection, he says: "They really seem to 'fall in love' with men; and I have known this affectionate interest to live for years, surviving lapse of time and separation." An illustration of the heroism inspired by such a friendship is given by this officer, as coming under his own observation. Three Bears and Feather-on-the-Head were attached friends, and were together as scouts in the United States service.

In the early gray of a cold morning in the late autumn of 1876, the government force to which these scouts were attached made a surprise attack on an Indian village in a cañon of the Big Horn Mountains. The horse ridden by Three Bears becoming unmanageable dashed ahead of the attacking party, carrying his rider into the very heart of the village, where all were now aroused for the defense of their homes and lives. Seeing his friend's desperate peril, Feather-on-the-Head urged forward his pony, in order to save his friend or to die with him. Throwing himself from side to side of his pony to avoid the thick-flying shots of the enemy as he dashed on, Feather-on-the-Head reached the center of the village just as the horse of Three Bears had fallen under him. Sweeping past the spot where his imperiled friend stood, at the full speed of his pony, Feather-on-the-Head caught up Three Bears and mounted him behind himself. Then together the two hero-friends flew unharmed through the shower of bullets out of that valley of death, and regained their place with their command in safety. Who will say that this act of Indian heroism through friendship is undeserving of mention alongside of the heroic exploits in the legends of Greece and Rome and the Norseland?

Nor need it be supposed that the progress of Christian civilization has tended to lessen the potency of friendship, as an incentive to such heroism as has been its outcome in the days of classic story, or among later primitive peoples. In the best days of medieval chivalry, the very bravest Christian knights were those who had bound themselves together in a covenant of sacred friendship for life and for death. "*Vraye fraternité et compagnie d'armes,*"—" True brotherhood and companionship-in-arms," this loving relation between knights was called. These knightly friendships were formally ratified in Christian churches, in the presence of relatives, and with the sanction of ecclesiastics; and they were the basis of the most heroic exploits of the most heroic Christian knights. Referring to these knightly friendships, Mills, the historian of chivalry, says: " The knights vowed that they would never injure or vilify each other, that they would share each other's dangers; and in sign of the perfection of love and true unity, and in order to possess, as much as they could, the same heart and resolves, they solemnly promised true fraternity and companionship-in-arms. They then received the holy sacrament [becoming sharers in each other's life through being sharers alike in the life of Christ], and the priest blessed the union. . . . This form of attachment was the strongest tie of chivalry." So powerful, indeed, was this bond of knightly friendship, that it was reckoned as taking precedence even of the chivalrous obligation to stand or fall in the defense of holy womanhood—if the choice must be made between the two. " A lady might in vain have claimed the protection of a cavalier, if he could allege that at that moment he was bound to fly to the succor of his brother-in-arms."

A typical romance of the earlier days of chivalry is that of Amys and Amylion, two knightly friends, who have been called the Damon and Pythias, and again the Pylades and Orestes, of medieval story. Their friendship as heroes, and their heroism through friendship, are the burden of all that is said or sung of them. Born the same day, of lordly parentage, Sir Amys and Sir Amylion came to love each other while children, and they were early pledged in a covenant of friendship:

> "On a day the childer war and wight
> Trewethes togider thai gan plight,
>   While thai might liue and stond;
> That, both bi day and bi night,
> In wele and wo, in wrong and right,
>   That thai schuld frely fond,
> To hold togider at eueri nede,
> In word, in werk, in wille, in dede,
>   Where that thai were in lond;
> Fro that day forward neuer mo,
> Failen other for wele no wo;
>   Therto thai held vp her hond."

From that time onward Sir Amys and Sir Amylion were together foremost in heroic adventures wherever they went. Sir Amylion at the risk of his own life rescued Sir Amys from deadly peril. And when Sir Amylion became an outcast leper, Sir Amys gave the heart's blood of his two children in order to restore his friend to health. In this sacrifice the mother of the children joined cheerfully, because it was at the call of a sacred friendship; and Heaven showed its approval of the sacrifice by bringing the two children to life again, while granting a cure to him for whom their blood had been shed. And this is but one story of many in proof of the hold that the sentiment of friendship had on the most heroic minds in the best days of Christian chivalry.

Friendship and heroism and religion combine, in the marvelous story of Roland and Oliver and Archbishop

Turpin, on the bloody field of Roncesvalles, in the days of Charles the Great, a thousand years ago. Roland and Oliver were such equal and inseparable friends, that their very names have come down the ages as the synonym of impersonated likeness; "a Roland for an Oliver,"— equal for equal. And such stalwart Christian believers were these hero-friends, that the brave and godly Turpin, the archbishop, was ever ready with his blessing for them as friends and heroes. Never men fought as these friends are said to have fought, when betrayed by a false comrade, and outnumbered by a countless host of unbelieving Spanish foes. Hundreds fell by the hand of the Christian friends; and still they battled on, until Oliver fell by the side of Roland, and as his eyes grew dim with death he reached out lovingly toward his friend, and said: "It is so dark I cannot see thy face; give me thy hand. God bless thee, Roland! God bless Charles and France!" So saying, he fell upon his face, and died. "Dear comrade!" said brave Roland, as he lifted his dead friend tenderly in his arms, "thou wast ever a good and gentle friend to me; better warrior brake never a spear, nor wielded sword. . . . God rest thy soul! A sweeter friend and truer comrade no man ever had than thou." And only when Roland was the last of his host, "a lonesome man in the Valley of Death," did he also fall down to die. No wonder that the great Charles should, according to the story, embalm the bodies of the hero-friends,—Roland and Oliver,—and carry them about with him in marble coffins wherever he went, as a memorial of their hero-friendship.

In the story of the first crusade there stands out the

figure of a hero-friend, and the record of exploits of heroism through friendship. Tancred is the hero of heroes of that expedition. "The annals of chivalry present no model more accomplished," says Michaud; "poetry and history have united to celebrate him, and both have heaped upon him the same praises." And Tancred was induced to join the first crusade largely through his warm friendship for his cousin Bohemond of Tarentum, whose motives in that undertaking were those of selfish ambition, to an extent beyond the conception of his pureminded kinsman. It was while Tancred was moving on heroically under the incitement of his friendship for Bohemond, that he came to know and love Godfrey of Bouillon, as one worthier of his devotion; and then it was that the nobler friendship assumed the higher place in his affections, without making him untrue to that friendship which had given him a start in this direction.

With Godfrey, and for Godfrey, Tancred multiplied his acts of heroism, in the campaigns and sieges that preceded the siege of Jerusalem. Inspired by that friendship he distinguished himself at the siege of Nicea. It was his gallantry that saved the army of Godfrey from destruction at Dorylæum. He led triumphantly the advance guard of the army through Asia Minor; and his courage and fidelity shone transcendently in the siege of Antioch. Before Jerusalem, the "Tower of Tancred" was a center of conflict and of hope in the many weary days of that prolonged siege; until at last the walls of the Holy City were surmounted, and Tancred had done his part in making his friend Godfrey its king. Meanwhile and subsequently Tancred showed himself a hero-friend to Bohemond, as he was pre-eminently the hero-friend of Godfrey.

What more beautiful illustration could be given of heroism under the incitement of friendship, than that of Sir James Douglas, "the hero of seventy fights," in his loving effort to rescue from the Saracens the heart of his dead friend, King Robert Bruce!

> "The Good Sir James, the dreadful blacke Douglas,
> That in his dayes so wise and worthie was,
> Wha here and on the infidels in Spain
> Such honor, praise, and triumphs did obtain."

After many a deed of heroism with and for the king whom he loved so royally, Sir James had been summoned to the bedside of the dying king, and enjoined to take the king's faithful heart, as soon as it had ceased to beat, and carry it to Jerusalem, to be deposited with humility and reverence at the sepulcher of our Lord. It was in pursuance of this mission of friendship that Douglas set out against the Saracens in Spain, as Bruce had purposed doing. Taking from its place, suspended about his neck, the casket containing the memorial of his friend, Douglas would throw it before him toward the enemy, exclaiming as he did so, "Onward, brave heart that never failed! Douglass will follow thee or die." And Douglas both followed and died. The blazoned arms of the proud house of Douglas, to-day, is a bleeding heart,—the heart of a royal and a hero-inspiring friend.

Down along the centuries, and up along the scale of Christian civilization, the sway of an unselfish personal friendship as an incitement to noble personal heroism shows itself in similar yet varying illustrations, in proof of the truth that there is good in human nature, and that human nature is at its best in this direction. It were needless to specify particular instances, as if only they could be noted; for the records of busy life abound with them everywhere.

It was the spirit of friendship, rather than of loyalty or patriotism, that bound the staff-officers of Napoleon to their chief, and that prompted their many heroic acts in his behalf. Marmont, an aide of the emperor, speaking of this feeling on their part, said: "A genuine friendship held us together, and our mutual attachment amounted to devotion." At the battle of Arcole, Muiron, one of these staff officers, "bound to Napoleon by those mysterious ties of affection which this strange man inspired, seeing a bomb-shell about to explode, threw himself between it and Napoleon, saving the life of his beloved general by the sacrifice of his own." And on that same day General Lannes, whom Napoleon called one of his few real "friends," also interposed his body between Napoleon and the enemy, and received three wounds that would otherwise have been his, even then refusing to leave his commander until the battle was over. And such acts of heroism as this were frequent on the part of those who loved Napoleon with the love of a friend.

In our Civil War many a soldier, on either side of the conflict, gave or risked his life to save a soldier-friend; and more than once or twice a soldier who was summoned to a place in a squad of prisoners going out from a gloomy prison-pen, pushed into that place a friend whom he loved dearer than life, and remained a prisoner in his stead. A sailor on a sinking ship has urged his friend into the boat that gave the last hope of life, when only one person could be safely added to its living freight. A miner has lost his own life in striving to rescue his friend from the deadly fire-damp. The hunter, the factory-hand, the railroad man, has proved himself the hero-friend in an emergency, because of the hero-inciting power of friendship. So it has been many a time, so it is; and so it shall continue to be.

Fiction has its illustrations of this truth as vivid and as real as fact; for the noblest ideals of the novelist are but the portraitures of that which has already had an existence in reality. No individual character pictured by Charles Dickens is more admirable and exalted than that of Sydney Carton, in its exhibit of sublime heroism under the incitement of self-abnegating friendship. Sydney Carton lived an aimless, useless life, wasting all his opportunities and powers, until he was aroused to a sense of something better and holier by a sentiment of the purest friendship for Lucie Manette. It was no craving love, no love with the hope or desire of possession, that uplifted and enlarged the soul of Sydney Carton, as it went out toward Lucie Manette in an unselfish friendship for her,—because of what she was in herself, and not because of what she was or ever could be to him. It was a love that included hers for her sake, and that had a steadily transforming power on him whom it swayed. The time came when Charles Darnay, the husband of Lucie Manette, was sentenced to the guillotine, during the reign of terror, in the French Revolution. Then it was that Sydney Carton managed to enter the cell of the condemned man, and to exchange places with him, sending him out to rejoin his wife and child in liberty,—all unconscious of the cost of this escape,—he going in his stead to the deadly block. And as this hero-friend passed along the streets to his execution, he was ministering religious comfort, in the spirit of self-forgetful friendship, to a gentle girl who was his fellow-sufferer; and his last words to her were the assuring words of the Friend of friends: "I am the Resurrection and the Life, saith the Lord: he that believeth in me, though he were dead, yet shall he live: and whosoever liveth and believeth in me shall never die." "They said of him, about the city that night, that it was the peacefullest man's face ever beheld there. Many added that he looked sublime and prophetic." And what could better show a man at his best than such an act of heroism, incited by such a friendship; for greater love hath no man than this, that a man lay down his life for his friend!

IMPELLING RELIGIOUS MOVEMENTS.

REAT religious movements, whether in behalf of truth or error, with their limitless results of influence on successive generations, have, again and again, pivoted on or been mainly impelled by the personal friendships of their pre-eminent leaders. Divinely given illustrations of this truth appear in the Bible record. When God would begin a new religious movement in the race, in the days of greatest degeneracy after the Flood, he chose one man to be his peculiar "friend," and he declared that in that friend, and because of that friendship, all the nations of the earth should find a blessing. When, again, the Son of man would make a new beginning in the line of God's covenant with Abraham, he chose to himself one of his disciples to be his peculiar friend; and the words of that friend, as a result of that friendship, are a means of spirit and life to all the followers of Jesus everywhere to-day.

The twelve apostles were sent out by our Lord, for the

proclaiming of his truth and for the extension of his work, not one by one, but two by two, in order that each one should have the impelling and cheer which only a close personal friendship can secure. It was the same with the seventy others appointed by our Lord; they went two by two, because, in the very nature of things, two are more than two—in all loving service for God or man. Peter and John were friends and fellow-helpers in their common work for their common Master, from the time when they alone of the twelve were together within the walls of the high-priest's palace at the time of that Master's trial. They cheered each other, and together they cheered their fellows, when they ran in company to the tomb of their risen Lord to gain proofs of his resurrection. Together they two went to the temple at the hour of prayer, and wrought a miracle in the healing of the cripple at the gate Beautiful. Together they were arrested and imprisoned because of their widespread influence through their common wonder-working. They strengthened each other in the faith, and together they were bold in their Christian confidence before the very rulers who had condemned their Lord; and the cause of Christ had increased power over the people in Jerusalem, in those earliest days of the Christian Church, because Peter the leader of the apostles, and John whom Jesus loved, were attached and helpful friends.

Paul, the apostle to the Gentiles, was as strong and self-reliant as it is possible for any man to be; but when God would sustain him in his appointed work, he saw to it that Paul should not be without the gain of friendship as a means of grace. When Barnabas proved to

Impelling Religious Movements.   177

be not the man for Paul's friend, Silas took his place. Luke also was permitted to be in that position for a time; and finally Timothy became so close a friend to Paul that the great apostle could count him dearly beloved, as both friend and son. It was because of the special friendship between Paul and Timothy that the letters from the one to the other have in them so much of tender sympathy and of affectionate counsel as a means of good to appreciative readers to the end of time. And it is because of Paul's evident sense of the value of friendship that Dean Stanley characterizes him as "the great Apostle who 'had a thousand friends, and loved each one as if he had a thousand souls, and died a thousand deaths when he parted from them.'"

If our knowledge were fuller of the personal lives of all the early leaders in the Christian Church, we should have evidence of the particular friendships which were shaping factors in those lives severally; for, because friendship is what it is, no great life can be at its best without its impelling power. But here and there along the centuries we have gleams of the friendships that have helped to make the more marked epochs of religious history, and that which we see is a suggestion of the more that is unseen.

Origen, of Alexandria, who was born before the close of the second century, has been called "the first great preacher, the first great commentator, the first great dogmatist, of Christianity," after the days of the Apostles. Origen's Hexapla, a comparative view of the Hebrew text and the various Greek versions of the Old Testament, was the beginning of critical study of the Bible text in the

Christian Church. His formal defense of Christianity against the attacks of Celsus, a Platonist philosopher, has been the basis, or starting-point, of Christian apologetics all down the centuries. His commentaries and homilies were multiplied to an extent that had no precedent, and that was a marvel for centuries afterward. Jerome suggestively asks: "Who has read as much as Origen has written?" His work "On First Principles" was "the earliest attempt to form a system of Christian doctrines, or rather a philosophy of the Christian faith;" and it became a center of interest and of theological controversies for generations following. The friendships of Origen are as noteworthy as is his place in religious history. It was while Origen was still a young scholar in the famous catechetical school at Alexandria that he formed a close friendship with a fellow-pupil named Alexander,—a friendship which had its influence over both friends during their lifetime. When Origen, who had come to be at the head of the school in Alexandria, was in Palestine during a season of violent persecution in Egypt, at the beginning of the third century, his old friend Alexander, who had become Bishop of Jerusalem, encouraged him to expound the Scriptures in the public services of the church, though he had not been ordained. This action called forth the censure of the Bishop of Alexandria, and it was the cause of heated discussions between ecclesiastics which had their part in making history, and in turning the life course of Origen. Bishop Alexander remained a true friend to Origen in all these difficulties, and he owes much of his place in religious history to this fidelity in friendship.

But even more influential on the life-work of Origen was the friendship of Ambrose of Alexandria, an early pupil and a devoted admirer of Origen. Ambrose had money as well as a warm and tender heart, and all that he had was at the disposal of his friend. It was Ambrose who urged Origen to begin his work of the written exposition of Scripture, and he it was who furnished means for the prosecution of this work. At Ambrose's cost, seven shorthand writers were provided to take down the comments of Origen as they were spoken, and other scribes were at hand to copy out for general use the notes of the shorthand reporters. The many exegetical works of Origen are, in fact, a monument to the friendship of Ambrose. It was at this friend's request that Origen composed his famous reply to Celsus. Meanwhile, at peril and sore cost to himself, Ambrose gave sympathy and cheer to Origen, until he was taken from the side of his friend, to suffer, if not to die, for friendship's sake. "Ambrose left no writings of his own except some letters," says Bishop Westcott, "but it is evident that he exercised a powerful influence upon Origen, who called him his 'taskmaster;'" as, in fact, every true friend is a "taskmaster," or spur to well-doing, in the life of him whom he loves. If, indeed, there had been no friendship of Origen with Ambrose, there would have been no such work of Origen as made his life and labors an epoch in religious history.

Closely following Origen came Eusebius of Cæsarea, as a new center of historical interest in the religious world, and as a beginner in a new sphere of religious writing. Eusebius is called "The Father of Ecclesiastical History." He wrote a history of the first three centuries of Christianity, a life of Constantine, a universal history, a work on Christian evidences against Paganism, and many other works. He was on terms of intimacy with the Emperor Constantine, and was designated by the latter to make the opening address at the epoch-making Council of Nice. Apart from all questions as to the correctness of his theological opinions, it is an unmistakable fact that the influence of Eusebius was exceptionally potent in his day; and it is equally clear that his character and course felt profoundly the sway of a personal friendship. Pamphilus, a native of Phœnicia, was the friend who put his impress on this great Christian scholar. Like Ambrose the friend of Origen, Pamphilus had ample means; and, like him, he employed his means in aiding the literary labors of his friend, and in multiplying copies of the Scriptures and of valuable religious writings. He was himself a scholar, and he gathered a library of rare value, which was, of course, at the disposal of the friend whom he loved. Together the two friends transcribed and annotated copies of the Scriptures from the best manuscripts available to them; and, in addition to this work, they promoted the translation of portions of the Bible, in order to extend their influence to those who were unfamiliar with the Greek.

Pamphilus seems to have been the leading spirit of the two, and to have advanced the character as well as the scholarship of Eusebius. "Eusebius owed far more to Pamphilus," says Bishop Lightfoot, "than the impulse and direction given to his studies. . . . To the sympathy of the friend he united the courage of the hero. He had also the power of impressing his own strong convictions on others. Hence, when the great trial of faith came [in the days of persecution for Christ's sake], his house was found to be not only the home of students, but the nursery of martyrs. To one like Eusebius, who owed his strength and his weakness alike to a ready susceptibility of impression from those about him, such a friendship was an inestimable blessing." Pamphilus was cast into prison as a Christian. For two years Eusebius watched by him, studied with him, and gained from him. Soon after the beginning of the fourth century, Pamphilus met a martyr's death together with eleven holy companions. Eusebius mourned his friend as more than his other self. "My lord Pamphilus," he termed him; "for it is not meet," he added, "that I should mention the name of that holy and blessed Pamphilus without styling him 'my lord.'" And from that day onward Eusebius insisted on being called by the name of his dead friend. "Eusebius Pamphili," "Pamphilus's Eusebius," he wrote his name; and it is by this name that he is known to history. And Eusebius was right in thus styling himself; for all that was best in him and in his work came from and through the friendship of Pamphilus.

A new movement in religious thought was made by Augustine in the generation after Eusebius. His personality gave shape to a system of doctrine that has put its impress on the Christian thought of the world ever since. "The Protestant emulates the Romanist in paying him honor," says the historian. "He is the dividing line between the Church of the persecution and the Church of the empire. He ended the old and began the new period of her development." That the character and course of Augustine were largely shaped by his personal friendships, the pages of his own " Confessions" bear unmistakable witness. While yet a careless unbeliever, Augustine had a young friend, a fellow-townsman, and schoolmate in his birthplace, Tagaste. One of the first serious impressions on the mind of Augustine seems to have been made by the earnest words of this young friend on his death-bed; and the memory of that friend, and of those words, was an abiding force in his life thenceforward. The friendship as a friendship could not be forgotten. " I wondered," says Augustine, "that the rest of mortals could live, because he was dead whom I had loved as if he were never to die; and I much more wondered that I myself—who was *another he*—could live when he was gone." Confessing to the struggles of mind which followed the loss of this friend, Augustine records: " I was restless, and sighed and wept, and was distracted and bereft both of ease and counsel. For I carried about with me a soul all wounded and bleeding—impatient to be any longer carried by me, and yet where to lay it down to rest I did not find. . . . I still remained to myself an unhappy place, where I could neither be nor yet get away. For whither could my heart fly from my heart? whither could I fly from myself? and where would not myself follow me? However I fled from my own country, for my eyes missed him [the dead friend] less where they were not used to see him; and from Tagaste I came to Carthage."

If this friendship had been the only one to have an

influence on the character and opinions of Augustine, it would be evident to the careful reader of his Confessions that it was an important factor in the shaping forces of his whole being. But in addition to this, another friendship came in to hold and sway him wonderfully, until he could look back upon that first great life sorrow, and say reverently: "I was weighed down by the grievous burden of my misery, which by thee, O Lord, was to be lightened and cured;" and he could look up in the light of his new friendship, saying: "Ah! blessed is he that loveth thee, O Lord! and his friend in thee." It was Alypius, another native of Tagaste,—one who had been the pupil of Augustine there,—who afterwards came into closest friendship with him at Carthage. "He loved me much, because he thought me to be learned and good," says Augustine; "as also I loved him for his great inclination to virtue, which considering his age was very eminent." Even while the two friends were yet unbelievers, each influenced the other to nobler purposes. Again they were together in Rome, and there, says Augustine of Alypius, "he stuck close to me with a most strong bond of friendship; and he went with me to Milan that he might have my company." At Milan the two friends heard Ambrose preach, and were impressed by his preaching. Afterwards they were there brought together into the church by baptism. During the spiritual struggles of Augustine, Alypius was his companion and sharer. Even when the former would be by himself in prayer and communion with God, the latter could be with him. "For I counted not myself less private for his being there," says Augustine; "nor would he leave me alone, seeing me in this commotion." It was in such intimacy that the two friends, who had inspired each other toward a higher ideal while they were yet out of Christ, were led along together in the path of the Christian life. Alypius became the saintly Bishop of Tagaste, and Augustine the godly and renowned Bishop of Hippo. The power of either of these in its world-wide sweep is the power of both; and in the work of Augustine we may see incorporated the work of his friend Alypius.

The religious movement led by Muhammad, in the seventh century, was widely different from that led by Augustine two centuries before, yet it has proved hardly less potent and far reaching among the sons of men; and the course and life-work of Muhammad as a religious leader were shaped and impelled by a personal friendship, as truly as were those of the great Christian dogmatist. Muhammadanism owes a large share of its success as one of the world-religions to the sympathy, the companionship, the unswerving fidelity, and the never-failing aid of Aboo Bekr, the earliest, the latest, and the ever dearest friend of its founder. Aboo Bekr, whose earlier name was Abdallah (Servant of God), or, as some claim, Abd-el Kaaba (Servant of the Holy House), was of the same tribe and clan with Muhammad, and of nearly the same age. There is reason for believing that these two were fellow-pupils of Zayd, a famous truth-seeking teacher at Mekka, who put his impress on them both. From their very youth Muhammad and Aboo Bekr were bosom friends, and the latter shared with the former in his struggles toward truth. When Muhammad announced himself in his own family as a heaven-sent prophet, and had as yet not a single believer in his claims save his wife and their two adopted sons, Aboo Bekr was the first person to give him his confidence, and to pledge him support. Of this promptness in trusting,—which is a characteristic of friendship,—Muhammad said gratefully: "I never invited any to the faith who did not at the first show hesitation and perplexity, excepting only Aboo Bekr. But he, when I had propounded unto him Islam, tarried not, neither was perplexed." When the prophet fled for his life from Mekka (an event that marks the beginning of his religion as a religion), Aboo Bekr was his sole companion—the prophet's only earthly hope. The two were together in the cave on Mount Thôr, when, according to a Muhammadan tradition, their pursuers were turned from it by a spider-web freshly spun across its entrance. Then it was that the prophet said to his friend: "We are three; for God is with us;" and thenceforward, as at that time, the hope of Muhammad seemed to rest on God and Aboo Bekr. So generally was this recognized that Aboo Bekr was often called the "Second of the Two;" as he was also called "Es-Sadeeq"—"The True Friend." His name Aboo Bekr, "Father of the Virgin," was assumed later in life, when his daughter Ayeshah was married to the prophet at nine years of age.

It was a close personal friendship, not a mere "modal alliance," that bound these two to each other. "Ah, thou for whom I would sacrifice father and mother, white hairs are hastening upon thee," said Aboo Bekr tenderly, when he saw that the prophet's beard was graying. Of Aboo Bekr's place in the prophet's heart the poet Hassan sang:

> "And the Second of the Two in the glorious cave,
>   While around the foes were searching;
>   When the Two had ascended the mountain together.
>   And they knew that the prophet loved him above all
>   the world besides;
>   He held no one equal to him."

It is said that when Muhammad heard these lines from the poet he "laughed so heartily as to show his back teeth, and said, 'Thou hast spoken truly, O Hassan! It is just as thou hast said.'" Such a friendship could not but have been a potent factor in the prophet's life-work, and the most careful historians have emphasized the fact that it was so. Gibbon, in reviewing the case, says: "The wealth, the moderation, the veracity of Aboo Bekr confirmed the religion of the Prophet, whom he was destined to succeed. By his persuasion ten of the most respectable citizens of Mekka were introduced to the private lessons of Islam. They yielded to the voice of reason and enthusiasm"—at a time when personal support at Mekka was all-important to the prophet's cause. Sir William Muir, whose exceptional familiarity with the facts and lessons of Muhammadanism gives a peculiar value to his opinion, says: "Abû Bekr early cast in his lot with the Prophet, and through all the changing scenes of his life to the end was to him a pillar of strength." "His nature was mild and sympathetic, but not incapable of firm purpose where important interests were concerned. Impulse and passion rarely prompted his actions; he was guided by reason and calm conviction. . . . He was popular throughout the city [of Mekka]. . . . To gain such a man as a staunch adherent of his claims was for Mahomet a most important step."

Sprenger, who wrote his authoritative life of Muhammad after a careful study, in the East, of original sources of information, is yet more unqualified and emphatic in his testimony to the importance of Aboo Bekr's friendship. "The first believers in Mohammad after his family, and those who contributed most towards the progress of the new doctrine, were Abú Bakr and his friends. . . . Abú Bakr . . . was staunch as a friend, and made by nature to work out the ideas of others. . . . He was to all appearance the confidant and friend of the prophet, with whom he discussed, during the transition period, his doubts and speculations. . . . The faith of Abú Bakr is, in my opinion, the greatest guarantee of the sincerity of Mohammad in the beginning of his career; and *he did more for the success of the Islám than the prophet himself.* His having joined Mohammad lent respectability to his cause; he spent seven-eighths of his property, . . . when he embraced the new faith, towards its promotion at Makkah; and he continued the same course of liberality at Madynah; and six of the earliest and most talented and respectable of converts who joined Mohammad did so at his persuasion; and they had been, evidently, prepared by him long before the mission."

Nor was it only in the beginning of Muhammad's mission that Aboo Bekr's power was manifest as the "Second of the Two." Always the friend and counselor of the prophet, and his right arm in times of conflict, Aboo Bekr was, during the prophet's last illness, deputed by Muhammad to take his place in leading the public prayers, when the prophet was no longer able to perform this service himself. And when at last the tired head of

Muhammad rested in death on the bosom of Aboo Bekr's daughter, and the despairing cry went forth that the "Prophet of God" was dead, then, more than ever before, the Second of the Two stood out for both himself and his friend, in the beauty and potency of a deathless friendship. Omar, the strong-armed supporter of Muhammad, who was a rival with Alee (the prophet's son-in-law) for the succession to the prophet's power as khaleef, was afraid to admit the fact of the prophet's death, lest his followers should be in despair; and his cry was that the prophet was only in a trance, from which he would shortly awake. But Aboo Bekr was too true to his friend and to his friend's faith for such a falsehood. Love led him first to his friend's cold body, and then to the defense of his friend's mission. Hastening to the door of Ayeshah's apartments, "he drew aside the curtain, entered, and, stooping down, kissed the face of his departed friend. 'Sweet wast thou in life,' he said, 'and sweet thou art in death, dearer than father and mother to me! Yes, thou art dead, and [referring to Omar's wild words without] thou art too precious for the Lord to give thee to drink the bitter cup a second time.'" And then Aboo Bekr covered the face of his dead friend, and rose up to carry on that dead friend's life-work. "Is it Muhammad, or the God of Muhammad, whom you worship?" he asked of Omar and of the panic-stricken multitude. "Whosoever among you has believed in Muhammad, let him know that Muhammad is dead. But he who has believed in the God of Muhammad, let him continue to serve him; for he is still alive, and never dies.' Even Omar recognized in this the power of

Muhammad's other self, and he instantly gave deference to Aboo Bekr as the prophet's successor. Alee also acquiesced in this, and he who had been the life-long bosom friend of Muhammad continued Muhammad's life-work.

It was Aboo Bekr who compiled and edited the detached suras of the Qurân, which, up to the time of the prophet's death, had been kept, as originally recorded, "on palm-leaves, and the shoulder-bones of mutton," and on other stray materials, without order or connection, in a chest in the custody of one of the prophet's wives. And when Aboo Bekr's personal work was done, he designated Omar as his successor in the khaleefate, and so the sway of his influence passed on to the generations following. There is a double fitness in the term by which the theologians of Islam call a Muhammadan El-Habeeb, The Friend; for the Muhammadans are the followers and representatives of The Friends,—Muhammad El-Ameen, and Aboo Bekr Es-Sadeeq: The Faithful One, and The True Friend. Those two have already numbered more than four thousand millions in the passing centuries, and "the end is not yet."

It was while Muhammad was starting out on his mission, with the aid and stimulus of Aboo Bekr's friendship, early in the seventh century, that there grew up in the ancient city of Tarsus a lad named Theodore, who was destined to do a great work for Christendom in the then far West, under the impelling power of a friend's affectionate devotion. Trained in the best schools of Tarsus and Athens, Theodore found his way to Rome,—possibly in company with the Emperor Constans. There he won the friendship of an abbot named Hadrian, and this friendship it was that shaped his life-course. A strong man was just then needed to make new beginnings of religious activity in Britain. Pope Vitalian selected Hadrian to be the Archbishop of Canterbury, as peculiarly suited to this work. Hadrian said that his friend Theodore was a better man than he for the place; but when the pope pressed the position on Theodore, the latter was unwilling to accept it unless his friend Hadrian would go with him, to give him sympathy and stimulus and counsel. Then it was that the two friends went together from Rome to Canterbury, as if to illustrate and emphasize the power of friendship in impelling a religious movement of importance.

Theodore of Tarsus was the seventh Archbishop of Canterbury. Hadrian was his friend and co-worker from the beginning. Together they journeyed through the ecclesiastical realm, and together they planned for its advancement in one line and another. Schools were founded, learning was promoted, Christian work was organized, the interests of the church were looked after closely. "It is difficult, if not impossible, to overstate the debt which England, Europe, and Christian civilization owe to the work of Theodore," says Bishop Stubbs. "He was the real organizer of the administrative system of the English Church, and in that work laid the foundation of English national unity. He brought the learning and culture of the Eastern empire into the West, and, with the aid of Hadrian and Benedict Biscop, established schools from which the scholars and missionaries of the following century went out to rekindle the light of Christian culture in France and the recently converted parts of Germany; and thus ... formed a most important link between ancient and modern life. ... Both his character and his work seem to place him among the first and greatest of the saints whom God has used for the building up of the church and development of the culture of the world." Whatever was thus done by Theodore as Archbishop of Canterbury was an outcome of the friendship of Hadrian; for it was through that friendship that he came to that exalted position. And the best work done by Theodore in that position was done the better because of the presence and sympathy of the friend without whom he would not have undertaken the work.

An important movement in religious thinking, in the eleventh century, is represented by Anselm of Aosta, successively Abbot of Bec and Archbishop of Canterbury; and in a pre-eminent degree the impelling force in the life of Anselm was personal friendship. Anselm has been called "the father of orthodox scholasticism," "the second Augustine," "the one philosopher of the eleventh century." His method of argument for theism has been a favorite pattern for Christian thinkers from that day to this. His book on the Atonement first gave shape to the Church's thought on that great doctrine. The conflict that he waged, single-handed, with the kings of England, had its echoes, in religious warfare, for five centuries thereafter. Anselm was an original thinker, a dauntless hero, and a peerless friend. Because of these qualities it was that he made his impress on his own age and on ages following.

Lanfranc of Lombardy, prior of the monastery at Bec in Normandy, seems to have been the first friend who was an impelling force in the career of Anselm. Anselm came, as a young man, from Aosta to Bec to study under Lanfranc, who was then a famous teacher. Young as Anselm was, he was already a stronger thinker than Lanfranc, but Lanfranc was more energetic in practical affairs. "Teacher and pupil," says Dean Church, "besides being both Italians, had much to draw them together; and a friendship began between them, which, in spite of the difference between the two men, and the perhaps unconscious reserve caused by it, continued to the last genuine and unbroken." Anselm came to love and trust Lanfranc without reserve, and submitted himself to his guidance. It was through Lanfranc's counsel that Anselm became a monk. Lanfranc secured a position for Anselm as teacher at Bec. When Lanfranc was appointed to the archbishopric of Canterbury, by the choice of William the Conqueror, Anselm succeeded to his place as prior, and subsequently became abbot, of Bec. Visiting Canterbury as the friend of the archbishop, Anselm came to be known in England, and finally to be looked upon, when Lanfranc was dead, as the natural successor of his friend as the ecclesiastical head of the Church in England. And so it followed that Anselm's friendship for Lanfranc was the means of bringing Anselm into the exalted position that enabled him to exhibit his peculiar power, and to do his peculiar work in the world.

Friendship was a prevailing sentiment in Anselm's nature, and it shone transcendently there. When he was promoted over his seniors at Bec, at the time of Lanfranc's going to England, there was no little jealousy on the part of those who were thus slighted. Among others there was a young monk named Osbern, who was particularly bitter against the new prior. In a spirit of love, Anselm first bore patiently with this opposer, then he gave extra attention to him; finally he watched over him with unwearied devotion in a siege of sickness, and thus came to be his truest and tenderest friend. And when that new charge of his heart was dead, Anselm was overwhelmed with sorrow lest Osbern had died unforgiven of God. Then it was that he showed what it was for him to be a friend. Writing to a dearly loved and highly honored Christian brother, he asked that whatever prayers would be offered for his soul, when he was dead, by those who loved him, might now be offered for the soul of Osbern, even though he himself must suffer for their lack. "I beseech you and all my friends,— words I know come short, and feeling is more than I can express," he wrote,—" wherever Osbern is, his soul is my soul. Let me receive then in him, while I am living, whatever I might have hoped for from my friends when dead, so that when I am gone they may have no more to do. . . . I pray and pray and pray, remember me, and forget not the soul of Osbern my beloved. If I seem to be too burdensome to thee, forget me and remember him."

Such a friend as Anselm would be showing his friendship as long as he lived. When Osbern was dead and Lanfranc was dead, it was Eadmer of Canterbury toward whom Anselm's friendship went out for the remainder of his lifetime. It was on his first visit to Canterbury that Anselm made the acquaintance of Eadmer, who was then but a youth. Afterwards the two became united in closest friendship. Eadmer was the loved and trustful companion of Anselm, at home and abroad, in the most momentous experiences of the great thinker's life; and when Anselm's worn body finally rested by the side of his first friend Lanfranc at Canterbury, his latest friend Eadmer wrote his life-story for future generations. Because of Anselm's friendship for Lanfranc, Anselm came to the eminence that gave him scope for his great powers. Because of Anselm's friendship for Osbern, Anselm rose to a height of sacred self-abnegation that only friendship could reach. Because of Anselm's friendship for Eadmer, the record of Anselm's elevation of personal life was passed down the ages in the words of Eadmer. Moreover, the epoch-making work of Anselm on the Incarnation and Atonement (*Cur Deus Homo?*) is said to have been planned primarily as a means of giving light to the troubled mind of Eadmer.

Early in the thirteenth century there arose two new workers for Christ and for their fellows,—" Francis in Italy and Dominic in Spain,—who came, full of the primitive spirit of the gospel, to renew the religious life and bring a fresh flood of genuine spiritual influence upon the world." The influential orders of mendicant friars, the Franciscans and the Dominicans, were founded by these two men; and, for a period, the work of these orders was a potent factor in the teachings and doings of the Christian Church. Friendship had its part in impelling and directing the religious movements thus inaugurated.

Francis of Assisi was brought up in wealth and pleasure-seeking, but, in consequence of a severe illness, and of a vision that gave him specific direction in duty, he determined to devote his life to evangelizing and reforms. While his plans for a new order of evangelists were still incomplete, a friendship formed by him with a young girl of noble family, in his native town, did much to influence his life and hers, and to promote the larger lifework of both. Francis of Assisi was thirty years old, handsome, eloquent, full of piety and zeal. Chiara Sciffi, afterwards known as St. Clare, was not yet eighteen when she was moved to leave her home and come to the saintly leader whose praise was on all lips, telling him that she was ready to commit herself to his guidance, and to be in God's service as he should direct. "This circumstance threw great luster over both his person and his enterprise," says the historian Engelhardt; and it had much to do with securing the wonderful start gained by the Franciscans on the one hand and by the Clarisses on the other. Within fifty years from its founding, the Order of Franciscans numbered eight thousand monasteries, comprising two hundred thousand friars; and it was one of the world-forces.

Mrs. Oliphant, as a biographer of St. Francis, referring to the first coming of this "devout, spotless, saintly maiden" to the earnest and devoted man of God, says appreciatively: "This was the beginning of one of those tender and touching friendships which are to the student of history like green spots in the desert; and which gave to the man and the woman thus voluntarily separated from all the joys of life a certain human consolation in the midst of their hardships. They can have seen each other but seldom, for it was one of the express stipulations of the Franciscan rule that the friars should refrain from all society with women, and have only the most sparing and reserved intercourse with their sisters in religion. . . . But he sent to her to ask enlightenment from her prayers when any difficulty was in his way. He went to see her when he was in trouble. . . . Once the two friends ate together at a sacramental meal, the pledge and almost the conclusion on earth of that tenderest, most disinterested, and unworldly love which existed between them. That he was sure of her sympathy in all things, of her prayers and spiritual aid, whatsoever he might be doing, wheresoever he might be, no doubt was sweet to Francis in all his labors and trials." " The world has jeered at the possibility of such friendships from its earliest age," continues Mrs. Oliphant, " and yet they have always existed —one of the most exquisite and delicate of earthly ties. Gazing back into that far distance over the graves, not only of those two friends, but of a hundred succeeding generations, a tear of grateful sympathy comes into the student's eye. He is glad to believe that, all those years, Francis could see, in his comings and goings, the cloister of Clara; and that this sacred gleam of human fellowship,—love purified of all self-seeking,—tender, visionary, celestial affection sweetened their lives." Nor can it be doubted that much of the best exhibit of saintliness in the beginnings of the Franciscan and Clarissan orders was due to the power of this friendship between St. Francis and St. Clare.

Foremost among the representative men in the new

orders of Dominicans and of Franciscans, during the first century of their existence, were Thomas Aquinas of the Dominicans and Bonaventura of the Franciscans. These two great men were attached personal friends, and their friendship was a shaping force in their lives and teachings. Thomas Aquinas is known as the Angelic Doctor, and Bonaventura as the Seraphic Doctor. The two men were near of an age, and they were attached friends almost from boyhood. "They both had dedicated their lives to God in the same year," and they were helpers of each other's faith, while working toward the same end in their rival orders. "Each was different from the other," says a Roman Catholic biographer of the first-named of the two, "and each found in the other that which was wanting in himself, and in that sweet discovery experienced the full harmony of his entire being. Bonaventura loved to look into the placid, earnest soul of Thomas as into a deep glassy sea with its marvelous transparency and awful stillness; whilst Thomas was roused and brightened by the ardent, outpouring nature of his friend. St. Thomas was angelical, St. Bonaventura was seraphic,—the one the deep thinker, the other the tender poet. Thomas was famous in the schools for the keenness of his thought and for his depth and clearness; Bonaventura, for his eloquence and vivacity in exposition. . . . Thomas was essentially a child of contemplation; Bonaventura, of activity."

The friends visited each other from time to time, while they were representatives of widely different schools of thought, until they died in the same year. On the same day they were made doctors of theology in the University of Paris; and they were side by side while putting upon others the impress of their interdependent yet independent natures. Each gained from the other that without which he could never have been his best self, or have done his best work. Thomas, being the stronger character of the two, was enabled to gain most from this friendship, and therefore to be its best representative; but Bonaventura was himself a great gainer through being a means of greater gain to his friend. Thomas Aquinas was a prince of scholastic thinkers. His thinking, as tinged by the color of his friend's saintly feeling, has become the thinking of the Roman Catholic Church for to-day. It is his liturgy, in the office and mass for the solemn feast of *Corpus Christi*, that gives expression to the profoundest feeling of the devout worshipers of that communion, in their holiest adorations; and this liturgy seems to have had a measure of its inspiration from the suggestion of Bonaventura to Thomas as to the source of his own inspirings. When Thomas asked Bonaventura out of what books he obtained the sublime thoughts that appeared in his writings, Bonaventura pointed to a figure of the body of Christ, saying, "There is the book!" Afterwards, Thomas gave himself to writing about the Holy Body of Christ. It is said, indeed, that Pope Urban IV. had given instructions to the two great teachers, at the same time, for the construction of this liturgy for the feast of *Corpus Christi;* but that, when Bonaventura saw the work of Thomas while it was still in progress, he cast into the flames, as unworthy in comparison, that which he had himself prepared.

It was a great religious movement, for its time, that was begun by Francis of Assisi; and Clare of Assisi was an impelling force in that movement through her loyal friendship for its leader. It was a great religious movement in the realm of thinking and feeling, for a longer time than that of his own day, that was begun by Thomas Aquinas; and an impelling force in that movement was the friendship for its leader by Bonaventura.

Among the agencies which quickened the spiritual life in the Christian Church at the time, and which prepared the way for the Renaissance of literature and art in the fifteenth century, and for the great Protestant Reformation of the sixteenth century, was the association of spiritual-minded Christians known as Brothers of the Common Life; the best known representative or product of which is Thomas à Kempis, author of the "Imitation of Christ." This association was founded by Gerhard Groot, at Deventer, in the latter fourth of the fourteen century. Groot's conversion to the truth was distinctly a result of "a close and intimate friendship" formed by him, at the University of Paris, with Henry Aeger, known also as Henry von Kalkar. To this friendship is due, under God, all the mighty results of Gerhard Groot's devotion to the cause of truth, and of his work in and through the association that extended itself so widely after its beginning by him. On this point the words of Gerhard himself, as cited in his Life by Thomas à Kempis, are explicit and conclusive.

Close personal friendships, among those who were brought under the influence of the Brothers of the Common Life, had much to do with inspiring and shaping the best work of the best workers in that sphere. This was peculiarly the case with Thomas à Kempis. "There were two valuable friendships which Thomas à Kempis formed whilst dwelling with 'The Brothers of the Common Life,'" says his latest and most trustworthy biographer. "The chief companion of Thomas à Kempis at Deventer, and the earliest of his most intimate friends, was Arnold of Schoonhaven, a youth of fervent piety, who from childhood was singularly devoted to God." These two friends occupied, as schoolmates together, "one little chamber and one bed." "The example of his young friend Arnold's glowing piety made a deep impression upon à Kempis;" and the ideal thus presented to him of a lovingly consecrated life seems to have been the germ, as it were, of his outreaching desire for a closer likeness to his Saviour, that found its expression in the pages of his marvelous book. "Here was the very companion every way suited for Thomas à Kempis in his early life to promote his growth in grace and holiness, and one in whose congenial society he could always find refreshment and delight. The one became very dear to the other, for they found in each other that harmony of soul and sympathy of disposition that earnest minds most crave after and desire." This is the impartial testimony of à Kempis's biographer; and, in view of the facts he records, he ejaculates: "How hallowed is the sacred tie which thus binds one soul to another! What a safeguard! How healthful, cheering, and strengthening!" So long as Arnold lived, he and à Kempis were devoted friends. When Arnold died, à Kempis wrote his story, thereby setting "before us the example which Thomas himself admired and was animated by; for it appears from the account which he gives us that in his own estimation—ever thinking humbly of himself—he fell short of his friend's stature in grace, and that, in comparison with him, he was not satisfied with his own zeal in devotion."

"The other intimate friend and companion of Thomas à Kempis in his early years . . . was John Cacabus, or as he was otherwise called John Kessel, Kettel, or Ketel." He also was a pupil with à Kempis at the home of The Brothers of the Common Life; and he also was an example and an inspiration to him, as a result of the warm intimacy early formed between them, "which quickly grew into a great friendship." John Ketel, like Arnold, died before à Kempis, leaving the memory of his consecrated living as an incitement to his surviving friend, and as a factor in that friend's highest ideal.

These were the friendships which aided in the shaping and impelling of the religious movements begun, or prepared for, by the association of The Brothers of the Common Life, and the writings of Thomas à Kempis. It was because of the friendship of Gerhard Groot and Henry von Kalkar that The Brothers of the Common Life were led to keep alive a love of truth by the study and teaching of the Word of God in communities which God was preparing for the great reformations approaching. It was because of the friendship between Arnold of Schoonhaven and John Ketel and Thomas à Kempis that the survivor of these three friends was enabled to present to the world such an ideal of Christian aspiring and such an exhibit of Christian devotion as are found in his "Imitation of Christ;" a book which Matthew Arnold calls "the most exquisite document, after those of the New Testament, of all that the Christian spirit has ever inspired," and which Canon Liddon characterizes as a work "which more than any other has caught the spirit of the evangelists," and has "touched the heart of the world;" a book of which Dr. Johnson declared: "It is said to have been printed, in one language or another, as many times as there have been months since it first came out;" and of which De Quincey affirmed: "Excepting the Bible, but excepting that only in Protestant lands, no book known to man has had the same distinction. It is the most marvelous bibliographical fact on record."

The very men who might seem to have withdrawn themselves most religiously from the sway of human affection, and to have given themselves up most devotedly to an exclusively spiritual communion with God, are found, all along the centuries, to have been inspired to and shaped in their holiest aspirations by their sacred personal friendships. What better proof than this could there be that friendship's fullest play has been found, not in the dimmer light of Greek paganism, but in the glow of the purest Christianity?

A young lad under the care of The Brothers of the Common Life in Deventer, in the last quarter of the fifteenth century, was afterwards known to the world as Desiderius Erasmus of Rotterdam. From his humble beginnings of learning in that school of friendship, Erasmus grew to be, unmistakably, "the greatest teacher of his age," and "one of the most gifted men that Europe has ever seen." Moreover, he was the most learned and brilliant representative of a movement for the correction of ecclesiastical abuses, and for the making of the Holy Scriptures the guide in religious teaching, that prepared the way for the great Protestant Reformation under Martin Luther and Henry the Eighth. The monks said bitterly, that "Erasmus laid the egg and Luther hatched a cockatrice;" and the historian Froude, in reviewing the work of the two reformers, says: "Without Erasmus, Luther would have been impossible; and Erasmus really succeeded—so much of him as deserved to succeed—in Luther's victory." The work of such an epoch-marker as Erasmus is worth studying in its causes and impulses; and it needs little study to show that that work, as in so many other cases, was inspired and impelled by the influence of a close personal friendship. Given a start in classical learning at Deventer, Erasmus went, after varying experiences, to the University of Paris, and thence to Oxford University—in pursuit of increased advantages in the study of Greek. At Oxford, Erasmus formed a friendship with John Colet, a young Englishman, son of a lord mayor of London, who had been studying Greek in the new classical atmosphere of Italy; and that friendship proved a shaping force in the life and life-work of Erasmus. Colet's name is less known to the world than Erasmus's, but Erasmus owes no small measure of his best fame to the inspiration and influence of his friend Colet.

John Richard Green, the historian of the English people, says concerning the power of Colet: "The awakening of a rational Christianity, whether in England or in the Teutonic world at large, begins with the Italian studies of John Colet; and the vigor and earnestness of Colet were the best proof of the strength with which the new movement was to affect English religion. . . . The knowledge of Greek seems to have had one almost exclusive end for him, and this was a religious end. Greek was the key by which he could unlock the Gospels and the New Testament; and in these he thought that he could find a new religious standing-ground. It was this resolve of Colet to throw aside the traditional dogmas of his day, and to discover a rational and practical religion in the Gospels themselves, which gave its peculiar stamp to the theology of the Renascence. His faith stood simply on the person of Christ." Speaking of Erasmus, Green adds that "his theology . . . he derived almost without change from Colet." And Drummond, the biographer of the Rotterdam scholar, affirms that "the man who possessed most interest for Erasmus," while at Oxford, and exercised most influence over him, was Colet." "When I listen to my friend Colet," wrote Erasmus from Oxford, "I can fancy I am listening to Plato himself." And the record shows that Erasmus's Greek Testament, the publishing of which was the most important work of his life, was an outcome of his friendship with Colet. Meanwhile, of course, the influence of such a man as Erasmus could not but have its effect on such a man as Colet. Marquard von Hatstein spoke for others as well as himself when he wrote to Colet, long years after the first coming of Erasmus to Oxford: "I seem to myself to see that each of you owes much to the other, but which of the two owes most to the other I am doubtful."

From its beginning the acquaintance of Colet and Erasmus was a friendship. Before they had yet met, Colet wrote to Erasmus, welcoming him to Oxford, with the assurance that he had already heard so much of him from others that he was prepared to be his friend. "As soon as I have seen you I will be my own pleader, as others have been yours in your absence," he said; "and I will commend myself to you and to your wisdom. That others should have commended you to me was unbecoming; for the less ought to be commended to the greater, the more unlearned to the more highly cultured. However, if there is anything within my small means, in which I can be either agreeable or useful to you, it shall be as readily and ungrudgingly at your service as your high merits can desire or claim." In answer to this letter, Erasmus wrote: "If I recognized anything at all in myself, most courteous sir, deserving of even slender praise, I should certainly rejoice, like Hector in Nævius, at being praised by you, the object of all praises. For I set so high a value on your opinion, that your single approbation of me is far pleasanter than if the whole forum of Rome were shouting its applause, or an ignorant multitude were admiring me, vaster than the fabled army of Xerxes. . . . In truth, my dear Colet, so far from your praises having made me conceited, I am even more dissatisfied with myself than ever, being naturally a little more fastidious. For when qualities are affirmed of me which I revere in others but miss in myself, it seems like admonishing me what sort of person I ought to be." Then, giving an outline of his own qualities, as he sees himself, he declares that he is "a stranger to ambition, but for friendship most ready; one whose acquaintance with literature is but scanty, but his admiration of it most ardent; one who worships integrity in others, but counts his own as none; yielding readily to all in learning, but to none in loyalty; ... a man of few words; in short, one from whom you would expect nothing but qualities of heart." "If you, Colet," he concludes, "can love such a man, and deem him worthy of your acquaintance, then set Erasmus down as your own, completely your own."

And from that beginning the two scholars were friends, in an unbroken friendship and in intimate companionship or close correspondence, until, twenty-one years later, Colet died in London, and Erasmus closed a letter concerning him from Louvain with the tender words: "Thus far have I written, grieving for the death of Colet; a death so bitter to me that the loss of no one for the last thirty years has afflicted me more. ... In the public interest I cannot but lament the loss of so rare a pattern of Christian piety, so unique a preacher of Christian doctrine. And on my own private account I lament so constant a friend, so matchless a patron. For what alone remains, in lieu of funeral obsequies, this duty I will discharge for him; if my writings are of any avail, I will not suffer the memory of such a man to die out among posterity." "I long," again wrote Erasmus, "to dedicate his memory to posterity;" ... "such a teacher, such a patron, such a friend!" One of Colet's latest letters to Erasmus shows how tenderly he ever bore his friend in remembrance during their prolonged separations. Erasmus had sent a new book to the Bishop of Rochester, together with a letter containing some kindly greetings to Colet. At this Colet wrote reproachfully: "I am half angry with you, Erasmus, for sending greetings to me in letters written to others, and not to myself. For, though I have no mistrust of our friendship, yet this indirect greeting in letters to other people makes others conclude that you are not so attached to me as you really are. . . . I take such pleasure in your affection that I am pained when I see you less mindful of me than of others."

And these two friends—helped and cheered mutually in their common life-work by and through their friendship—did much to prepare the way for the great Reformation approaching. The writings and sermons of Colet had power over the leaders of church and state and popular sentiment in England in the direction of needed reform. The issuing, by Erasmus, of the first Greek Testament ever published—in the very line of Colet's wishing and teaching from the days of his sojourn in Italy—was the opening of a new standard of religious truth to the Christian scholars of the world; and his parallel Latin translation, published with that Greek Testament, "became," as has been said, "the starting-point of modern exegetical science." How much, indeed, the Christian Church owes to-day to that friendship of Erasmus and Colet!

Foot-hills of the great mountain range of the Protestant Reformation were these subordinate reformations, in the revival of spiritual life through the work of The Brothers of the Common Life, on the Continent, and in the revival of Bible study and biblical criticism, as led by Erasmus and Colet in Great Britain. And as each of these foot-hills is shown to have been surmounted by means of a close and loving friendship between those who could never have been what they were, or have done what they did, without the inspirings of that friendship; so it will be found that the lofty summit-peak of that Reformation range, in the work of Martin Luther, was capped and turned by means of the same sacred sentiment of human friendship, with its pre-eminent and surpassing power over the sons of men.

The stamp of Luther's personal friendships is on every phase of his life-work, from his earliest peaceful school-days to the close of his stormiest career as a reformer; and to track the record of Luther's struggles and successes is to disclose the hidings of his friendship's power. While Luther was yet a student at Erfurt, his close personal friendships with members of a "circle of young humanists" began to have a shaping influence on his life and character. One of these friends was John Jäger, known as Crotus Rubianus; and another was George Spalatin (or Burkhardt of Spelt). Subsequently Spalatin, as court preacher and private secretary, and yet more as trusted friend and adviser, of Elector Frederick of Saxony, was a strong arm of support to his never-forgotten friend Luther. "But what am I not indebted to you!" wrote Luther to Spalatin after long years of abiding confidence in him. Crotus, also, proved an effective helper of Luther, in the stormiest days of the reformer's life, by his brilliant writings in behalf of his course and cause, in both Germany and Italy; and in those days he reminded Luther of the "close intimacy" in which they had lived as friends at Erfurt. Like St. Augustine, Luther was first aroused to profound anxiety concerning his spiritual condition by the sudden death of a loved friend. This event it was that decided him in his choice of a monastic life. He had entered the university with a purpose of studying law.

In the convent at Erfurt, the heavy-hearted Luther quickly won the confidence and sincere friendship of his ecclesiastical superior, John von Staupitz. It was Staupitz who first led Luther toward the light, when he was groping helplessly in spiritual darkness; and, again, Luther was a helper of Staupitz in making progress in the new life which they lived together as friends in Christ. Luther, as Köstlin tells us, spoke of Staupitz, throughout his life, with grateful affection as his spiritual father, and thanked God that, by this friend, he had been helped out of his temptations, when, without him, he would have been swallowed up in them, and perished. On the other hand, Staupitz, in the very last year of his life, wrote to Luther in affirmation of his "unchanging love, 'passing the love of woman;'" and in grateful acknowledgment of the fact that this dear friend first led him "to the living pastures, from the husks for the pigs." It was Staupitz who secured the appointment of his young friend Luther, at twenty-five years of age, as Professor of Philosophy at Wittemberg, and so gave to the reformer a pedestal from which he might command the world's attention. It was Staupitz whose entreaties induced that friend to enter the pulpit and begin the preaching that still echoes around the world. It was Staupitz, again, who induced that friend to be made a "Biblical Doctor," and so to take that oath of fidelity to the Holy Scriptures which D'Aubigné looks upon "as one of the causes of the revival of the Church"—to a recognition of the one infallible standard of truth. In short, it was Luther's friend "Staupitz who was the instrument of God to develop all the gifts and treasures hid in Luther,"—as only friendship could have aided to their developing.

Spalatin, Crotus, Staupitz, and the unknown friend whose death was so impressive an event in Luther's history, all had their parts as friends in directing and shaping the career of the great reformer; but it was Philip Melanchthon who was his transcendent friend, and whose friendship was the force of forces in swaying wisely his mighty personality from the beginning to the close of his life as a reformer. Indeed, Luther was Luther because Melanchthon was Melanchthon, and because Luther and Melanchthon were friends.

It was at Wittemberg that the two reformers, as fellow-professors, became friends. Melanchthon was appointed Professor of Greek in that university at twenty-one years of age, Luther having already been ten years in his professorship. Their friendship, like that of David and Jonathan, seems to have been "love at first sight," and to have continued with growing fervor until death. "Luther at once," says Köstlin, "recognized with joy the marvelous wealth of talent and knowledge in his new colleague. . . . We know of no other instance where Luther formed a friendship so rapidly; and the more intimately he knew him the more highly he esteemed him." It was only six days after Melanchthon's arrival at Wittemberg that Luther wrote to Spalatin of the "astonishment and admiration" which the new professor had excited, and which led all to "wonder and rejoice over him." Less than a month after this Luther went from Wittemberg to appear before the Diet at Augsburg; and, in writing to Melanchthon of his purpose to stand by his convictions at any cost, he said, in loving positiveness: "I will rather die, and, what is the hardest fate, lose for ever the sweet intercourse with you, than revoke anything that it was right for me to say." Already death itself was a lesser matter than the interruption of that new and dear friendship! And Melanchthon wrote of his new-found friend: "If there is one whom I dearly love, and whom I embrace with my whole heart, it is Martin Luther."

As is natural in such a friendship, each friend esteemed the other better than himself; each looking up to the other in that affectionate reverence that is a factor in every true friendship. When sneeringly told that Melanchthon was only a "grammarian," Luther responded vigorously: "I, the doctor of philosophy and theology, am not ashamed to yield the point if this grammarian thinks differently from myself. I have done so often already, and I do the same daily; because of the gifts with which God has so richly filled this fragile vessel, I honor the work of God in him." Again he said: "Philip is a wonder to us all. If the Lord will, he will beat many Martins as the mightiest enemy to the Devil and scholasticism." And yet again: "This little Grecian is even my master in theology." Long after this he wrote: "I am the rough woodman who has to make a path; but Philip goes quietly and peacefully along it, builds and plants, sows and waters, at his pleasure." Meanwhile, in a similar spirit of devotedness, Melanchthon said: "Luther supplies the place of all my friends. He is greater and more admirable in my sight than I dare express. You know how Alcibiades admired Socrates; but I admire Luther after another and a Christian fashion. . . . As often as I contemplate Luther, I find him constantly greater than himself."

To each friend the life of the other was dearer than his own life. When Luther would face death at Worms, Melanchthon begged to go with him. Only when Luther insisted that both lives must not be needlessly risked together, did Melanchthon consent to stay behind; and even then his regretful cry was: "Would to God that he had allowed me to go with him!" While Luther was a restless captive at the Wartburg, Melanchthon moaned out: "If he dies, what hope will remain for us? Would to God that, at the cost of my own wretched life, I could retain in the world that soul which is its fairest ornament! Oh, what a man! We never appreciated him rightly." When, on the other hand, Melanchthon seemed at the point of death, and longed to be at rest, Luther felt that he could not let him go, and that he would not. "No, no, Philip; we cannot spare you yet," he said. And, with prayer and soup, Luther struggled for Melanchthon's life. The prayer Melanchthon could not hinder. When he refused the soup, Luther said in vehemence: "Philip, take this soup, or I will excommunicate you." Luther prevailed, and Melanchthon recovered. "God gave me my brother Melanchthon back, in answer to my prayers," said Luther joyously to his wife; and Luther deemed life better worth living because his friend Melanchthon was to share it with him. Nor was it only in love and reverence and sympathy that these friends were fellow-helpers in the great Reformation. Each did his own work, while the two worked together as neither could have worked by himself in that epoch of religious history. Luther's individual work the world is familiar with; but Melanchthon's work, apart from, as well as with, his friend Luther, is not as well known as it should be.

While Luther was a prisoner at the Wartburg, Melanchthon prepared his *Loci Communes*, or "Common Places of Theology," in which he presented a system of theology as drawn directly from the Scriptures. This work in itself was of vast importance in shaping the theological opinions of the newly awakened scholars of that day. Erasmus, while avowing his dissent from its author at a number of points, characterized the work as "a wondrous army drawn up in battle array against the tyrannous battalions of the false doctors." Calvin commended it most warmly, as he presented it subsequently to the French people. Köstlin says that in this work Melanchthon "actually laid the foundation for the dogma of the Evangelical Church;" and D'Aubigné declares that "next to the Bible, this is the book that has possibly contributed most to the establishment of the evangelical doctrine." That this systematic arrangement of Bible teachings had its influence on Luther's opinions, as well as on those of Calvin, and, through Calvin, on those of his friend Knox, will hardly admit of a question. Throughout Luther's life, says D'Aubigné, "this work was the object of his admiration. The disconnected sounds that his hand, in the deep emotion of his soul, had drawn from the harp of the prophets and apostles, were here blended together in one enchanting harmony. . . . Hence he never ceased recommending the study of this work to the youths who came to Wittemberg in search of knowledge. 'If you desire to become theologians,' he would say, 'read Melanchthon.'"

Melanchthon was a sharer with Luther in the great work of giving the Bible to the common people of the German race in a fresh vernacular translation. Melanchthon brought to the aid of Luther profounder scholarship for its prosecution. Both the knowledge and the graceful style of Melanchthon gave increased value to that translation, beyond all that the sturdy vigor, the sound wisdom, and the unflinching fidelity to truth inherent in Luther's nature, could impart to it. Much, very much, of the wonderful hold that Luther's translation of the Bible has had on the German mind, down to the present hour, is due to the fact that it was made by Luther and Melanchthon working together as helpful friends. Again it was Melanchthon who drew up the regulations and instructions for the new ministers and people in Saxony, comprising "the fundamental principles of evangelical doctrine as they were henceforth to be accepted by the congregations;" which, with a preface by Luther, were formally published, by the elector's command, in 1528. More than this, it was Melanchthon who wrote the famous Augsberg Confession, that, as Dr. Schaff says, "struck the key-note to other evangelical confessions, and strengthened the cause of the Reformation everywhere." It was of this document that Luther wrote, when it had been sent to him for his revision: "I know of nothing by which I could better it or change it, nor would it be becoming; for I cannot move so softly and gently."

Finally, it was Melanchthon and Luther who together outlined the Saxon school system, which became the foundation of the magnificent school system of all Germany, and which has proved a germ of many of the best educational methods, Protestant and Romanist, all the world over.

How much, indeed, this world owes to the fact that the rugged nature and imperious will of Martin Luther had the counterbalance and check of the gentle spirit and wise heart of Philip Melanchthon, in the surpassing friendship of these two reformers! How well it was for the cause of truth, that all the finer qualities of Melanchthon's nature were made available for a service they could never have performed by themselves, through his being appreciated and loved by such a stalwart and fearless Christian warrior as Luther!

Correspondent with the friendship of Luther and Melanchthon as an impelling force on the mountain height of the Protestant Reformation, there was the friendship of Knox and Calvin as a factor in shaping the religious thought and ecclesiastical polity of a large portion of the Anglo-Saxon race. John Calvin's view of religious truth brought into prominence the place and privilege of the individual Christian in his relations to both church and state, in a light that was new to his times if not indeed new in the world's history. His system of doctrine was linked with a system of ecclesiastical government and responsibility and discipline that had its bearing on the life of the community as well as of the individual. "It was this system," says John Richard Green, "that Calvin by a singular fortune was able to put into actual working in the little city of Geneva, where the party of the Reformation had . . . called him in 1536 to be their spiritual head. Driven out, but again recalled, his influence made Geneva from 1541 the center of the Protestant world. The refugees who crowded to the little town from persecution in France, in the Netherlands, in England, found there an exact and formal doctrine, a rigid discipline of manners and faith, a system of church government, a form of church worship, stripped, as they held, of the last remnant of the superstitions of the past. Calvin himself, with his austere and frugal life, his enormous industry, his power of government, his quick decision, his undoubting self-confidence, his unswerving will, remained for three and twenty years, till his death in 1564, supreme over Protestant opinion."

In 1554, John Knox, an exile from his own land, found his way to Geneva, and made the acquaintance and won the friendship of Calvin. The two reformers were drawn to each other from the start, and their friendship deepened and strengthened during the remaining years of the life of Calvin. Knox's opinion of Geneva was expressed when he spoke of it, in a letter to an English correspondent, as "this place, where I fear nor shame to say is the most perfect school of Christ that ever was in the earth since the days of the apostles." Knox decided to remain near his new-found friend during his enforced exile from his home; and while under the influence of that friend's teachings and example he wrote suggestions to his co-workers in England and Scotland concerning important matters of both doctrine and practice. Thus it was in accordance with an appeal from Knox at Geneva that, in 1557, the Protestant nobles in Scotland united with other Protestant leaders there "in an engagement which," as Green suggests, "became memorable as the first among those covenants which were to give shape and color to Scotch religion," and which "marked a new epoch in the strife of religions," in its pledge to maintain the liberty of conscience in spite of all demands of the state. From this beginning the work in Scotland went on toward its completion; and, as the same historian declares, Knox was the "one well-known figure [who] embodied the moral strength of the new movement;" and "the moral power which Knox created was to express itself through the ecclesiastical forms which had been devised by the genius of Calvin."

Pointing out the importance of the movement, which, through the leadership of Knox in accordance with the views of Calvin, led to the formation of the Scotch Kirk, Green says, emphatically: "In that mighty elevation of the masses which was embodied in the Calvinist doctrines of election and grace, lay the germs of the modern principles of human equality. . . . It is the Scotch people that rises into being under the guise of the Scotch Kirk. . . . Strange to modern ears as their language may be, bigoted and narrow as their temper must often seem, it is well to remember the greatness of the debt we owe them. It was their stern resolve, their energy, their endurance, that saved Scotland from a civil and religious despotism, and that, in saving the liberty of Scotland, saved English liberty as well." Whether one agrees or disagrees with this historian as to the relation of Calvinism to the individual and to the state, it will be admitted, as proven, that Scotland came to its plan of church government and to its prevalent system of doctrine by way of John Calvin; and that all this was brought about directly through the relations of Knox and Calvin as personal friends.

It could, indeed, be shown that John Calvin's earlier religious life was largely shaped by his friendship with Nicholas Cop and Louis du Tillot, and that John Knox's conversion and religious life-direction were due in great measure to his enthusiastic friendship for George Wishart; but this would only be added evidence of the truth that religious reforms owe much to the impelling force of personal friendships. It is enough, in this instance, to point out the train of consequences from the friendship of Knox and Calvin.

On the hither side of the mountain range of the Great Reformation, there rises a rival peak of religious activities and influence in the record of Jesuitism; and it would even seem that, if it had not been for that newly raised barrier to progress, the power of Protestantism would have been unchecked and limitless, after the work of the lesser and greater reformers in the fifteenth and sixteenth centuries. That rival peak also stands as a monument to friendship, as do all the peaks of the range that it confronts.

Ignatius Loyola, a Spanish soldier-convert to a religious life, was the founder of the "Company of Jesus." This organization, which has proved to be the most potent agency of influence ever conceived by the mere human mind, was immediately the outgrowth of a close personal friendship between Loyola, on the one hand,

and Peter Faber (or Le Fèvre) and Francis Xavier on the other. Only through such a friendship could such results have been a possibility. It was at the College of St. Barbara, in Paris, that this friendship had its beginning. Faber and Xavier were already there, and already friends and room-mates, when Loyola entered as a student. Each of these three men had fine qualities of character in and of himself; but no one of them was likely to do any such work as the three together were enabled to do; nor could they have been such fellow-helpers in their common work if they had not first become such friends. Faber and Xavier were about the same age, while Loyola was sixteen years their senior; but as the latter had begun life as a soldier he was behind his juniors in college studies. Faber was, for a time, an instructor of Loyola in philosophy; and this led to their closer acquaintance and friendship.

"It was an advantage to both parties," to be thus brought together—as student-instructor and student-learner, says Bartoli, the Jesuit biographer of Loyola. "The relations thus established between them led to a more intimate acquaintance, from whence reciprocal attachment and esteem soon arose; for each possessed the species of merit which the other most loved and admired. Ignatius could not have desired to meet with one more capable of serving his designs, nor Faber with a friend more according to his heart." Faber was suited to be a friend; Loyola was suited to welcome and use a friend. Faber's warm heart ached for the strong support of a friend in whom he could confide freely. Loyola's active mind and vigorous nature were outreaching toward a friend who would trust implicitly, and who would be willing to co-work untiringly with him whom he trusted. Faber opened his heart to Loyola, and Loyola responded with helpful sympathy. The spiritual struggles of Faber, and the courageous devotedness of Loyola, were a means of bringing the two into a common sense of mutual need and mutual joy in friendship. "It is a spectacle," says Bartoli, "to observe these two souls thus penetrating into each other, thus perfecting each other under the all-powerful action of divine grace"—operating through their friendship.

It was after two years of this intimacy as friends that Loyola disclosed to Faber, in strictest confidence, his purpose of giving himself to a life of peculiar religious service, and of going as a missionary to the Holy Land, or of putting himself at the call of the Pope for any mission among infidels and unbelievers. Faber instantly responded to the self-sacrificing impulse of his friend; "and, throwing himself into his arms, he conjured him to receive him as his associate in this noble and perilous enterprise." In that embrace of friendship, with its pledge to consecrated co-work, was the beginning of the power-fraught movement toward the mighty sway of organized Jesuitism.

After Faber had left the College of St. Barbara, his earlier friend and room-mate, Francis Xavier, came into relations of friendship with Loyola; and after a time Loyola made Xavier also a sharer of his plans for the future, and Xavier responded to them with no less warmth than Faber. Both Faber and Xavier were friends of Loyola before they were linked with him in his purposes of peculiar service; and each of them became a sharer in the work of Loyola because of being his friend. Subsequently there were joined with these friends, in this new covenant, four others : Diego Laynez, Alfonso Salmeron, Nicolas Alfonso de Bobadilla, and Simon Rodriguez. And these seven composed the Company of Jesus, or Society of Jesuits, at its beginning.

As a consequence of that first compaćt between Ignatius Loyola and his personal friends at St. Barbara, with its subsequent linkings of friendship in that place of learning, Protestantism was hindered in its progress, and Romanism was given a new lease of power. Through the labors of the Society then brought into being, popes have been made and unmade; thrones have been set or overturned; institutions of learning have been multiplied, far and near; the gospel has been preached to many a heathen land; persecutions for righteousness' sake have been set afoot; the policy of the Church of Rome has been shaped and re-shaped anew; and to-day the ends of the earth thrill with the vibrations of the plans and purposes of Loyola and his college friends.

An important religious movement in the seventeenth century was led by George Fox, in the formation of the Society of Friends; and friendship showed its impelling force in that movement, as in all such movements. The work of the Society of Friends was far greater in the community outside of its bounds than within its own denominational lines. It did much to promote the principles of peace, of religious toleration, of simplicity in dress and manners, of regard for the spirit above the letter in Bible study, and of ready submission to the divine guidance from within the illumined soul. It had a mission, and it fulfilled it; and such a mission must needs be aided by friendship.

In 1652, when Fox was twenty-eight years old, and was still young in the work of his religious reform, he visited Swarthmore Hall, and was welcomed by its hostess Margaret Fell, in the absence of her husband, Judge Thomas Fell. She was some ten years older than her guest, a woman of an earnest religious nature, already seeking the light, and unsatisfied with the religious teachings she had so far received. No sooner had she heard George Fox, than she gave him her confidence; and it was not long before he had her assured friendship. This friendship had much to do with the progress and successes of the Society of Friends, during the first half-century of its existence. Because of her friendship for George Fox, Margaret Fell exerted herself in his behalf, and in behalf of his fellow-Friends. She interested her husband in him and in them; and although her husband never joined himself to their Society he had a kindly feeling toward its members, to the close of his life. In public and in private Margaret Fell did what she could to prove her friendship for George Fox. When he was in prison she sought to secure his release. When he was at liberty she gave him encouragement and counsel. His friends were her friends. She was ready to do her utmost for their welfare. Her social position enabled her to seek aid in high places; and her advocacy of Fox and of the Friends was known in Parliament and in palace, as well as in the lower courts of justice. Meanwhile she was showing her womanly tenderness of feeling in her untiring ministry of sympathy to the followers of her friend Fox in their times of persecution and distress. "It is remarkable," says one of their later biographers, "with what high esteem and Christian love Margaret Fell appears to have been regarded by our early and most eminent Friends. She seems to have been generally acknowledged as the faithful nursing-mother of the flock; and she often addressed them when they were in bonds, or otherwise tried, with letters of consolation and encouragement. It is also probable [that] she contributed largely to the relief of their outward necessities."

Six years after the friendship began between George Fox and Margaret Fell, the latter was left a widow; and her sorrow tended to deepen her interest in the truths that that friendship had first led her to appreciate. Her earnestness in this behalf brought her also into prison for conscience' sake, and she and George Fox were at the same time held in durance. Her trials, like her advocacy, won friends to the cause of the Friends; and that cause made progress by means of its hindrances, as well as by the impelling of this friendship. When George Fox and Margaret Fell had been friends for seventeen years, they became also husband and wife, eleven years after the death of her first husband. For twenty-one years they continued in this new relation; but that in no degree lessens the force of the truth that they were friends for wellnigh forty years; and that because they were friends the cause of the Friends was mightily advantaged in their day.

No new religious movement of the eighteenth century was comparable in importance with that which resulted in what is known as Methodism, or Wesleyanism, with its world-wide sweep of influence; and that movement had its inception and its chief impellings in the potency of personal friendships. It may be said, indeed, that it was as friends, rather than as brothers,—for a brother can be also a friend,—that John Wesley and Charles were workers together and fellow-helpers in the cause of truth as represented in that movement; and it was through the friendships made with others by these brother-friends severally that the movement extended itself from that beginning.

Even back of the common work of these two brothers at Oxford, there were impellings of personal friendship, direct and indirect, felt by each of the two separately. Charles Wesley was the gainer by his friendship at Westminster School with James Murray, afterwards the famous Lord Mansfield. John Wesley's early religious experience received impulse and direction from the writings of the friendship-inspired Thomas à Kempis, and from the earnest words spoken to him directly by a young friend at college. Charles Wesley had no such strength and positiveness of character as his brother John, but he had quite as much attractiveness of spirit and manner; and it was by this means of attraction that he won and held to himself the young students at Christ College who formed the nucleus of the little society which his brother was enabled to make use of as the beginning of his greater work. It was while John Wesley was absent from Christ College, assisting his father in the curacy of Wroote, that Charles entered that college and began his work of winning friends to himself and to the prayerful study of the Bible. John Gambold, one of his college friends, and subsequently a Moravian bishop, writing concerning his characteristics and spirit, said: "I shall say no more of Charles but that he was a man made for friendship; who by his cheerfulness and vivacity would refresh his friend's heart; with attentive considerateness would enter into and settle all his concerns; so far as he was able would do anything for him, great or small; and by a habit of openness and freedom leave no room for misunderstanding." Already Charles Wesley and his little band of friends at Oxford had won the designation of "Methodists," because of their strictness in method of conduct and life, when John Wesley returned to college from his three years' absence, and became the friend and leader of them all.

The Bible-loving friends at Oxford, of whom Charles and John Wesley were the leading spirits, included, besides themselves, William Morgan, Robert Kirkham, John Clayton, Benjamin Ingham, John Gambold, James Hervey, and George Whitefield. Although Bible-study and prayer and religious communings were a common basis of intercourse between these college friends, friendship rather than any correspondence of religious opinions was the tie that held them together while in college, and that intensified their power in any work that they did individually or collectively while thus associated. Tyerman, a biographer of John Wesley, and of the other Oxford Methodists, has laid emphasis on the truth that it was not Wesleyanism alone that had power in the revival at Oxford, or in the work for the world that was then begun there. He points out that these college friends who were so dear to one another as friends, included "the Hanoverian and Jacobite, the Methodist and Moravian, the Churchman and Dissenter, the Arminian and Calvinist, the itinerant evangelist and the parish priest;" and that their influence for good told upon the Church of England and the Moravian Church, as well as in the new field of Methodism.

Friendship was an impelling force in that Oxford revival, as in other great revivals; and it was because of Charles Wesley's power of friendship, quite as truly as because of John Wesley's genius for administration and evangelism, that a religious movement had its beginning then and there, with its possibilities of indefinite extension in time and space and numbers and spiritual power. Methodism is indeed only one result of the friendships which bound men together at Oxford under the lead of one man who chose the world for his parish, and who was resolved that every nook and corner of his parish should be evangelized.

Modern missions had their most notable beginning in the sending out of Moravian missionaries from Herrnhut, to the West Indies in 1732, and to Greenland in 1733. And this movement had its primary origin in the schoolboy friendship, at Halle, of Count Zinzendorf and the Baron von Watteville, which led them to covenant together for evangelistic effort in behalf of the heathen, and to form a Christian brotherhood, with a view to such effort, under the name *Senfkorn-Orden*, "The Order of the Grain of Mustard Seed." It was thirteen years after the first forming of this order that the attention of one of its leaders was called to the needs of the West India

Impelling Religious Movements. 227

slaves in one direction, and of the Greenlanders in another. Within a year or two more, two friends, under the influence of this leader, were led to declare that they would, if necessary, be sold into slavery in order to preach Christ to the slaves in the West Indies ; and soon, with three dollars apiece in their pockets, and a bundle on the back of each as their only outfit, they were on their way, afoot, for the capital of Denmark, six hundred miles away, seeking a passage to the West Indies as missionaries of Christ. Denied a passage from Denmark, they sought and found one from Holland. It was but six months later that another party of Moravian missionary friends was on its way to Greenland. And from that beginning of friendship's missionary work to the present day the Moravians have transcended all other bodies of Christian believers in the missionary spirit and work.

Early in this nineteenth century a pregnant movement in the direction of foreign missions from America, had its potent impelling in a warm college friendship. Samuel J. Mills, Jr., son of a Connecticut clergyman, was dedicated, from childhood, by his godly mother, to the work of Christian missions,—just then brought into new prominence by the labors and appeals of William Carey, the pioneer English missionary to India. A knowledge of that dedication impressed young Mills with a sense of the importance of the foreign missionary work ; but there was still needed the quickening force of a personal friendship to bring out of his impressions a purpose, a plan, and ultimate action. Mills entered Williams College in 1806. There he formed a close personal friendship with Gordon Hall and James Richards. After a time, in the intimacy of this friendship, he told of the thought of his heart, and was cheered by a sympathetic response from his friends. From that time onward the three college friends talked much together over the possibilities of missionary work among the heathen; and the idea gained and grew in hearts that were opened toward one another, and Christward, in friendship.

The geography of Asia came into the college studies of these friends. This turned the attention of Mills to Asia as a missionary field, and he waited his opportunity of laying it before his friends for their approval and coöperation. "At a stated prayer-meeting, held at hours when most students are engaged in sport or are doing nothing," says Dr. Mark Hopkins, "this idea [of evangelizing Asia] was presented [by young Mills]. Driven by an approaching thunder-storm from the grove where the meeting had usually been held, they took shelter behind a neighboring haystack, and there—in the language of one who was present—' Mills proposed to send the gospel to that dark and heathen land, and said we could do it if we would.' The subject was then discussed, and as the storm was passing away Mills said, ' Come, let us make it a subject of prayer, under this haystack, while the dark clouds are going and the clear sky is coming.' So they prayed, and continued to pray and consult together through that and the following season. Then a society was formed, the object of which was, in the language of its constitution, ' to effect in the person of its members a mission to the heathen.' This was the first foreign missionary society on this continent. A similar society was soon formed at Andover, by Mills and those who went with him [to the Theological Seminary there], and from that the proposition was made that resulted in the formation of the American Board of Commissioners for Foreign Missions."

From this beginning there followed all the many denominational missionary societies in this country, which, together with the parent organization, have girdled the world with a belt of light. Young Mills was largely instrumental in securing the formation of the American Bible Society and of the American Colonization Society; and other beneficent organizations followed these by the score, all having their germ, as it were, in the college friendship of Mills and Hall and Richards. Of these three friends, Mills went to Africa, Hall to India, and Richards to Ceylon. A marble monument marks the site of the haystack where their college friendship culminated in that initial missionary society; and wheresoever by the agency of any of these societies the gospel of Christ shall be preached in all the world, this result of their friendship should be told for a memorial of them.

It were needless to continue the search along the centuries for proofs of the impelling power of friendship in great religious movements; but illustrations in this line would disclose themselves wherever the search was pursued. In what are known as the Broad Church movement and the Anglo-Catholic movement, having their center in Oxford University during the second quarter of this century, personal friendships were a factor of unmistakable importance. Back of these movements, the friendship of Coleridge and Wordsworth would have to be recognized as opening a new era in religious thought in England. Then there would come into prominence the friendships of such leaders or prompters as Whately, Arnold, Milman, Thirlwall, Julius Charles Hare, Bunsen, Maurice, Stanley, and Kingsley; Rose, Keble, Newman, Hurrell Froude, and Pusey. It may, indeed, be too soon to say which of the friends in these groups severally were the pre-eminent leaders, and which of them had most impelling power in their lines of thought and feeling; but it is not too soon to say that their friendships as friendships were potent in giving direction and impetus to the great movements in which they bore a part.

Because religion is the expression of man's profoundest nature, and friendship is the holiest out-going of the human heart, therefore a great religious movement is sure to have as its leader a man whom friendship inspires and impels. The head is never at its best unless swayed by the heart; and the heart is never swayed so powerfully as when swayed by friendship.

ADVANCING CIVIL LIBERTY.

INITIAL movements in the direction of civil liberty have had their promptings in, or have gained fresh force from, strong personal friendships. A reason for this is found in the fact that no sentiment is purer or stronger than that which impels a man to be unselfishly devoted to the highest interests held before him in the ideal of one who has his love and his reverence; and that when this sentiment is superadded to a generous desire for the good of one's fellows, a man will do or die with his friend in behalf of the liberties of all.

The Athenians ascribed their deliverance from regal tyranny to the joint endeavors of the two friends, Harmodius and Aristogiton. Hippias and Hipparchus, sons of Pisistratus, held tyrannically the chief power in Athens, in the sixth century before our era. Harmodius and Aristogiton, devoted friends, were young Athenian citizens. Harmodius being outraged by an insult to his sister, on his account, from the tyrant Hippias, turned to his friend Aristogiton for sympathy and assistance. A wrong done to either of these friends was a wrong done to both, and both were aroused to a purpose of vengeance. On the occasion of the great feast of Panathenæa they slew Hipparchus, intending also to slay Hippias. Harmodius was instantly stricken down by the royal guards; and Aristogiton was taken and executed. This tragedy was a means of arousing the Athenians against the tyranny of the reigning dynasty, and Hippias was soon expelled from his country; and it is said that he afterwards perished at Marathon, while treacherously acting as a guide to the Persians against his countrymen. "Harmodius and Aristogiton were afterwards," says the historian Grote, "commemorated as the winners and prototypes of Athenian liberty. Statues were erected in their honor, shortly after the final expulsion of the Pisistratides; immunity from taxes and public burdens was granted to the descendants of their families; and the [Athenian] speaker who proposed the abolition of such immunities, at a time when the number had been abusively multiplied, made his only special exception in favor of this respected lineage."

The bronze statues of these two friends, made by Antenor, and set up in the Agora of Athens, having been carried away by Xerxes, new ones by Critias were erected in their stead; although the originals were afterwards sent back to Athens by Alexander. It was of the first-named statues that Antipho made mention when, in answer to the tyrant Dionysius's question which was the finest kind of brass, he replied, "That of which the statues of Harmodius and Aristogiton are formed." An ancient

Greek song, ascribed to Alcæus, voices the sentiment of the Athenians concerning these liberty-loving and tyranny-hating friends, in the words:

> "Bright shall your fame be through the ages,
> Dearest Harmodius and Aristogiton;
> For ye twain slew the lordly despot,
> And gave just laws again to Athens."

It is true that historians are not agreed in wholly condemning the Athenian rulers whose overthrow was wrought by these friends, or in approving the spirit of these friends in their conspiracy against those rulers; but the fact remains that it was a personal friendship which brought Harmodius and Aristogiton to conspire against the Pisistratides, and that the overthrow of the Pisistratides as a result of that conspiracy was the beginning of better days for the liberty of Athens. Indeed, if it were true, as some students of history would have us suppose, that the Pisistratides were "the persons who in good truth gave Athens her freedom, far more than Harmodius and Aristogiton," it is worthy of note that Pisistratus, the father of Hippias and Hipparchus, and the founder of the dynasty bearing his name, came into power originally, and won the Athenians to their renewed struggle with the Megarians, through his intimate personal friendship with Solon the Sage. So whether it were through the action of Harmodius and Aristogiton, or of Pisistratus and Solon, that the beginning of Athenian liberties was made, in either case it received its impulse from friendship.

Legend and history intermingle in the early days of Rome, as of Greece; and in both cases the story that gained currency and credence gives a foremost place to a personal friendship in bringing about the struggle that advanced the liberties of the commonwealth. Those were dark days for Rome, when Tarquin the Arrogant had trampled on the rights of both patricians and plebeians, and was ruthlessly swaying imperial power for the gratifying of his personal ambitions and hatreds. Then it was that Tarquin's son Sextus blindly followed his lusts in the treacherous and cowardly outrage on Lucretia the wife of his kinsman Collatinus, madly confident that justice could have no power over a son of Rome's ruler. And it seemed, at the time, as if Sextus might be right in his daring reliance on the wrong. But Tarquinius Collatinus had a friend, in his kinsman Lucius Junius Brutus, who had been feigning idiocy in order to save his life from the royal tyrant's hatred. To that friend Collatinus turned in his hour of need, and the two friends hasted together from the camp before Ardea, when the husband was summoned by his wife to hear the terrible story of her wrong, as she made ready to die by her own hand. It was the sympathy of friend with friend that made Brutus then rise up for the avenging of his friend's great wrong, by the overthrow of the tyrant ruler whose tyranny had made possible this wrong. And that outcome of friendship brought new liberty to Rome.

Shakespeare, following the narrative of Livy, tells the story of that scene by the bedside of the dead Lucretia, when her husband and father vied with each other in their despairing grief; and that husband's friend aroused them both to vigorous action, and pledged them both to this oath of vengeance:

> " 'Now, by the Capitol that we adore,
>   And by this chaste blood so unjustly stained,
>   By heaven's fair sun, that breeds the fat earth's store,
>   By all our country's rights in Rome maintained,
>   And by chaste Lucrece' soul that late complained
>   Her wrongs to us, and by this bloody knife,
>   We will revenge the death of this true wife.'
>
> " This said, he struck his hand upon his breast,
>   And kissed the fatal knife, to end his vow;
>   And to his protestation urged the rest,
>   Who, wondering at him, did his words allow:
>   Then jointly to the ground their knees they bow,
>   And that deep vow, which Brutus made before,
>   He doth again repeat, and that they swore.
>
> " When they had sworn to this advised doom,
>   They did conclude to bear dead Lucrece thence;
>   To show her bleeding body thorough Rome,
>   And so to publish Tarquin's foul offence:
>   Which being done with speedy diligence,
>   The Romans plausibly did give consent
>   To Tarquin's everlasting banishment."

And on the ruins of the overthrown monarchy there arose the fabric of Rome's republic. Tarquinius Collatinus and Lucius Junius Brutus, the two friends who had brought about this change, were fittingly made the first consuls, or prætors, of the new government. When, finally, Brutus fell in a struggle with the deposed house of Tarquin, the matrons of Rome wore mourning for him for a twelvemonth; a statue was erected in his honor; and he was called the Avenger of Woman's Honor, because of what he had done with and for his friend, in the time of that friend's extremity.

English history gives similar testimony to that of

Greece and Rome, in exhibit of the power of friendship at the turning-point of conflicts for civil liberty. John Hampden stands out as a prominent leader in the earlier struggles for English constitutional liberty. By his wise and courageous firmness in resisting the aggressions of Charles I. on the rights of Parliament, and the king's arbitrary tax-levies on the people, Hampden "became the turning-point of the course of the history of England." And John Hampden was a leader and a reformer, as the close personal friend of Sir John Eliot, and of John Pym. It was what these three were to each other as friends, which enabled them to be what they were, as patriots, to the English nation. Hampden was not twenty-seven when he took his seat in the Parliament of 1621, "and became the friend of Eliot and of Pym;" the former of whom was then twenty-eight, and the latter thirty-six. The intimacy of these friends became a shaping power in the career of each and all of them, and in turn a shaping power in the course of their country and of the world. "Eliot and Pym," says a recent historian, "formulated the grievances against absolutism, a contemplation of which led to the revolution that established Anglican liberty on its present basis." Of these two friends of Hampden, Hallam characterizes Eliot as "the most illustrious confessor in the cause of liberty whom that time produced;" and Green affirms that "the earlier struggle for parliamentary liberty centers in the figure of Sir John Eliot." Forster, on the other hand, calls John Pym "the first great popular organizer in English politics." Clarendon thinks that Pym was, for a time, "the most popular man, and the most able to do hurt that hath lived at any time." And Green is sure that, when both Eliot and Hampden had fallen, Pym remained "the greatest, as he was the first, of parliamentary leaders;" and that, when he was dead, his already formed plans for the future were carried out by Cromwell and his army.

Yet, between Eliot the earlier leader, and Pym the later one, Hampden is conspicuous above both of his friends. "In the earlier days of his parliamentary career," says Gardiner, "he was content to be overshadowed by Eliot, as in his later days he was content to be overshadowed by Pym, and to be commanded by Essex. Yet it is Hampden, and not Eliot or Pym, who lives in the popular imagination as the central figure of the English revolution in its earlier stages. It is Hampden whose statue, rather than that of Eliot or Pym, has been selected to take its place in St. Stephen's Hall, as the noblest type of the parliamentary opposition, as Falkland's has been selected as the noblest type of parliamentary royalists." Macaulay sums up the claims of Hampden to the place of pre-eminence in his day. He cites Richard Baxter as saying, that "Mr. John Hampden was one that friends and enemies acknowledged to be most eminent for prudence, piety, and peaceable counsels, having the most universal praise of any gentleman that I remember of that age." Macaulay also shows that when Eliot wrote, in his prison, a treatise on government, he submitted it to "his friend" Hampden, by whom it was kindly criticised and revised as by a master; that when, after Eliot's death, Pym and Hampden were leaders together in Parliament, "by the universal consent of friends and enemies, the first place belonged to Hampden;" that Hampden "alone had discovered [in ' his kinsman Oliver Cromwell, over whom he possessed great influence'], under an exterior appearance of coarseness and extravagance, those great and commanding talents which were afterwards the admiration and the dread of Europe;" and finally, that "in Hampden, and in Hampden alone, were united all the qualities which, at such a crisis, were necessary to save the state;—the valor and energy of Cromwell, the discernment and eloquence of Vane, the humanity and moderation of Manchester, the stern integrity of Hale, the ardent public spirit of Sydney; . . . the sobriety, the self-command, the perfect soundness of judgment, the perfect rectitude of intention, to which the history of revolutions furnishes no parallel, or furnishes a parallel in Washington alone."

And this leader of leaders in that crisis-time of English history swayed and was swayed by his intimate friendships. It is not merely that Hampden was a close counselor with his chief co-workers, but that he was a friend, in affectionate personal relations, first with Eliot, afterwards with Pym, and for a time, meanwhile, with both. Macaulay points out, that while Eliot was writing from his prison, to give his views of government to Hampden, Hampden was caring, in tenderness, for the two sons of Eliot, as if they had been his own; moreover, that, after the death of Eliot, Hampden "lived in habits of the closest intimacy," with Pym. Again, Green says of Hampden, at the opening of the second stage of the great governmental conflict: " He had been the bosom-friend of Eliot, till the victim of the king's resentment lay dead in the Tower. He was now the bosom-friend of Pym."

And the influence of those two bosom-friendships has been a factor in the wisest movements for the promotion of true civil liberty in the last two centuries and a half; and all mankind has reason to thank God for them to-day.

Among the historic conflicts for civil liberty, that of the American people stands out in a unique pre-eminence, not by its severity and magnitude as a conflict, but in its successful issue in the founding of a new nationality on the basis of principles of justice and equity that stand the test of time, winning and holding the admiration of the world. In its permanent results rather than its current contests, this struggle has its prime importance on the pages of human history; and its central characters are those who did most for its ultimate success, apart from the measure of their share in its initiating. George Washington and Alexander Hamilton stand out all by themselves in their greatness, as chief actors in that struggle for liberty which culminated in the fully established government of the United States of America. Each of these men was more of a power in this struggle than any one else except the other; and each of them was enabled to be what he was and to do what he did in this struggle, through his relations of friendship with the other. On this point the verdict of history is explicit, as every careful student will have reason to perceive.

Lord Brougham characterizes Washington as "the greatest man of our own or any age." Earl Russell says: "To George Washington alone in modern times has it been given to accomplish a wonderful revolution, and yet to remain to all future times the theme of a people's gratitude and an example of virtuous and beneficent power." Mr. Gladstone's testimony is: "Washington, to my mind, is the purest figure in history." M. Guizot sums up Washington's life-work in the declaration: "He did the two greatest things which in politics man can have the privilege of attempting. He maintained by peace that independence of his country which he had acquired by war. . . . Of all great men he was the most virtuous and the most fortunate. In this world God has no higher favors to bestow." And these utterances are the expression of the world's conviction concerning Washington.

Of Alexander Hamilton, so acute and discerning an observer of his fellows as Prince Talleyrand said, according to the testimony of Mr. George Ticknor, "that he had known nearly all the marked men of his time, but he had never known one, on the whole, equal to him." Professor Francis Lieber quotes the historian Niebuhr as saying: "Alexander Hamilton was one of the most powerful minds of modern times. He had resources within him such as none of his contemporaries had." In the opinion of M. Guizot, "Hamilton must be classed among the men who have best known the vital principles and fundamental conditions of a government." Said Fisher Ames: "The name of Hamilton would have honored Greece in the age of Aristides." Justice Story said of him: "I have deemed him a giant among his contemporaries, of whom it might truly be said, '*Toto vertice supra est.*'" Looking back over the pages of history, Charles Francis Adams says of Hamilton: "Among all the remarkable men of the Revolution, we

Advancing Civil Liberty. 241

know of no one who, for the attributes which usually mark genius, was more distinguished." And the historian Hildreth, passing upon the death of Hamilton, pronounces it "a loss second only to that of Washington;" adding, in a comparison of these two great men: "Hamilton possessed the same rare and lofty qualities, the same just balance of soul, with less, indeed, of Washington's severe simplicity and awe-inspiring presence, but with more of warmth, variety, ornament, and grace. If the Doric in architecture may be taken as the symbol of Washington's character, Hamilton's belonged to the same grand style as developed in the Corinthian—if less impressive, more winning." Of no other associate of Washington are such words spoken by such judges.

And that it was the friendship of these two men which secured to their common country, and to the race, those blessings of a good government which they severally perceived and together worked for, is as patent as that each of them had no peer but the other, in the struggle in which they contended side by side, and that each was in a peculiar sense the other's complement and balance in the progress and issues of that struggle. Washington and Hamilton were fitted to be friends; they were friends; and they were mutually helpful, and potently useful, in and through their friendship. Hamilton was enough younger than Washington to have been his son. It was while Hamilton was yet in his teens that the attention of the new commander-in-chief of the army was called to his ability and efficiency as a young artillery officer, first by the veteran General Greene, and afterwards by personal observation. An interview with the young officer seemed to win to him Washington's sincere regard; for Hamilton was always remarkable for the measure of personal attachment that his words and ways secured to him. Washington speedily proffered him an appointment on his staff. This was not an attractive position to Hamilton, as he preferred an independent command; but as his biographer, John T. Morse, expresses it, " Hamilton entertained such sentiments of respect and affection for his chief, that he could not easily determine to refuse the request, preferred with no small degree of warmth and earnestness." Hence, when just turned of twenty, Hamilton was appointed a personal aide of Washington, with the rank of lieutenant-colonel; Washington being then forty-five.

The close personal relations thus formed between Washington and Hamilton became closer and closer. The spirit and ability of the young man won the confidence and admiration of his superior. Hamilton became the confidential secretary, as well as the favored aide, of the commander-in-chief. " His principal occupation was in the conduct of Washington's immense correspondence," involving the treatment of questions of great importance, and of yet greater delicacy; and he was soon "the depositary of the most secret thoughts of his chief, and the organ of their promulgation." Washington deserves all credit for his pre-eminent part in directing and using this service so effectively; and it was because he here loved and trusted one who was so worthy and so capable, that so few mistakes were made in this portion of his career. Henry Cabot Lodge sums up the case for Hamilton, when he says for him: " As his enthusiastic comrade, the gallant Laurens, said, he certainly held the pen of Junius in the American army; and to that gifted pen, employed as freely in another's service as in his own, and to the versatile and original mind of its possessor, Washington owed much, and gave every proof that he appreciated the debt."

Again and again Hamilton was sent by Washington on some special mission of peculiar importance and delicacy; and his action always justified the wisdom and the confidence that had selected him. Meanwhile his abounding and unfailing cheerfulness, in times of greatest general depression, was a source of stimulus and encouragement to the sore-pressed and sadly beset commander-in-chief. Moreover, young Hamilton was ever looking forward with the eye of a prophet, and with the spirit of a born leader, to the possibilities and needs of the future; and there can be little doubt that the conferences of Washington and Hamilton, during this period of their early intimacy, did much to shape the opinions and action of both in the subsequent days of the young Republic. Neither friend could have done what he did for his country, without the friendship and help of the other. Judge Shea, writing in the latest edition of the Encyclopædia Britannica, says emphatically: " The first suggestion toward the establishment of an adequate and permanent government [for the American colonies] came, as it is now conceded, from Hamilton. It was contained in a letter written by him, September 3, 1780 [while he was still an aide of Washington], to James Duane, a delegate from New York to the Congress at Philadelphia." After mentioning a second letter written a few months later, by

Hamilton, Judge Shea adds: "These letters are indeed the *principia* of the American government in its organization and administration."

If, indeed, the friendship of Washington and Hamilton had gone no farther than this, it would be evident that America owes much for all time to the suggestions and incitements of that friendship. But, fortunately, it did not stop here. Washington loved Hamilton, perhaps more than Hamilton loved Washington; and Washington was faithful as a friend even when Hamilton was unduly sensitive to reproof, and resigned from the staff of the Commander-in-chief, after four years of important service there. Lafayette, writing to Hamilton of the estimate in which Washington held him, said: "I know the General's friendship and gratitude toward you, my dear Hamilton; both are greater than you perhaps imagine." And Washington Irving, in narrating the circumstances of the retirement of Hamilton from the staff of Washington, says of the latter's continued attachment to his over-sensitive young friend: "The friendship between these illustrious men was destined to survive the Revolution, and to signalize itself through many eventful years, and stands recorded in the correspondence [of Washington] almost at the last moment of his life."

Hamilton remained in the army until after the surrender of Cornwallis at Yorktown. Later, he studied law and entered on its practice in New York. He was elected to Congress from New York; and again he was a delegate to the convention that framed the Constitution of the United States. Meanwhile, he was doing, by pen and voice, a work of preparation for the new government such as no one else could have done; and in all his labors he was in pleasant relations and co-work with Washington. Guizot says of this period of Hamilton's labors: "There is not in the Constitution of the United States an element of order, of force, or of duration, which he has not powerfully contributed to introduce into it, and caused to predominate." And it is now admitted by statesmen of Europe as well as of America, that Hamilton's writings in elucidation of the principles of federal government stand at the head of authorities in that sphere. After a while, the Constitution of the United States was completed and confirmed, and the government under it was inaugurated with George Washington as its first president. Then, again, Washington called his friend Hamilton to his aid, and proved his wisdom in so doing. Nominally Hamilton was Secretary of the Treasury. In reality he was the organizer and inspirer of the new government. In his immediate sphere his work was marvelous. Daniel Webster says of him in this position: "He smote the rock of the national resources, and abundant streams of revenue gushed forth. He touched the dead corpse of the Public Credit, and it sprang upon its feet. The fabled birth of Minerva from the brain of Jove was hardly more perfect than the financial system of the United States as it burst forth from the conception of Alexander Hamilton."

In our foreign policy, as in our domestic, the views of Hamilton had such weight with Washington that it came to be a charge against the President, that he was unduly swayed by the opinions of his friend, the Secretary of the Treasury. More than once it was specifically asserted, by the critics of the first Administration, that "the fame of Washington was more indebted to Mr. Hamilton than to any intrinsic merit of his own." Thomas Jefferson, the Secretary of State, after vainly opposing Hamilton in the councils of the Cabinet, resigned his position, rather than remain a subordinate figure in it. And the administration of George Washington was so largely a success, in the troublous times of its beginning, because Washington was what he was, and Hamilton was what he was, and Washington and Hamilton were friends. Henry Cabot Lodge, as a biographer of Washington, emphasizes the fact that the Cabinet relations of Hamilton with the President were those of friendship quite as surely as of politics. "Washington was not much given to professions of friendship," he says. "But it is a mistake to suppose that . . . he was . . . without friends. In war and politics . . . the two men who were nearest to him were Hamilton and Knox, and his diary shows that when he was President he consulted with them nearly every day, apart from the regular Cabinet meetings. They were the two advisers who were friends as well as secretaries, and who followed and sustained him as a matter of affection as much as politics."

As to the relative importance to the country of these two friendships, there is no room for serious question. It was not until Hamilton felt that Washington could spare him from the Cabinet that he also retired from that position; and even then he was ever ready at the call of his friend for any special service, and he had frequent occasion to respond accordingly. "Continually did Washington consult him, and cause the secretaries to consult him in all matters of difficulty," says Hamilton's biographer, Morse; referring to the period after Hamilton's retiring from the Cabinet: "Whenever he was hard pushed for advice or assistance, he turned to Hamilton as to a friend in whose ability and kindliness he could fully trust; and never did Hamilton hesitate to put aside his own private affairs and devote his time to the service of Washington." When at last Washington decided to retire permanently from public life, he sought the assistance of Hamilton in the preparation of his Farewell Address; and that immortal paper has greater force and greater finish from the work done upon it by Alexander Hamilton. The new government was now in good working order, and the long struggle for its establishment in which these two friends had battled and endured side by side was practically at an end. Two years after this, however, the prospect of a war with France led to the formation of a provisional army with Washington at its head as lieutenant-general; and in accepting this appointment Washington nominated his friend Hamilton as first on the list of major-generals. President Adams preferred to give this position to General Knox, who had been the senior of Hamilton in Revolutionary service; but Washington pivoted his own continuance in office on the appointment of Hamilton, who was kept at the head of the list accordingly. This was the close of Washington's public career. It was but a brief season before he lay down to die, leaving as a precious legacy to his country and to the world the memory, the influence, and the practical results of his friendship and cowork, for more than twenty-two years, with Alexander Hamilton.

Whether or not the French Revolution be deemed a success as a movement in the direction of civil liberty, there can be no question that it was a terrible struggle in that direction; hence it is a movement to be looked at as illustrative of the sway of friendship in the sphere of such a struggle. "It was not only a period of destruction, but a period of construction," says one of its latest historians. "Nearly every expedient, whether socialistic or purely democratic, which has been proposed, of recent years, for benefiting the condition of the people, was tried between 1789 and 1799; and, if history has any value at all, it is this period, which ought to be examined before any other"—for lessons in the realm of civil liberty. A personal friendship which was a power in the French Revolution was the friendship of Camille Desmoulins with Georges Jacques Danton. One of these friends was the beginner of that revolution, the other was for a time its central figure. Together the two friends were leaders and shapers of the best thought and purposes of its stormiest periods; and the death of the two friends, side by side, on the guillotine, was the end of its brightest hope as a movement for human welfare.

On the 12th of July, 1789, young Camille sprang upon a table at one of the cafés of the Palais Royal, and announced to the listening crowd of restless idlers the dismissal by the king of M. Necker as prime minister, calling that act "the tocsin of the St. Bartholomew of the patriots," and sounding the cry, "To arms! To arms!" It is admitted that "this scene was the beginning of the actual events of the Revolution." Two days later the Bastile was stormed, and the era of violence was fairly open. Camille was the pamphleteer, the editor, the popular voicer of the period. There was reason in the recognition of him as the "Attorney-General of the Lamppost;" yet he was more than a mere inciter to vigorous action; he was a thinker with a purpose in his thinking. Lord Brougham says of him: "The merit of Camille rises very much above any literary fame which writers can earn, or the public voice can bestow. He appears ever [after the Revolution had begun] to have been a friend to milder measures than suited the tastes of the times." And it has been said that his latest work, in the *Vieux Cordelier*, was "the noblest expression of revolutionary thought." At the beginning of his revolutionary career, Camille was the friend of Robespierre, who had been his fellow-student at the College of Louis the Grand in Paris; and the two friends were workers together in the Jacobin Club. But Camille was more of a man, a truer man, with nobler instincts, than Robespierre; and it was not long before Camille formed a worthier friendship with Danton; and from the beginning of their acquaintance until their death together, Camille and Danton were devoted friends. "If any man," says Brougham, "can more than another be termed the author of the French Revolution, it is Danton;" and Guizot suggests that "the indomitable, inexhaustible genius of the Revolution resided in that unequal nature" of his. Danton was alike admired by the populace and feared by the strong thinkers of his day. He was called "the Mirabeau of the *sans culottes*," a "Titan," and "Jove the Thunderer." And Danton has been rightly called the "inspirer" of Camille.

When Danton was made Minister of Justice, Camille was made his secretary-general. Thenceforward the two friends were as one, in their thinking and doing. Together they voted in the Assembly for the death of the king. When Danton was at the head of the Triumvirate in the Reign of Terror, Camille was his mouthpiece and advocate in all efforts at shaping public sentiment or directing public thought. When Robespierre would be rid of Danton he must be rid of Camille as well; for the two were one, and either was the other. So it was that they were sent together to the scaffold, on April 5, 1794, to die together as friends; and that "with them died also the hope of the Revolution." Nor was it merely a coincidence that these two men were in political affiliation in their revolutionary career. They were friends to the last. Guizot records that when they went to execution Danton "wished to embrace Camille Desmoulins at the foot of the scaffold, but the executioner separated them. 'Wretch,' said he, 'you will not hinder our heads from kissing in the basket presently.'"

These representative illustrations from the course of Greek and Roman and English and French and American peoples, in their contests for liberty, are sufficient to indicate the prevailing power of this sentiment in this field of human endeavor. Added research would supply added proof in the same direction.

AFFECTING PHILOSOPHIC THOUGHT.

T might, at first thought, seem that calm philosophy would be less likely than any form of practical action to exhibit the influence of personal friendship; but when we consider that philosophy is human thinking concerning the relations of things, we can see that the spirit of the individual thinker will naturally affect the manner of his thinking; and that, therefore, philosophers are liable to feel the sway, in all their reasonings, of the most potent of human sentiments. As a matter of fact it is found that philosophies, ancient and modern, have given large prominence to the element of friendship; and that the authors of those philosophies have been peculiarly open to its immediate influence.

Tradition assigns to the Greek Pythagoras, in the sixth century before our era, the claim of being the first to call himself a philosopher, or "lover of wisdom." We know but little of the personal history, or even of the specific teachings, of Pythagoras; but the numerous stories concerning his influence over his contemporaries go to show that he was a man who loved and was loved. And the one saying of his that has been preserved to us in classic records, is his reference to "a friend" as "the half of one's soul." Out of the choicest of his followers, Pythagoras is said to have formed a select brotherhood, or society of friends whom he drew close to himself in the privileges of confidence and affection; and within this sacred circle of sworn friends there were inner circles, one within another, until the innermost was reached by those nearest and dearest to himself.

In the brief writings ascribed to Pythagoras, under the name of "Golden Words," probably composed by one of his disciples as embodying the great master's more important teachings, there is an appeal to all to choose wisely in friendship; and this appeal immediately follows the injunction to duties that look God-ward, as if friendship were the highest duty in purely human relations. And a modern historian of classic times, summing up the influences of Pythagorean philosophy, says: "As regards the fruits of this system of training or belief, it is interesting to remark, that wherever we have notices of distinguished Pythagoreans, we usually hear of them as men of great uprightness, conscientiousness, and self-restraint, and as capable of devoted and enduring friendship." Damon and Pythias were representative Pythagoreans, and their undying friendship seems to have been in the line of the teachings of this first of the Greek philosophers.

Confucius was a contemporary of Pythagoras, in that wonderful sixth century before our era. While his philosophy was mainly limited to the principles that should govern men in their development of personal character, and in their purely social relations, it had in it enough that was of permanent value to make its impress on, and to hold its power over, one-third of the human race for now twenty-four centuries; and friendship was a permanent element in the philosophy of Confucius. It is said that when Tze-kung once asked the sage "if there were any one word which would serve as a rule of practice for all one's life," Confucius replied "Yes," and then named the word, or composite character, *shu*, meaning literally "as heart." This he explained by showing that we were to look out upon others in that sympathy with them, and that regard for them, which our hearts would prompt us to have for ourselves. An unselfish affection, which is the very essence of friendship, Confucius made the active principle of his system of social ethics. The more ancient Chinese classics which were studied by Confucius, made the cultivation of friendship a means of spiritual attainment; and the most eminent followers of Confucius named friendship as the first of social relations. Throughout the writings of Confucius the influence on himself of his personal friendships is plainly disclosed; and he explicitly declared that his ideal in that direction was beyond his attainment.

After Pythagoras there came Socrates and Plato as new beginners in the realm of speculative philosophy, whose influence has been on all the ages since; and in the lives and teachings of both these philosophers friendship bore an important part. Socrates was dependent, from the beginning, on the help of a devoted friend in securing the possibility and means of the best intellectual training that

Athens could then afford. Socrates was the son of a sculptor, and he was trained to his father's art as a means of support. But Crito of Athens, a young friend of Socrates, had large wealth, and he supplied both books and teachers for his friend, so that he could become a student of philosophy; and then he studied with him and under him, while remaining true as his friend. This friendship of Crito for Socrates was unbroken to the last. When Socrates was condemned to death, Crito was one of his bondsmen, and he sought the privilege of securing his escape by the use of his large wealth. When Socrates refused to avail himself of this proffer, Crito remained with him in affectionate converse during the last hours of the philosopher's life; and finally he who had helped to open the eyes of Socrates to the light of truth, lovingly closed those eyes to the light of earth. The influence of this friendship of Crito is seen in all the thought of Socrates. Its value in his eyes is indicated when he declares to Lysis: "I have a passion for friends. . . . Yea, by the dog of Egypt, I should greatly prefer a real friend to all the gold of Darius, or even to Darius himself. I am such a lover of friends as that." And he discloses his understanding of the scope of his friend's friendship for him, when he says to Menexenus and Lysis, of their relative wealth: "Friends have all things in common; so that one of you can be no richer than the other, if you say truly that you are friends." And in all the searchings of the great philosopher after truth absolute, hardly any question has larger prominence than the nature and possibilities of friendship.

Plato, like Socrates, was largely indebted to friendship,

and largely influenced by it. Among the stories that gained credence concerning Plato's life-course is one, deemed probable by Grote and Ueberweg and Erdmann, that tells of his visit to Syracuse with his friend Dion, and of the bearing of this journey on all his future. Offending the tyrant Dionysius by his plain speaking, Plato was sold as a slave by the tyrant's order; and his mission as a philosopher would have ended abruptly had it not been for the interference of his friend Anniceris, the Cyrenian, who gave of his wealth to ransom his friend. And, as the story goes, when, subsequently, other friends of Plato would have refunded to Anniceris his outlay on this account, Anniceris refused to accept the payment, and the money raised for his reimbursement was devoted to the purchase of grounds for the Academy at Athens. So it came to pass, according to this story, that this world-center of philosophic teaching was itself a monument and memorial of a personal friendship. Certain it is that unselfish friendship had such prominence in the mind of Plato, as a main factor in his philosophy, that it has been characterized, in all the ages since, as "Platonic love;" a love that is noblest and purest and most Godlike among human sentiments. To separate friendship from the teachings of Plato would be to destroy the integrity and life of Platonism.

But in addition to all that we know of the influence of personal friendship on Socrates and Plato individually, we find that the friendship of Plato and Socrates was the main cause of the power of each and both in the world's philosophy. What should we have known of Socrates as a philosopher, had not Plato been his friend? What would Plato have done without that material which he gathered for use through his friendship with Socrates? Emerson brings out this truth when he says: "Socrates and Plato are the double star, which the most powerful instruments will not entirely separate. . . . It was a rare fortune that this Æsop of the mob and this robed scholar should meet, to make each other immortal in their mutual faculty. The strange synthesis in the character of Socrates capped the synthesis in the mind of Plato. Moreover, by this means he was able, in the direct way, and without envy, to avail himself of the wit and weight of Socrates, to which unquestionably his own debt was great; and these derived their principal advantage from the perfect art of Plato." The fountain of philosophy at Athens sent out its waters of truth into all the world through its twin streams of Socratic and Platonic wisdom, gaining their force and flow in the friendship of those great teachers, who had learned from the friendship of others how to be friends to each other.

Greater even than Socrates or Plato in intellectual power, and more influential in the realm of systematic philosophy, stands Aristotle, the greater pupil of the great master of the Academy; and in the life and thought of Aristotle, friendship is again an important factor. While yet a lad, Aristotle was an attached friend of the young prince who subsequently became Philip of Macedon; Aristotle's father being the favorite physician of Philip's father, king Amyntas II. This friendship had its shaping influence on the career of Aristotle. After the early death of his father and mother, young Aristotle was cared for and educated by Proxenus of Atarneus in Mysia, a devoted friend of his father; and it was as a result of this legacy of friendship that Aristotle came to be a pupil, and so to become a friend, of Plato at Athens. Still later Aristotle won the friendship of Hermias, dynast of Atarneus, the home of his father's friend; and this friendship was a life treasure to him. By means of it he was aided in his studies and prompted in his thinking. And when Hermias was killed by the Persians, Aristotle gave expression to his ardent love for him in a poem that has survived until the present; and he caused a statue to be erected to his memory at Delphi. His love for Hermias, Aristotle seems to have transferred to the adoptive daughter of his friend, whom he had married; and he appeared to love her with the love of friendship in addition to conjugal love. Long years after her death he directed by his will that her ashes should be placed by his own in his tomb. Because of Philip's friendship for Aristotle he committed to his care the instruction of his son Alexander, and Alexander became the friend as well as the pupil of the philosopher. It was by the princely aid of Alexander that Aristotle was enabled to pursue his investigations in the realm of nature to an unparalleled extent, and to gather his wonderful collection of specimens for purposes of comparative study. Friendship is a theme of themes in the teachings of Aristotle; and in the world's literature, to-day, there is hardly a truer exhibit of the nature and scope of friendship than in his essay on that transcendent virtue. Nor can any one doubt that Aristotle made so much of friendship because friendship was so much to Aristotle.

After the days of Socrates and Plato there came a sharp

division in Greek philosophy, separating the Epicureans from the Stoics; and it is a noteworthy fact that, widely as these two schools of thinking differed in other respects, they were agreed in recognizing the surpassing importance of friendship. The Stoics held that the supreme end of life, or the highest good, is virtue; while the Epicureans held that the highest good is defined as happiness, or enjoyment. But both were agreed that friendship was desirable; the one school claiming that its cultivation was a duty, and the other that it was in itself a good. Zeno, the chief of the Stoics, taught that man exists for society rather than for himself; hence that unselfish friendship is the truest exhibit of personal virtue. Epicurus, on the other hand, taught that a man ought to seek personal advantage and enjoyment by every means in his power; and, holding this view of life, he is reported by Cicero as claiming "that, of all things which philosophy brings together for the happy life, nothing is greater than friendship, nothing more enriching, nothing more delightful." Diogenes Laertius says that Epicurus "had so many friends that even whole cities could not contain them." Among the closest and most influential friends of Epicurus stood the poet Menander. Alike in the realm of abstract truth and in the realm of practical utility, friendship had a foremost place in the philosophies of ancient Greece—and beyond.

As with ancient philosophy, so with modern, friendship has been a potent factor in its shaping and outbringing. It were needless to follow down the centuries for detailed proof of this proposition at every period; but it suffices to pass from the beginnings of ancient speculative philosophy to the beginnings of the more modern thinking in this realm. "Modern philosophy rigorously defined," says Lewes, "commences with Bacon and Descartes;" and although eighteen centuries intervened between their Greek prototypes and these founders of new schools of systematic speculation, human nature is found much the same in these later days as in the earlier, and friendship is as influential now as then.

Francis Bacon is known as "the Father of Experimental Philosophy." He first brought into due prominence in the world's thinking the place and method of inductive reasoning as a basis of philosophic study. And the record of Bacon's life-course shows that he owed much to friendship for the opportunities of investigation in the line of his special researches, and for the quickening of his thought in the materials gathered by him. Left in a dependent state, by the death of his father, while only eighteen years old, with the disadvantage of expensive tastes in a prominent social position, and without the means of maintaining himself creditably in such a sphere, Bacon had need of help in order to pursue the studies for which his genius and inclinations preeminently fitted him. In this emergency Bacon was befriended by the warm-hearted, generous, and brilliant young Earl of Essex, who was a few years his junior, and who became devotedly attached to him. With all the faults of this unfortunate peer there was a noble side to his nature, and that side was always turned toward Bacon. Dean Church says of Essex, appreciatively: "He began life with great gifts and noble ends; he was a serious, modest, and large-minded student both of books and things, and he turned his studies to full account. He had imagination and love of enterprise, which gave him an insight into Bacon's ideas such as none of Bacon's contemporaries had." Of the relations of Essex with Bacon, Church adds: "Their friendship came to be one of the closest kind, full of mutual services and of genuine affection on both sides. It was not the relation of a great patron and useful dependant; it was, as might be expected in the two men, that of affectionate equality. Each man was equally capable of seeing what the other was, and he saw it."

Essex knew how to be a friend, better than Bacon did. He was watchful of the interests of Bacon, and ever ready to promote them, in public or in private, at any cost or risk to himself. When Bacon sought the office of Attorney-General, Essex made Bacon's cause his own, regardless of the enmities provoked thereby. "Resolutely, against all the world, I stand for your cousin, Francis Bacon," he said to Sir Robert Cecil, when to announce that determination was to set himself in opposition to one high in royal favor. And when Sir Robert would fain turn him from his purpose by suggesting that a proposal for another appointment for his friend would "be of easier digestion to the Queen," Essex responded with unabated vigor: "Digest me no digestions. The attorneyship for Francis is that I must have; and in that I will spend all my power, might, authority, and amity, and with tooth and nail procure the same for him against whomsoever; and whosoever getteth this office out of my hands for any other, before he have it, it shall cost him the coming by." The sturdy efforts of Essex in behalf of Bacon in this instance, as again in a later effort to obtain for him the place proposed by Sir Robert, were unsuccessful; and Essex felt the disappointment hardly less keenly than Bacon. But his ministry of friendship did not end here. Finding that he could not secure for his friend a public appointment that was fittingly remunerative, Essex presented to Bacon a personal estate near Twickenham, worth nearly two thousand pounds,—a much larger sum for that day than for now; and this gift was made, as Bacon afterwards confessed, "with so kind and noble circumstances, as the manner was worth more than the matter." Then and thus it was that Bacon first obtained the means of leisurely study, and was enabled to begin the preparation and publication of those writings which have linked his name with immortality. Their beginning was an outgrowth and a memorial of friendship, and friendship was a theme of prominence in their pages.

Again and again, after this, Essex exerted himself in behalf of Bacon's welfare; and Bacon was the gainer by his friendship. But there came a time when Bacon found that he must choose between self and friendship, when to be true as a friend to Essex would cost him his position and his prospects, and he chose selfishly, with all its consequences to his character as well as his reputation. "The lamentable truth must be told," says Macaulay. "This friend so loved, so trusted, bore a principal part in ruining the Earl's fortune, in shedding his blood, and in blackening his memory." In spite of all that has been done to explain away or excuse the conduct of Bacon toward Essex, by such admiring biographers as Montagu, Spedding, and Aldis Wright, the fact remains, as shown by Dean Church, that Bacon "was willing to be employed to hunt to death a friend like Essex, guilty, deeply guilty to the state, but to Bacon the most loving and generous of benefactors." This latest conscientious and fair-minded biographer of Bacon sums up the case as it stands, when he says: "The question was not whether Essex was guilty. The question for Bacon was, whether it was becoming to him, having been what he had been to Essex, to take a leading part in proceedings which were to end in his ruin and death. . . . Bacon had his public duty; his public duty may have compelled him to stand apart from Essex. But it was his interest, it was no part of his public duty, which required him to accept the task of accuser of his friend, and in his friend's direst need calmly to drive home a well-directed stroke that should extinguish chances and hopes, and make his ruin certain. No one who reads his anxious letters about preferment and the Queen's favor, about his disappointed hopes, about his straitened means and distress for money, . . . can doubt that the question was between his own prospects and his friend; and that to his own interest he sacrificed his friend and his honor."

It was through his winning a friend that Bacon gained a start in his life-work. It was through his failing as a friend that his character began to fail him, and that he was on the way to his final downfall. It is in the varying phases of that character that made friends for him, and that made him untrue as a friend, that Bacon appears in history so great in his glory and in his shame. But Essex was not the only friend who aided Bacon in his philosophic studies, and who had a shaping influence upon his work for the world. Bishop Lancelot Andrewes was Bacon's close friend and counselor, from his young manhood to his life's close. Bacon called him his "Inquisitor-General," as he was accustomed to examine and criticise inquiringly whatever Bacon proposed to lay before the public. Saintly George Herbert was warmly attached to Bacon, and gave him no little help in his studies. Yet closer than any other in helpful friendship was Toby Matthew, a son of the Archbishop of York, who had seen much of learned men in Italy, and whose judgment and fidelity were highly valued by Bacon. It is even said that all of the translating of Bacon's works into elegant Latin was done by his personal friends, as much of it is known to have been. Thus it is that he refers to one of these translations as made "by the help of some good pens which forsake me not."

Of the gain which the keenest mind can acquire only through the intercourse of such friendship as he enjoyed, Bacon says felicitously: "Friendship maketh indeed a fair day in the affections, from storm and tempests: but it maketh daylight in the understanding, out of darkness and confusion of thoughts. Neither is this to be understood only of faithful counsel, which a man receiveth from his friend; but before you come to that, certain it is, that whosoever hath his mind fraught with many thoughts, his wits and understanding do clarify and break up, in the communicating and discoursing with another: he tosseth his thoughts more easily; he marshalleth them more orderly; he seeth how they look when they are turned into words; finally he waxeth wiser than himself; and that more by an hour's discourse than by a day's meditation." And as if he were epitomizing his own experience in the intellectual as in the political world, Bacon says of the best man's effort to play his part in life's drama, "If he have not a friend, he may quit the stage."

Descartes was nearly a contemporary of Bacon, but his influence as a philosopher was far greater, both in his own day and later. He was the pioneer, in the realm of modern analytic or deductive philosophy, even more surely than was the other, in the realm of modern empirical, or inductive, philosophy. "There have been disputes," says Lewes, "as to Bacon's claim to the title of Father of Experimental Science; but no one disputes the claim of Descartes to the title of Father of Modern Philosophy." Comparing Descartes with Bacon in point of influence on his times, Hallam says positively: "He worked a more important change in speculative philosophy, than any who had preceded him since the revival of learning; for there could be no comparison in that age between the celebrity and effect of his writings and those of Lord Bacon." The friend who did most to affect and develop the philosophic thinking of Descartes, was Marin Mersenne, whom he met as a fellow-student at the Jesuit school of La Flèche, at Anjou, and who continued his devoted friend for nearly forty years. Mersenne was some eight years the senior of Descartes, and was already deeply interested in both mathematics and philosophy when he made the friendship of the young student, not yet more than twelve or fourteen years old, through whom he was destined to do his best work in the world. In addition to what has been called the psychological side of Descartes' philosophy, having its starting point in his famous epigram "*Cogito, ergo sum*,"—"I think, therefore I am,"—the mathematical, or deductive, side of that philosophy was what gave it pre-eminent force among men; and that this combination of methods was largely due to the personal influence of Mersenne, with his peculiar tastes and acquirements, will hardly admit of a doubt.

Neither Mersenne nor Descartes ever married. The one entered the priesthood, and the other was for a time a soldier; but they continued in correspondence while separated by distance, and they were much together, at other times, in mutual studies. In Paris, soon after his leaving La Flèche, Descartes was engaged in close mathematical study with Mersenne, and with a still more eminent mathematician, Claude Mydorge. A little later, while Descartes was in winter quarters, at Neuburg, as a soldier in the Bavarian service, the foundations of his system of philosophy came before his mind as by a revelation. He did not, however, pursue his studies without intermission, in the line of his new thinking; for he was again in Paris, six years after his Neuburg revelation, "and, in company with his friends Mersenne and Mydorge, was deeply interested in the theory of the refraction of light, and in the practical work of grinding glasses of the best shape suitable for optical instruments." It was when he was about thirty-two years of age that Descartes, at the request of Cardinal de Berulle, decided to devote himself to philosophic studies, and removed to Holland for this purpose, leaving all his financial affairs in France to the care of the Abbé Picot, and making his friend Père Mersenne "his literary and scientific representative." For twenty years Descartes remained at his studies in Holland, visiting France on only three occasions meanwhile. During all that time his work was going on with the help of his friend Mersenne. Descartes would state his views and his difficulties to Mersenne; and Mersenne would raise objections in the one case, and suggest solutions in the other. Descartes would ask for fresh investigations in one line or another; and Mersenne would pursue the desired researches and report on them. Each fresh work, in its issue, was forwarded by Descartes to Mersenne; and the latter secured criticisms upon it from other scholars, and forwarded them, with his own, to his friend. By this means each successive edition of the works of Descartes was in substantial advance on that which had before appeared.

Other friendships than those of Mersenne and Mydorge had their influence on the studies of Descartes. His warm friendship with Guez de Balzac had its effect on his style of thought and expression. His friendship with the Princess Elizabeth, daughter of Frederick V., Elector Palatine, was, as Professor Mahaffy says, "one of the most sincere and affectionate he ever formed;" and his extended correspondence with her included a close discussion of the metaphysical and mathematical phases of his system, and of the elements of other philosophies. After the death of Mersenne and Mydorge, Descartes came into relations of friendship, first with Claude Clerselier, the French translator of one of his important works, and then with Pierre Chanut, the French ambassador at the court of Sweden. Through his friend Chanut, Descartes became known to Queen Christina of Sweden, daughter of Gustavus Adolphus; and she entered into a correspondence with him on the nature of love and friendship. After a while the Queen became desirous of having Descartes take up his residence at Stockholm; and she even sent an admiral to wait on him, with the proffer of his ship to bring him to her shores. Accepting the royal invitation, with certain important conditions, Descartes made his home with his friend Chanut at the Swedish capital. Queen Christina not only desired the counsel of Descartes for her personal guidance in study, but she wished him to aid her in founding a learned Academy, while she urged him to undertake the work of editing a completed edition of his papers. Hardly, however, had he entered upon these new duties, when Chanut was taken dangerously ill with inflammation of the lungs; and, through devotion to him in his illness, Descartes was stricken down with the same disease, and died, while Chanut recovered.

From his earliest life to its close, Descartes was helped upward and onward, in his thinking and in his doing, by friendship. Great as he was, he could never have done all he did for the world, without the inspiration and aid of the friends he had. And who can doubt that one reason why Descartes so transcended Bacon in the influence of his life work, as a man and as a philosopher, is to be found in the fact that he had the character that enabled him to *be* a friend so truly, as well as the attractiveness and ability that won to him and held the friendship of others?

Next after Descartes, as a pioneer thinker in the realm of speculative philosophy, stands John Locke. John Stuart Mill calls Locke "the unquestioned founder of analytic philosophy of mind." And one of his recent biographers says of his place among modern thinkers: "To trace Locke's influence on subsequent speculation would be to write the history of philosophy from his time to our own. In England, France, and Germany, there have been few writers on strictly philosophic questions, in this century or the last, who have not either quoted Locke's 'Essay' [Concerning Human Understanding] with approbation, or at least paid him the homage of stating their grounds for dissenting from it. In the last century, his other works, especially those on Government and Toleration, may be said to have almost formed the recognized code of liberal opinion in this country, besides exercising a considerable influence on the rapidly developing speculations which, in the middle of the century, were preparing no less than a social revolution in France." And John Locke, power as he proved to be in the world's forces, may almost be called the creature of friendship; as he was unmistakably an illustration of its helpfulness in the realm of philosophic thought.

Before Locke had begun his philosophical writings, and while he was pursuing medical studies at Oxford, he had occasion to deliver a message of regret, or apology, from a physician with whom he was connected, to Lord Ashley, afterwards the Earl of Shaftesbury, who had come to Oxford to drink the Astrop waters, found in that region. That simple call proved a turning-point in the life of Locke. He seems to have won the favor of Lord Ashley at the start. He was invited to stay and sup with him that evening, and "the result of this short and apparently accidental interview was the beginning of an intimate friendship, which seems never afterwards to have been broken, and which exercised a decisive influence on the rest of Locke's career." Locke was soon invited to make his home with Lord Ashley's family. His counsel and attention were the means of saving Lord Ashley's life, and thereby winning his grateful affection. It was in the home thus opened to him that he gained time for his philosophical studies, while its associations enabled him to extend his acquaintance into the outer world of thought and action. There it was that, at his friend's suggestion, Locke wrote his first essay on Toleration, the substance of which was so influential, in other forms, in later years. There also it was that, in an evening's discussion with "five or six friends" concerning the "principles of morality," Locke began "a careful examination of the exact limits of man's power to know the universe," as a means of finding a way out of the difficulties that presented themselves in the discussion. And this was the beginning of his famous "Essay Concerning Human Understanding," which Hallam calls "the first real chart of the coast," and which was given to the public twenty years after this beginning. "This work gave intellectual unity and a purpose to his life as a man of letters and philosophy," and its opportunity as well as its inspiration was a result of Locke's friendship with Lord Shaftesbury. Locke had the oversight of Lord Shaftesbury's son; and such confidence was reposed in him by his friend, that the duty of finding a suitable wife for the young lord was committed to him, and was satisfactorily discharged. When Lord Shaftesbury was made Lord High

Chancellor, he secured a lucrative appointment for his friend Locke; and it was by this means that the latter was brought into the activities and responsibilities of public life, where he was enabled to accomplish so much for his fellows. At every step of his progress it was a friendship that prompted to his best and most efficient service. Thus it was by way of counsel to one of his friends, Edward Clarke of Chipley, in the training of his children, that Locke first wrote the substance of his treatise on Education; and subsequently it was through this friend Clarke, as the leading manager on the part of the House of Commons in its conference with the House of Lords over the Licensing Act, that Locke was enabled to secure the adoption of his liberal views concerning the limits of censorship of the press; a step which, according to Macaulay "has done more for liberty and for civilization than the Great Charter, or the Bill of Rights."

In turn, Locke was on terms of special friendship with the great Sydenham, and his associate Mapletoft; with Sir Isaac Newton, and Robert Boyle; with Limborch, and Le Clerc; with Lords Somers and Monmouth and Pembroke; as well as with Edward Clarke, and Lord Shaftesbury, as above mentioned; and each of these friends had his influence on Locke's thinking and doing. The place that friendship held in the life-forces of Locke is evidenced in the way in which he spoke of a friend who for the time being had control of his mind and heart. William Molyneaux of Dublin, who represented the University of that city in the Irish Parliament, was such a friend. The two came to love each other through correspondence. Before they had yet met they were attached friends, and the feeling of affection between them had "become as intense," says a biographer of Locke, "as if they had lived together all their lives." In his second letter, Locke wrote to Molyneaux: "You must expect to have me live with you hereafter with all the liberty and assurance of a settled friendship." And when, two or three years later, the possibility of a visit from Molyneaux was in Locke's mind, he wrote: "I cannot but exceedingly wish for that happy day when I may see a man I have so often longed to have in my embraces. . . . You cannot think how often I regret the distance that is between us; I envy Dublin for what I every day want in London." As to the bearing that such a friendship would have on his philosophic thinking, Locke wrote to Molyneaux: "There is one place vacant that I know nobody would so well fill as yourself; I want one near me to talk freely with, *de quolibet ente*, to propose to the extravagancies that rise in my mind; one with whom I would debate several doubts and questions to see what was in them."

After six years of this friendship without a meeting, Molyneaux visited Locke in England, and the two friends had rare enjoyment in their unrestrained converse. "I will venture to assert to you," wrote Molyneaux after his return, "that I cannot recollect, through the whole course of my life, such signal instances of real friendship as when I had the happiness of your company for five weeks together in London." It was not long after this that Molyneaux died, and that Locke wrote of him: "His worth and friendship to me made him an inestimable treasure, which I must regret the loss of, the little remainder of my life, without any hopes of repairing it any way." Then, as showing that Locke's friendship was real friendship, he went on to ask his correspondent if there was any service he could render to the son of Molyneaux. "They who have the care of him cannot do me a greater pleasure than to give me the opportunity to show that my friendship died not with his father."

It would seem as if Locke must have a friend to love, and to give himself out to. After the death of Molyneaux, Locke made the acquaintance of young Anthony Collins, who subsequently became prominent as a Deistical writer; and he was warmly drawn to him by the young man's apparent desire to know the truth, in lines of philosophic and religious study. The new acquaintance ripened into friendship. "Why do you make yourself so necessary to me?" wrote Locke to Collins, only a year before his death. "I thought myself pretty loose from the world; but I feel you begin to fasten me to it again; for you make my life, since I have had your friendship, much more valuable to me than it was before." And he added, in illustration of the practical value of friendship to a thinker: "If I were now setting out in the world, I should think it my great happiness to have such a companion as you, who had a relish for truth, would in earnest seek it with me, from whom I might receive it undisguised, and to whom I might communicate freely what I thought true."

Yet another beautiful illustration of Locke's enjoyment of, and profit from, friendship, is found in his intimacy with Lady Masham. She was the daughter of Dr. Ralph Cudworth, author of the well-known work, "The Intellectual System of the Universe." Locke had known Damaris Cudworth, and been her friend, while she was yet unmarried. Her interest in his studies was an inspiration and a help to him, and when she became the second wife of Sir Francis Masham she welcomed Locke to her new home; and after a while he was induced to take up his residence with that friend; as he had, in the beginning of his career, made his home with his friend Lord Ashley. For the last fourteen years of his life Locke lived in close and delightful intimacy with this good friend. Her influence on his later writings, and on the revision of his earlier ones, was considerable; and the help of her friendship gave him increased power for good in his varied labors of love. Lady Masham was as a daughter to her fatherly friend Locke; and when at last he breathed out his gentle spirit in death, she was watching over him with tenderness and sympathy; and afterwards she aided to honor his memory and extend his influence by her reminiscences of his life-story.

Among the developments or outgrowths of Locke's theoretical philosophy, in the British mind, were the idealism, or phenomenalism, of George Berkeley, and the skepticism of David Hume, as philosophical systems. The apostles of these two systems, like all other representative philosophers, were influenced and aided by friendship in their thinking and being.

Professor Fraser, the biographer of the first named of these eminent men, says that "the early years and the ancestry of George Berkeley are curiously shrouded in mystery," and that "he comes forth the most subtle and accomplished philosopher of his time, almost from darkness." Yet in view of the "exquisite purity and generosity of character" that marked this man of such "extraordinary merits as a writer and thinker," it is not to be wondered at that in the first glimpse we have of him, as a boy eleven years old in the school or college at Kilkenny (which has been called the "Eton of Ireland"), he is found entering into a close friendship with Thomas Prior, a schoolmate some four years his senior, who is to prove his closest friend and constant helper for more than half a century. Berkeley and Prior were subsequently fellow-students at Trinity College, Dublin. It was there that Berkeley began his philosophical studies; and in them all he was sure of aid and sympathy from Prior. As the years went on, Prior was always at hand in any emergency. He was the man of affairs for his friend, caring for his business interests, and counseling him in all practical matters. Prior was one of the founders of the Royal Irish Society, and was interested in study as well as in business. He was an enthusiastic advocate of his friend Berkeley's tar-water theories, when the great philosopher thought that he had discovered in tar "an extraordinary proportion of the vital element of the universe," and that by means of this simple agency he would be able to mitigate human suffering, prolong human life, and materially advance the interests of humanity. Prior was intimate with Lord Chesterfield, when the latter was Lord Lieutenant of Ireland, and he interceded with the Earl in behalf of the tar-water projects of his friend Berkeley. Chesterfield testified to the worth of Prior "as one who had no view in life but to do the utmost good he is capable of." For fifty-five years the intimacy and correspondence between these two friends was kept up with unabated heartiness, until Prior died in Dublin; and Berkeley survived his friend only a little more than a year. To the last, Prior was "dear Tom" to the great philosopher and godly bishop, as he had been to plain George Berkeley in their early schooldays at Kilkenny; and none can question that his friendship was a factor in the life-work of the friend to whom he was so devoted.

Other friendships, early and later, had their part in influencing Berkeley. Thomas Contarini, "the good uncle of Oliver Goldsmith," a chum of Berkeley at Trinity College, aided him in a philosophical experiment to ascertain the sensations of a person in being hanged, by tying Berkeley to a beam of the ceiling and pulling a chair from under his feet, at almost the cost of his life. And this was but a specimen of the co-work of Berkeley's college friends in his investigations of natural phenomena. Samuel Molyneaux, son of William Molyneaux, a friend of John Locke, was an attached friend of Berkeley before the young philosopher had issued his first important treatises, and Berkeley dedicated one of his works to him. Molyneaux afterwards presented Berkeley to the Prince of Wales, and otherwise aided him into prominence. Sir John Percival, later the Earl of Egmont, was a warm friend and close correspondent of Berkeley for years. He did much in the way of obtaining important criticisms of Berkeley's works, that aided him in maturing and developing his views. Dean Swift also was a valued and valuable friend. He introduced Berkeley at the Court of Queen Anne, and he secured his appointment by Lord Peterborough as chaplain and secretary of the embassy to Sicily, thus enabling him to travel under advantageous circumstances. Among Berkeley's warm friends in London were Richard Steele, Joseph Addison, Alexander Pope, and Bishop Atterbury. By means of these friendships his fortunes as well as his studies were materially influenced. He formed friendships also with Archbishop Secker and Bishop Rundle and Bishop Benson, whose names are linked with his in the familiar lines of Pope:

> "Even in a bishop I can spy desert;
> Secker is decent, Rundle has a heart:
> Manners with candor are to Benson given,
> To Berkeley every virtue under heaven."

In fact, Berkeley's spirit was peculiarly the spirit of friendship, and his friendships had their part in shaping and in making influential his philosophical speculations.

David Hume has a place of importance in the history of modern philosophy, rather through that which his speculations led to, than in aught which they arrived at. "His destructive criticism," says Professor William Knight, "has been quite as helpful to the progress of the human mind, as the constructive efforts which it overthrew, chiefly because it cleared the atmosphere of mist. It took the mind of England, and subsequently that of Europe, away from secondary and outlying questions to those which are primary, and compelled it to probe the philosophy of experience to the core—thus preparing the way for the critical idealism of Kant, and rendering its rise inevitable." And Ueberweg says, in confirmation of this view, that "in Germany it was chiefly the Skepticism of Hume which incited Immanuel Kant to the construction of his Critical Philosophy." And David Hume was not wholly unlike George Berkeley, in the attractiveness of his personal character and in his dependence on personal friendships. The earliest extant letter of Hume's, written when he was about sixteen years old, was addressed to a very dear young friend, Michael Ramsay, of whom little is known save that he continued to be the valued and helpful friend of Hume for at least fifty-one years after this. This earliest letter is full of friendship. Hume tenderly chides Ramsay for his self-sacrificing endeavors in his behalf, while he suggests that he would have done much the same himself. The immediate subject of the correspondence was the philosophic speculations of Hume, upon which he had desired Ramsay's comments. Ramsay had evidently promised to visit Hume and talk the matter over with him, and this was a delight to Hume. "For," he added, "the free conversation of a friend is what I would prefer to any entertainment." From this time forward Ramsay was the trusted friend and confidant of Hume so long as they both lived. It is perhaps true, as one of his latest biographers asserts, that Hume "never loved any one intensely," and that "constitutionally he could not identify himself with the interests of others;" yet it is also certainly true that Hume from his early life was sure that "friendship is a solid and serious thing," and that the sentiment of friendship, in such measure as he was capable of, had an influence over his character and career as potent as any of which he felt the sway.

William Mure of Caldwell, afterwards Baron Mure,

"was among those who seem to have earliest secured and longest retained Hume's esteem;" and for nearly forty years the counsel and aid of Mure were of practical value to Hume. James Oswald of Dunnekier, who was a friend of Hume in his early life, and who remained so through his maturer years, is said to have been "infinitely serviceable to the speculative labors" of the distinguished philosopher. Then there were Matthew Sharp of Hoddam, Gilbert—later Sir Gilbert—Elliott of Minto, and yet others, who had their part as Hume's friends in aiding him in his philosophic thinking. Yet more important to him was the friendship of Adam Smith, begun when Smith was but seventeen years old and Hume was thirty, and continued until the close of Hume's life. The friendship of these two men was intimate, and its influence was real on both of them. It has been said, indeed, that Smith's "Wealth of Nations" would hardly have been written but for his friendship with Hume; and Hume expressed his indebtedness to Smith for his rare helpfulness as a friend. It is proof of the attractiveness of David Hume's personal character that a friend like Adam Smith could publicly say of him, after their long years of intimacy: "Upon the whole, I have always considered him, both during his life-time and since his death, as approaching as nearly to the idea of a perfectly wise and virtuous man, as perhaps the nature of human frailty will permit." If friendship could bring a man of David Hume's skeptical nature to be thus attractive to a lifelong friend, friendship certainly had its influence in his character and in his philosophy.

Leibnitz is called "the founder of the German philosophy of the eighteenth century;" and "the first and last of Locke's great critics." Although his philosophy had less of originality than was shown by some of his predecessors, his modifications of the theories of Locke and Descartes gained an ascendency in the German mind, and held it for a considerable period. It was through his friendship with the Baron von Boineburg that Leibnitz was led into the sphere of action that decided his career for life. He was hardly more than twenty years old when this friendship was formed. As a result of it he was brought into intimate relations with the Archbishop of Mentz; and by the great prince bishop he was set at the work of assisting in the codifying and reforming the body of civil law of the empire. This led to important discussions involving the metaphysical and political views of Leibnitz; and by the suggestion and with the co-operation of his friend Boineburg he made progress in bringing himself and his theories to public notice.

A political mission to Paris, undertaken by Leibnitz at the request of Boineburg, led to his pleasant intimacy with Arnauld and Malebranche, disciples of Descartes, and with the great mathematician and physicist Huygens. These associations had a determinative influence on the studies and final theories of Leibnitz. From Paris, Leibnitz went to London, and there, also, made acquaintances of value. It was while on this absence from his home that Leibnitz lost by death both his friend Baron Boineburg, and their common patron the Archbishop of Mentz. But the gain which friendship had already secured to him he never lost. It was after the death of his friend Boineburg that Leibnitz won the friendship of Queen Sophia Charlotte, wife of the first king of Prussia; which proved to be an impelling force in his philosophical studies. This friendship was a close one, and Schwegler is explicit in saying that it was at the prompting of Queen Charlotte that Leibnitz undertook his greatest work, the Théodicée. And it is Schwegler who, while confessing that Leibnitz owes so much to friendship, enthusiastically declares that "Leibnitz was, after Aristotle, the greatest genius in his reach of universal knowledge that ever lived."

Kant succeeded and transcended Leibnitz as the leader of German philosophy. He was the founder of the modern critical, or transcendental, school of metaphysics. So great was the influence of his works on European thought, that they have been placed, in the estimation of historical judges, "on a level with the great events of the French Revolution, as the most important factors in determining the characteristic features of nineteenth century culture." If ever there was a man, in modern times, who would seem able to do his own thinking, without the help of friendship, it was this man, who has been called "the most profound thinker with whom the history of the human mind has made us acquainted;" but Kant owed very much, even in his thinking, to personal friendship, and he recognized its practical worth in the line of his most important life-labors.

Kant's first impulse toward the studies of his lifetime was given to him by his friend, as well as teacher, Schultz, while he was under his instruction at the college in Königsberg. And when he was left dependent by the death of his father, with his university course yet incomplete, it was by the generosity of his attached friend Richter that Kant was enabled to go on with his studies. In this instance, as in so many another from the days of Socrates and Aristotle onward, the friend who had money shared his means with the scholar who had none; in illustration of the proverb of the ancients, that "the property of friends is common." Kant was never married, and he never traveled many miles from the place of his birth; but his very isolation from the outer world seemed to give intensity to his personal friendships within his limited sphere. Nearest and dearest of his personal friends was an English merchant named Green, who was resident in Königsberg. "For years," says Kant's biographer, Stückenberg, "the philosopher and the merchant were daily companions, regularly spending several hours together." And in proof of the fact that this close friendship had its shaping influence on the thoughts of the great philosopher, Stückenberg records the fact that Kant assured another friend, Jackmann, whom he desired to prepare his biography, that "*he did not write a sentence in the 'Kritik' which he had not first submitted to Green.*"

It were easy to continue such sketches of the friendships of great philosophers; for what has been shown of the few could also be shown of the many. But it must suffice to have given these more illustrious examples in detail, with the added assurance that a similar exhibit could be made in other cases, hardly less noteworthy, all along the record of the centuries. Thus, for instance, the three great names that followed Kant in the development of German philosophy, are Fichte, Schelling, and Hegel; and friendship shows its force in the case of each and all of these, as plainly as in the case of Kant. Fichte was indebted to the offices of his attached friend Weisse for a position at Zurich, when the death of his early friend and patron Von Miltitz had left him without the means of study; and at Zurich he won the friendship of Pestalozzi and Lavater, and received impressions that affected all his future. Schelling owed much to friendship; and, like Bacon, both the good side and the bad of his nature found quickening through his friendship with the Schlegels. Hegel, while still an undergraduate, formed ties of special friendship with two of his fellow-students—young Schelling, the philosophic thinker, and young Hölderlin,—whose poetic tastes tended to deepen Hegel's interest in Grecian literature and thought. It was after Schelling had given public proof of his interest in philosophy that Hegel wrote to him of his own growing interest in that theme, and of his desire to have such help, in bringing his thoughts to bear upon human life, as only a personal friend could supply. "Of all the men I see around me," he wrote, "you are the one in whom I should most desire to find a friend—as in other things, so especially in reference to this business of getting myself expressed, and brought into effective contact with the world." And for years these two philosophers helped each other through friendship.

And so it might be found in every portion of the field of speculative thought. The greatest philosopher is a gainer through having a friend; and even more so through being a friend.

INSPIRING POETRY.

OETRY is more to the world than philosophy; for poetry includes all that philosophy has to offer, and far more. Poetry swayed the mind of man before philosophy had a place there, and poetry is sure of an immortality that no system of philosophy can aspire to. Philosophy is from the intellect, and its appeal is to the intellect, while poetry is from the heart to the heart; and where heart-power and the power of intellect are in comparison, heart-power always leads, and will longest endure.

Love is thought to be the chief inspiration of poetry. The suggestion is:

> "Never durst poet touch a pen to write
> Until his pen were temper'd with love's sighs;"

and, on the other hand, it is claimed that

> "Poets are all who love."

But, as friendship transcends all loves, the inspiration of

friendship to a poet is an inspiration that no craving love can supply. Impassioned love gives a burning intensity to a poet's flame; while an unselfish friendship enables a poet's light to shine out with clear and far-reaching beams, like those of the never-failing stars. The poetry of the ages owes its inspiration to friendship, more than to love. In the world's literature, poetry precedes prose; as the nursery song has its place in a child's training before the matter-of-fact narration. The earliest literature of any people is found in its epic poems, with their story of the exploits and sayings of ancient heroes; and it is in these epics that the influence of primitive passions and sentiments may be traced historically. Foremost among the world's representative epics are the Iliad, of the Greeks; the Mâhabhârata, of the Hindoos; and the Nibelungenlied, of the Germans; and in all of these epics love shows itself as a discordant element, while friendship proves a conserving force.

In the Iliad, love is little more, at its best, than refined lust. It is because Helen of Sparta is a type of physical beauty that the heroes of Greece are her rival and jealous suitors, and that, when she has been won by Menelaus, Paris of Troy violates the rights of hospitality, and carries her away captive from the home where he was a guest. It is another phase of the same selfish passion that brings Agamemnon under the wrath of Apollo, by his desire for the daughter of Apollo's priest Chrysēs, and that again causes a breach between Agamemnon and Achilles over a common object of lustful craving. There is nothing ennobling or inspiring in such love as this, in the Grecian epic. But how different the influence of friendship's sentiment! There is inspiration in the self-abnegating affection of Diomedes and Ulysses; and their heroism through mutual love and fidelity is an incitement and example to succeeding ages. And the friendship of Patroclus and Achilles is the transcendent charm of the Iliad. When love for country is powerless to bring the aggrieved hero, Achilles, once more into the field against the enemies of Greece, the knowledge that his friend Patroclus has been slain, while giving battle in his name, arouses him to the purpose of rescuing his friend's body and avenging his friend's death; and on this impulse of friendship pivots the issue of the eventful war.

Friendship shows its surpassing beauty and its pre-eminent force, as it rises above the passions and selfish instincts of the battle-field, when Diomedes the Greek is drawn by friendship toward Glaucus the Trojan, and he proffers a covenant of love to him who is for the time his enemy.

> "'Henceforward I will be thy host and friend
> In Argos; thou shalt be the same to me
> In Lycia when I visit Lycia's towns.
> And let us in the tumults of the fray
> Avoid each other's spears, for there will be
> Enough for me to slay whene'er a god
> Shall bring them in my way. In turn, for thee
> Are many Greeks to smite whomever thou
> Canst overcome. Let us exchange our arms,
> That even these may see that thou and I
> Regard each other as ancestral guests.'
> Thus having said, and leaping from their cars,
> They clasped each other's hands, and pledged their
>   faith."[1]

[1] Bryant's translation.

So, all through the Iliad, while love provokes jealousy and leads to discord, friendship inspires to lofty purposes and noble doing.

The Mahâbhârata, like the Iliad, is the story of a war between rival peoples; and the prolonged conflict which its verses outline is finally decided by the influence of a personal friendship, while the loves that it records have in them no uplifting influence in comparison with that of friendship. In the Mahâbhârata, the love of the wifely heroine, Draupadî, is shared alike by five brothers; whereas the friendship of Krishna for the hero of heroes, Arjuna, is unfaltering and devoted from first to last. When war is inevitable between the Kauravas and the Pandavas, each party desires the assistance of the mighty Krishna, who is alike a kinsman of both. Duryodhana as leader of the Kauravas, and Arjuna as representing the Pandavas, visit Krishna at the same time, and solicit his aid. The answer of Krishna is: "I will put myself alone into one scale, and all the warriors of my army into the other scale, and you are welcome to take your choice between the two: but if you take me, remember that I shall not fight, though I will give counsel." Duryodhana prefers Krishna's army to Krishna, thinking within himself, "What comparison is there between a single man and thousands of heroes!" But Arjuna says promptly: "I at once decide upon taking yourself, for whether you go with arms or without, and whether you fight or do not fight, your presence will so fortify our hearts that it will be worth a hundred thousand armies." And when Krishna expresses surprise that Arjuna chooses him when he is unwilling to fight, Arjuna responds: "Although you will not join us in the battle, yet if you will but drive my chariot I am assured of victory." As, from time immemorial, he who drives the chariot is counted the closest friend of him who fights in the chariot, this choice of Krishna by Arjuna is the choice of a friend; and the result proves that the friendship of Krishna and Arjuna gives victory to the Pandavas, at the cost of destruction to the Kauravas. The heroism of Achilles, and the prevailing influence of his friendship for Patroclus, are not more prominent in the story of the Iliad than the heroism of Arjuna, and the overmastering influence of Krishna's friendship, in the story of the Mâhabhârata. The most sacred of the Brâhmanic scriptures, the Bhagavad Gîtâ, is but the record of one of the conversations between the peerless hero Arjuna and his charioteer-friend Krishna, in an interval of the great battle between the Kauravas and the Pandavas.

Throughout the Nibelungenlied, as in the Iliad and the Mâhabhârata, the destroying element is love, the conserving force is friendship. The epic opens with the jealous rivalry of Kriemhild and Brunhild for the love of the hero Siegfried. On the other hand, Siegfried gains Kriemhild as his bride through Gunther's friendship, and Gunther wins Brunhild through the friendship of Siegfried. Brunhild's love for Siegfried turns to hate, and she seeks his destruction; but she is powerless against him until, by an act of foul treachery on the part of his companion Hagen, Siegfried is slain in time of peace. Thenceforward the movement of the story is toward the vengeance of Kriemhild on the slayer of her husband. Years after Siegfried's death, Kriemhild consents to marry Etzel, king of the Huns, through the intercession of his dearest friend, Rüdiger von Bechlarn,—this friend binding himself by an oath to be her avenger. When, on the invitation of Kriemhild, Hagen comes with the other Burgundians to the court of Etzel, Kriemhild's long-laid plans of vengeance are matured. Then it is that the idea of fidelity in friendship becomes the chief inspiration of the epic. The brothers of Kriemhild are the friends of Hagen, and when, in the bloody conflict in the palace of the Huns, she offers them their lives if they will surrender the murderer of Siegfried, their united cry is that they will all die with Hagen rather than betray a friend. Thereupon Kriemhild calls on her sworn friend Rüdiger to make good his oath, and become her avenger. But Rüdiger has been the host of Hagen and his followers, and he is bound to them by ties of affection and honor; how then can he turn against them for their overthrow? There comes a struggle between conflicting duties, and when Rüdiger at last decides that his earlier oath of friendship to Kriemhild must outweigh every other consideration, he has no desire to survive the contest which he enters. In his sensitive regard for the rights of his former guest, to whom he must now give battle, Rüdiger states his case to Hagen, secures his approval of his course, transfers to him his shield to guard him, as he has before given a trusty sword to another of the party; and Hagen promises, like Diomedes to Glaucus, not to strike at Rüdiger personally, even when their companions and followers are in combat. Rüdiger, best and truest of men and of friends, falls dead under a blow of the sword he had given to the companion of Hagen. Because of Rüdiger's death, his friend, Sir Dietrich, who had stood aloof from the conflict until now, enters the lists and takes Hagen a prisoner, to deliver him captive to Kriemhild. The epic closes with the death of all the heroes, its main idea being the exaltation of the sentiment of fidelity in friendship, as illustrated by the beauty of that sentiment in its exercise, and the terribleness of its violation in treachery.

The source of a poet's inspiration is indicated in the highest aspiration that his poetry discloses. Not the baser but the nobler sentiments to which he gives expression, are those which have helped to make him a poet. Even though we may know little of his personal history, if we find a poet uplifting a lofty standard for the heroes of whom he sings, or giving highest praise to the loftiest sentiment of his song, we can be sure that his own nature has been stirred in the direction of that standard and by the power of that sentiment. When, therefore, we find in the earliest epics, and in later lyrics and dramas, the transcendency of friendship as an object of admiration and honor, we must recognize the proof that friendship is the inspirer of poetry and of poets. In an essay on "Friendship in Ancient Poetry," Principal Shairp calls attention to the fact that Pindar, greatest of lyric poets in Greece, brings out in its rare beauty the story of Castor and Pollux, in which Pollux, when bereft of his brother-friend Castor, cared not to live any longer, but was permitted because of his friendship to share his own immortality with his mortal friend; and that the tragic poet Euripides exalts in its admirableness the self-abnegating friendship of Orestes and Pylades, when each friend sought the privilege of dying in the other's stead. And the essayist adds, suggestively: "Had not the lyric poetry of Greece—all save part of Pindar's—perished, there would no doubt have come down to us frequent memorials of the love of friends."

First after Homer, in order of time among the poets of ancient Greece, comes Theognis, whose gnomic poems were a literary force in the golden days of that land of letters and art. We know little of this poet as a man; but we gather from his own writings that his friend Cyrnus, son of Polypas, was an inspirer of his poetry, and that his gnomic poems were brought together, and finished for the public, as a tribute to that friend.

Bion and Moschus stand out as poet-friends, in the days close following Theocritus—the last great poet of ancient Greece. Bion dwells with delight on the joys of friendship, as if he felt their inspiration. "Happy are they that love, when with equal love they are rewarded. Happy was Theseus when Pirithous was by his side; yea, though he went down to the house of implacable Hades. Happy among rude men and inhospitable was Orestes, in that Pylades chose to share his wanderings. And *he* was happy, Achilles Æacides, while his darling lived; happy was he in his death, because he shielded him from dread fate." And the choicest pastoral preserved to us from the work of Moschus is his lament over his friend Bion, of whom he tells as the inspirer of his poetry. "Every famous city laments thee, Bion, and all the towns. Ascra laments thee far more than her Hesiod, and Pindar is less regretted by the forests of Bœotia. Nor so much did pleasant Lesbos mourn for Alcæus, nor did the Teian town so much bewail her poet, while for thee more than for Archilochus doth Paros yearn; and not for Sappho, but still for thee, doth Mytilene wail her musical lament; and, in Syracuse, Theocritus. But I sing thee the dirge of an Ausonian sorrow,—I that am no stranger to the pastoral song, but heir of the Doric muse which thou didst teach thy pupils. This was thy gift to me; to others didst thou leave thy wealth, to me thy minstrelsy. . . . But ah! if I might have gone down like Orpheus to Tartarus, or as once Odysseus, or Alcides of yore, I too would speedily have come to the house of Pluto, that thee perchance I might behold, and if thou singest to Pluto, that I might hear what is thy song."

Cicero refers to the inspiring influence, on the popular mind, of the illustrations of unselfish friendship, portrayed in the drama by poets whom this sentiment had inspired. "If at any time any act of a friend has been exhibited, either in undergoing or in sharing dangers, who is there," he asks, "that does not extol such an act with the highest praise? What shouts of applause were lately heard through the whole theater, on the occasion of a new play by my guest and friend, Marcus Pacuvius, when, the king being ignorant which of them was Orestes, Pylades said he was Orestes in order that he might be put to death instead of him; but Orestes solemnly maintained, as was the fact, that he was the man! All stood up and applauded in an imaginary case; but what must we suppose they would have done in a real one? Nature herself excellently asserted her rightful power, when men pronounced that to be rightly done in another which they could not do themselves."

Down along the centuries, from the earliest epics to the most finished lyrics and idyls of every golden age of literature, the truest poets have felt the inspiration of the truest friendship, and have uplifted that sentiment as an ideal before those who might otherwise have failed to perceive its transcendent admirableness. Thus inspired they have become inspirers in the realm of this noblest and most God-like affection.

Ennius, who is called the father of Latin poetry, and whose impress was on the best literary work of his successors, so felt the inspiration of his friendship with Scipio Africanus, that, as Cicero reminds us, he felt that life would not be "worth living" without the joy that comes of having and being a friend. Terence, a leader in Latin comic poetry, and Lucilius, the pioneer in Roman satire, shared in the friendship of Lælius and Scipio; and the friendship which is immortalized in the *De Amicitia* of Cicero was directly an inspiration to these poets, while Terence certainly had aid in the composition of his comedies by the chiefest of these friends. Catullus could never have been the poet he showed himself in his passionate expressions of love, if he had not been the man he was through his friendship for Veranius, and through his unselfish devotedness to his brother-friend Hortalus.

When we reach the golden age of Latin poetry, in the days of Virgil and Horace, we find that friendship is the very center of the innermost poetic circle. Mæcenas inspires friendship in the hearts of the poets, and by inspiring their friendship he inspires their poetry. Varius, and Pollio, and Tibullus, and Virgil, and Horace, are of those who feel and show this inspiring influence. Virgil tells tenderly of his ever-growing love for his earliest friend and schoolmate, Gallus. He sings exultantly the praise of friendship, in the story of the hero-friends, Nisus and Euryalus. Two of his Eclogues are addressed to his friend Pollio. His most finished poems, the Georgics, are written at the special request of his friend Mæcenas. And at the approach of death he names his friend and fellow-poet Varius as one of his literary executors, to whom should be entrusted the care of his unfinished work and of his reputation. Neither Horace nor Virgil could have been what he was, without the other's friendship; and both of these poets owed much to Mæcenas as patron and friend.

Sir Theodore Martin, in his "Life of Horace," speaks of this poet's friendship with Mæcenas as "among the closest and most affectionate on record." "Throughout the intimate intercourse of thirty years which ensued" after the beginning of their friendship, he says, "there was no trace of condescension on the one hand, nor of servility on the other. Mæcenas gave the poet a place next his heart." And "Horace is never weary of acknowledging how much he owes to his friend. When he praises him it is without flattery. When he soothes his anxieties or calms his fears, the words glow with unmistakable sincerity. When he resists his patron's wishes, he is firm without being ungracious. When he sports with his foibles he is familiar without the slightest shade of impertinence." The Sabine farm near Tivoli was a gift of friendship from Mæcenas to Horace; which secured to the poet both a competency and the pleasures of a country life. "It gave him leisure and amusement, and opportunities for that calm intercourse with nature which he needed for his spirit's health." And "it at once prompted much of that poetry which has made Mæcenas famous, and has afforded ever-new delight to successive generations." It has been said that Horace "gave to friendship the ardor which other men give to love;" but it might better be said that Horace illustrates, in his life and verse, how much every true poet owes to the inspiration of friendship. When, indeed, the thought of losing the companionship of Mæcenas by death pressed home on the heart of Horace, his cry of agony went up:

> "Why wilt thou kill me with thy boding fears?
>   Why, O Mæcenas, why?
> Before thee lies a train of happier years;
>   Yes, nor the gods, nor I,
> Could brook that thou shouldst first be laid in dust,
> Thou art my stay, my glory, and my trust!
>
> "Ah, if untimely Fate should snatch thee hence,
>   Thee, of my soul a part,
> Why should I linger on, with deadened sense,
>   And ever-aching heart,
> A worthless fragment of a fallen shrine?
>   No, no, one day shall see thy death and mine!
>
> "Think not that I have sworn a bootless oath;
>   Yes, we shall go, shall go,
> Hand linked in hand, whene'er thou leadest both
>   The last road below." [1]

Mæcenas, dying, commended with almost his last words his friend Horace to his imperial friend Augustus; and Horace, within a few brief weeks, followed his friend, as

[1] Sir Theodore Martin's translation.

he had promised. Side by side the friends were buried on the Esquiline Hill in Rome.

Next, in order of time, after Horace, as a satirist, comes Persius; and, with all the intensity of his denunciation of the vices and follies of his age, there is, in the poetry of Persius an evidence of such sympathy with all that is pure and noble that his writings found exceptional favor among the early Christians, and have a peculiar charm to many to the present day. That it was the inspiration of friendship that gave Persius his best and truest impulses, his own emphatic words bear witness. He was only sixteen years old, when he became the pupil and the friend of Annæus Cornutus, the Stoic philosopher. Persius was of a noble family, while Cornutus was at the best only a freedman, and originally a slave from Libya; but Cornutus was a true friend to Persius, and Persius realized this fact with all that it might bring to him. "To thee," says Persius to Cornutus, in grateful confidence, "now, at the exhortation of the Muse, I give my heart to be searched out; and I long to tell thee, my sweet friend, how large a portion of my heart is yours." Recalling his debt of gratitude to his friend as his guide and teacher, Persius says: "When the path was doubtful, and ignorance of pitfalls of life was drawing trembling minds to the branching cross-roads, 'twas then I leaned on thee. Thou didst receive my tender years, Cornutus. Then the straight rule skilfully applied made straight my warped morals; . . . and my countenance came to be molded by thy thumb. . . . Our task was one, and together we arranged our times of rest. Thou canst not doubt that the days of us both have been set in unison by one fixed principle, and are derived from one star." Thrasea Pætus, "the noblest specimen of Stoicism which the Roman world produced in the first century of the Empire," was also an attached friend of Persius; as, again, was the young poet Cæsius Bassus, to whom he addresses his sixth satire; and both of these friends had their part in uplifting his ideals and in inspiring his best work. But it was the friendship of Cornutus that was the making of Persius; and when the poet died all his property was bequeathed to this friend, and his literary productions were committed to his keeping.

And so it is with the record of all the classic poets. Friendship is an inspiration to that which is best and noblest in poet and poetry.

It has been held by modern scholars that the peculiar prominence given to friendship among the ancient Greeks, and their Roman imitators, was a result of the absence of domestic love in its highest purity; and that the progress of Christianity brought other sentiments into the place of friendship, so that it could no longer have that pre-eminence which the Greeks accorded to it. Principal Shairp expresses the thought of many, when he says of the old-time views of friendship: " Affection of this kind was the highest moral power known to the Greeks, the central purifying power in Greek ethics. It was . . . to the Greeks not only an enjoyment, a pleasant ornament of life, it was a necessity for all higher souls, an essential element in their daily life, the antidote to selfishness and narrow-mindedness. It was the touchstone of Hellenic virtue while their greatness lasted. . . . It was the real soul of ancient life, shedding a grace and a bloom over its clear-cut outlines. It supplied at once that tender devotion which religion has engendered, and that imaginative romance with which Christianity and chivalry have combined to invest womanhood."

This view of the case is correct in its explanation of the prominence given to friendship by the Greeks; but it is a mistaken view in its suggestion that Christianity and chivalry have lessened the relative importance of the sentiment of friendship among personal and social virtues. Self-abnegating friendship still is, as it always has been, the transcendent human affection, man-ward and God-ward. Among the ancient Greeks, when woman was little else than an object of passionate desire, and a wife was rather a servant than a companion, the ties of family had no such sacredness or binding force as those of a voluntary affection resulting from a generous and lofty purpose; and then it was that the sentiment of friendship at its best was the one gleam of divine truth falling on men's pathway, to lead them onward and upward toward unfailing light. Even then there were suggestions of the possibility of friendship between husband and wife, as in the case of Hector and Andromache; between brothers, as in the case of Castor and Pollux; and between brother and sister, as in the case of Orestes and Electra; but such instances were exceptional in the history of the race, until Christianity intensified and extended the power of friendship within the family circle, as well as outside of it. It was through the uplifting sentiment of friendship, in its purity and its ennobling power, that chivalry did its best work in the world, and that Christianity came to exhibit its refining and elevating influence in the best social life of these later centuries. When Christian chivalry had elevated a man's unselfish friendship for a woman who could never be his wife, above any passion of love for a woman whom he sought for himself, a new era had begun in the world, and woman had a new and loftier place among men.

Chivalry was first known as pivoting on a devoted friendship of man for man,—two companions-in-arms being ready to do and dare and die for each other, because of their mutual love. But the progress of Christianity caused men to see the superiority of woman over man in purity and nobleness, and to honor and revere her because of that superiority in its revelation of God's likeness. Then came an advance in the relation of a knightly servitor to his mistress. He was no longer her suitor, but her friend. His chief desire was not to marry her, but to be worthy of her recognition of himself as brave and pure and true through his loyal devotion to her, or to the ideal which she held before him. Not because of any disrespect for the married state, but in order to keep the sentiment of unselfish friendship for his mistress above temptation or suspicion, it was held, in the best days of chivalry, that the highest and purest affection of a knight for his mistress was possible only where there was no thought of marriage between them as an outcome of their relation as friends. The laws of the Court of Love (which found their expression in the *Codex Amoris*, attributed to King Arthur, but probably put into form in the thirteenth century) affirmed that chivalrous love would be terminated by the marriage of the lovers to each other. Either party might marry another without the interruption of the friendship; but their union in marriage was not deemed consistent with that exalted and unselfish sentiment which should actuate and control a knight in his chivalrous love for the woman who was his inspiration to noble being and noble doing. "The only senses allowed to be the vehicle of chivalrous love," says Richard Simpson, "were the eyes and ears. The lover was forbidden to go beyond gazing on, or hearing, or thinking of, his love." These restrictions were deemed necessary in the effort to uplift an uncraving love above all selfish desire; and their result, as a means of training, was a purer life for man and a loftier position and worthier character for woman. This truth is emphasized by Charles Mills, in his historic review of the influence of chivalry, when he says: "Woman was sustained in her proud elevation by the virtues which chivalry required of her; and man paid homage to her mind as well as to her beauty. She was not the mere subject of pleasure, taken up or thrown aside as passion or caprice suggested; but, being the fountain of honor, her image was always blended with the fairest visions of his fancy, and the respectful consideration which she, therefore, met with, showed she was not an unworthy awarder of fame. Fixed by the gallant warriors of chivalry in a nobler station than that which had been assigned to her by the polite nations of antiquity, all the graceful qualities of her nature blossomed into beauty, and the chastening influence of feminine gentleness and tenderness was, for the first time in his history, experienced by man."

Such a sentiment as that which, in chivalry, conjoined

thoughts of God and an unselfish love could not be limited to the minds of martial knights. Illustrated and uplifted by these men of heroic action, it would be sure to lay hold of the better nature of men of profound thought and of profounder feeling, and inspire them to grander conceptions and loftier aspirings. And so it was that this Christianized view of friendship became the inspiration of modern poetry at its best; as a pure and sacred friendship had been the inspiration of the best classic and primeval poetry.

Modern poetry may be said to have begun with Dante. Dante was born at a time when chivalry in its best exhibit of heroic action was already on the wane; while the influence of its self-abnegating spirit, in its reverent loyalty to the ideal of pure womanhood, remained as its choicest legacy to the world. Impressibility of nature, purity of mind, and intensity of feeling, were the characteristics of Dante from his earliest youth; and these characteristics gave him his special susceptibility to the best influences of his day. As chivalry required a would-be knight to begin his special training at seven years of age, and to choose early the woman who was to be his inspiration to high thinking and noble achieving, young Dante was yet but nine years old when he was impressed with a sense of the loveliness and worth of a pure-minded maiden a year younger than himself, and loyally yielded to her the homage of his unselfish friendship. This recognition of Beatrice Portinari as the object of his uncraving love, is designated by Dante as the beginning of a "new life" to him; and in his *Vita Nuova* he tells the story of the growing inspiration which possessed his whole being through the ideal which she presented to him. From the first, Dante had so exalted an estimate and so overpowering a sense of the womanly purity and grace of Beatrice, that he could not be at ease, or seem "himself," in her presence. He suffered in the consciousness that he presented "so contemptible an appearance" before her, through his embarrassment; but his absorbing regard for herself as herself caused him renewedly to forget his failures and to seek anew the inspiration of her presence; "Therefore past sufferings," he said, "hold me not back from seeking the sight of her." Dante seems never to have sought Beatrice in marriage, or to have been on terms of intimacy with her. His whole thought was of her transcendent worth, and his desire was simply to live as became the friend of one so good and lovely as she,—in accordance with the sentiment of the purest chivalry concerning the duty of a true knight to the woman to whom he was a friend.

For a while Beatrice was accustomed to greet Dante with a gracious salutation as they met, and this always brought him to "the bounds of bliss." But by his very efforts to avoid causing her disturbance he caused her to so misunderstand him that she withdrew her salutations, and this abashed him more than ever when he met her, while it in no degree lessened his love for her. It was at this time that he was asked by a group of ladies, "To what end lovest thou this thy lady, since thou canst not sustain her presence? Tell us, for sure the end of such a love must be most strange." Thereupon his answer was: "My ladies, the end of my love was formerly the salutation of this lady of whom you perchance are thinking, and in that dwelt the beatitude which was the end of all my desires. But since it has pleased her to deny it to me, my lord Love, through his grace, hath placed all my beatitude in that which cannot fail me." This beatitude which could not fail Dante was the privilege of being her friend, of loving her and admiring her and sounding her praise, whatever her opinion of him might be. "And I proposed," he said, "to take for theme of my speech, always henceforward, that which should be the praise of this most gentle one." In pursuance of this resolve Dante told in poetry of the graces of Beatrice in her character and in her person, including, according to the customs of the times, her figure, her eyes, and her lips. But having done this he added, in assurance of the purity of his friendship—as uncraving love: "And in order that every evil thought may be removed hence, let him who readeth remember what is written above, that the salutation of this lady, which was an action of her mouth, was *the end of my desires*, so long as I was able to receive it."

There was an inevitable conflict of feelings in the mind of Dante, with, on the one hand, his desire to be worthy of the approval of the woman whose ideal inspired him, and, on the other hand, his oppressive sense of shortcoming in his best endeavors. Confessing to this conflict, he said: "The lordship of Love is good, in that it withdraweth the inclination of his liegeman from all vile things;" and again: "The lordship of Love is not good, because the more fidelity his liegeman beareth to him, so much the heavier and more grievous trials he must needs endure." Yet through all these mental struggles

Inspiring Poetry. 303

as a result of his unselfish love, Dante was conscious that he was himself the gainer through this friendship, and that all with whom he had to do were thereby advantaged. He longed to tell her how he was "disposed to her influence, and how her virtue wrought in" him. And in speaking of the effect upon him of a sight of her in her goodness, he said: "There no longer remained to me an enemy; nay, a flame of charity possessed me, which made me pardon every one who had done me wrong; and had any one at that time questioned me of anything, my only answer would have been 'Love,' and my face would have been clothed with humility."

Beatrice Portinari was married, and this, it would seem, without her ever knowing the measure of love she had inspired in Dante; and then she died. But neither her marriage nor her death made Dante any less truly her friend; for his friendship, like all true friendship, was conditioned, not on what the loved one was to her friend, but on what she was in herself. The inspiration of her memory was no less potent in Dante's mind than the inspiration of her presence. After her death, and after his triumph over a temptation to give her a lower place in his mind, Dante recorded this new purpose of his: "A wonderful vision appeared to me, in which I saw things which made me resolve to speak no more of this blessed one until I could more worthily treat of her. And to attain to this I study to the utmost of my power, as she truly knoweth. So that, if it shall please Him through whom all things live, that my life shall be prolonged for some years, I hope to say of her what was never said of any woman." The outcome of this purpose of Dante was the *Divina Commedia*, reflecting all the struggles of his tender nature, and all the varied experiences of his life of disappointment and trial, transfigured in the light of a sacred and inspiring friendship.

> "Ah! from what agonies of heart and brain,
>   What exultations trampling on despair,
>   What tenderness, what tears, what hate of wrong,
> What passionate outcry of a soul in pain,
>   Uprose this poem of the earth and air,
>   This medieval miracle of song!" [1]

Dante's simple narrative, in his *Vita Nuova*, of his feelings and experiences as the true-hearted friend of a woman, with whom his relations can never be aught but those of friendship, who commands his loving reverence, and whose lofty ideal inspires while it abashes him, is so true to nature that it has bewildered those critics and commentators who were unready to accept it in its simplicity. It has seemed, indeed, to be too simple for plain fact. Yet there is no better illustration, in all the ages, of the inspiring power, over a true man's mind, of a pure friendship for a true woman, without craving and without wavering. Moreover, to one who has had all of Dante's experiences, all the experiences of Dante seem most natural.

A noteworthy confirmation of the fact that in Dante's day the highest refinement of poetic sentiment was evidenced in a reverent admiration of a true woman, apart from all craving love or selfish desire, is given in one of Sordello's poems. Sordello was a predecessor of Dante, whom Dante admired and honored. He lived yet nearer

[1] Longfellow.

to the Crusades than Dante, and his writings are shaped by the influences of his age. "In the south of France the spirit of chivalry was beginning to express itself, and it found utterance in Provençal poetry. Sordello was a troubadour, if we may believe some of those who have written of him; and he had some of the finer, as well as some of the coarser qualities which were associated with chivalry." And this is Sordello's conception of an unselfish love:

> "I love a lady, fair without a peer,
> Serve her I'd rather, though she ne'er requite
> My love, than give myself to other dames,
> However richly they might pay their knight.
> Requite me not? Nay. He who serves a dame
> Whose honor, grace, and virtue shine like day,
> Can do no service which the very joy
> Of doing doth not bounteously repay.
> For other recompense I will not pine,
> But should it come, her pleasure still is mine." [1]

Close following Dante as a poet was Petrarch; and Petrarch's inspiration through friendship was not unlike that of Dante's. It was the same chivalrous recognition of a lofty ideal represented by a pure woman, to whom he could never be more, and to whom he would never be less, than an unselfish friend, that gave to each of these Christian knights that sense of personal lack and that purpose of high attainment which made him the poet he was, and which won him his exalted place in the world of literature. Petrarch, like Dante, dates the beginning of a new life from his first sight of the woman who so commanded his admiration and rever-

[1] F. M. Holland's translation.

ence that he became her friend for always. Laura de Noves was already the wife of Hugh de Sade when, on April 6, 1327, Petrarch first saw her in the church of St. Clara of Avignon. But the fact that Laura was married was no barrier to such a pure and unselfish friendship as Petrarch gave to her, and as accorded with the highest conception of the best Christian chivalry of the period. She was then about nineteen years of age, and he was not quite twenty-three. At once he was drawn away from himself and toward that which was purer and nobler than his earlier enjoyments, in order to become worthy of one so lovely, so admirable, and so good, as he deemed her to be. Petrarch's very reverence for Laura was, indeed, an embarrassment to him and to her; and their kindly intercourse was less immediately helpful to either than it might have proved to both, had his obvious estimate of her not been so exalted and peculiar. But with all the unrest and self-reproaches and manifold discomforts that were a result to him, and with all the mental pain that she may have endured in consequence of this friendship and its expression, it was an unfailing incitement and inspiration to him, and this is to her unfailing honor.

It was for what she was in herself, and not for what she was or ever could be to him, that Petrarch loved Laura with friendship's unswerving love. His warmest praises of her grace and beauty breathe this truth:

> " The stars, the elements, and Heaven have made
> With blended powers a work beyond compare;
> All their consenting influence, all their care,
> To frame one perfect creature lent their aid.

> Whence Nature views her loveliness displayed
> With sun-like radiance sublimely fair;
> Nor mortal eye can the pure splendor bear:
> Love, sweetness, in unmeasured grace arrayed.
> The very air illumed by her sweet beams
> Breathes purest excellence; and such delight,
> That all expression far beneath it gleams.
> No base desire lives in that heavenly light,
> Honor alone and virtue!—fancy's dreams
> Never saw passion rise refined by rays so bright." [1]

Of the origin of his surpassing friendship for her, he says:

> "Fair fame, bright honor, virtue firm, rare grace,
> The chastest beauty in celestial frame,—
> These be the roots whence birth so noble came.
> Such ever in my mind her form I trace,
> A happy burden and a holy thing,
> To which on reverent knee with loving prayer I cling." [2]

Because Laura is what she is, Petrarch would rather be her unrequited friend than have the fullest friendship of one less worthy of his devotion. In all his painful inability to prove himself the friend he longs to be—

> "One comfort rests—better to suffer so
>   For her, than others to enjoy." [3]

That his friendship for Laura was the inspiration of Petrarch's best poetry is obvious in the fact that his fame as a poet rests on his poems in her praise; and he himself is ever forward to give her credit for his highest attainments as a poet:

> "Blest be the year, the month, the hour, the day,
> The season and the time, and point of space,
> And blest the beauteous country and the place
> Where first of two bright eyes I felt the sway:

---

[1] Capel Loft's translation.   [2] Macgregor's translation.   [3] *Ibid.*

> Blest the sweet pain of which I was the prey,
> When newly doomed Love's sovereign law to embrace,
> And blest the bow and shaft to which I trace
> The wound that to my inmost heart found way:
> Blest be the ceaseless accents of my tongue,
> Unwearied breathing my loved lady's name;
> Blest my fond wishes, sighs, and tears, and pains:
> Blest be the lays in which her praise I sung,
> That on all sides acquired to her fair fame,
> And blest my thoughts! for o'er them all she reigns."[1]

After Laura's death, Petrarch finds himself striving in vain after his former attainment as a poet:

> "But she is gone whose inspiration hung
> On all my words, and did my thoughts beguile.
> My numbers harsh seemed melody awhile,
> Now she is mute who o'er them music flung."[2]

Best of all, in proof of the truth that it was an unselfish friendship, and not a craving love, for Laura that possessed and inspired Petrarch, is his oft-repeated declaration that his affection for her was the means of drawing his affections heavenward, and that, the more he loved her, the more he loved his God.

> "'Twas she inspired the tender thought of love
> Which points to heaven, and teaches to despise
> The earthly vanities that others prize:
> She gave the soul's light grace, which to the skies
> Bids thee straight onward in the right path move;
> Whence buoyed by hope e'en now I soar to worlds above."[3]

> "Lady, in your bright eyes
> Soft glancing round, I mark a holy light,
> Pointing the arduous way that heavenward lies.
>
> .   .   .   .   .

---

[1] Wrangham's translation.   [2] Wollaston's translation.
[3] Wrangham's translation.

> This is the beacon guides to deeds of worth,
> And urges me to seek the glorious goal:
> This bids me leave behind the vulgar throng,
> Nor can the human tongue
> Tell how those orbs divine o'er all my soul
> Exert their sweet control." [1]

Nor is it in impassioned verse alone that Petrarch bears this testimony to the spiritual uplifting which this friendship gave to him. In one of his prose dialogues with St. Augustine, he dwells on the influence of his friendship for Laura. "I never loved anything that was base," he said; "yea, I do not remember that I ever loved except the most excellent. . . . This one thing—whether you find my motives in gratitude or in folly—I will not pass over in silence. Whatever you see in me, be it little or much, is due to her; nor would I ever have attained to this measure of name and fame, unless she had cherished, by those most noble influences, that very feeble implanting of virtues which nature had placed in this breast. She recalled my youthful spirit from every kind of baseness, and drew me back, as they say, with a hook, and constrained me to give heed to lofty things. And why not?—since it is certain that love changes us into the likeness of what we love." It was twenty-one years after Petrarch's first meeting of her that Laura died, having lived a quiet and blameless life as a true wife and mother,—the mother of ten children, and the revered ideal of her friend Petrarch. With all his sorrow over her loss he was as truly her friend after her death as before; and he even felt that while still inspired by

[1] Dacre's translation.

her he was in a sense nearer to her and in closer sympathy than while she was here. In a vision she appears to him, and speaks words of comfort, in view of his grief and of her memory of the constraint that was between them in her lifetime here.

> "'Dear friend,' she says, 'thy pangs my soul distress;
> But for our good I did thy homage shun '—
> In sweetest tones that might arrest the sun." [1]

And his confidence in her recognition of his friendship, as it was and is and ever must be, finds this glad expression:

> "Who feared me once, now knows, yet scarce believes,
> I am the same who wont her love to seek,
> Who seek it still; where she but heard me speak,
> Or saw my face, she now my soul perceives." [2]

Petrarch had already been crowned poet laureate at Rome, because of what he had done and of what he was through the inspiration of his friendship for Laura. He wore his laurels gracefully for a quarter of a century after her death; but he was never less her friend than while in the zenith of his fame in her lifetime, and his place in history is secure for all time, because of what she was, as inspiring him to the friendship which made him what he was.

"Dante and Petrarch," says Hallam, "are as it were the morning-stars of our modern literature." Dante wrought the greater master-piece of poesy; but Petrarch had larger influence over his times and the poets who followed him. The inspiration of each was a sacred

---

[1] Macgregor's translation.   [2] *Ibid.*

friendship for a pure-minded and noble-hearted woman. But both Dante and Petrarch felt and evidenced the power in their lives of the sentiment of friendship, apart from its exhibit in the master passion which inspired their highest poetry; for he who is a true friend to one, can be a better friend to all.

When Dante wrote his earliest sonnet, before he had a poet's experience or a poet's name, young Guido Cavalcanti, a poet of tender heart and of appreciative sensibilities, recognized a brother spirit in Dante, and responded in sympathy to his heart-call in that sonnet. "Among those who replied to it," says Dante, "was he whom I call *the first of my friends*. . . . And this was, as it were the beginning of the friendship between him and me." Guido Cavalcanti is described by his contemporaries as a noble knight, brave and courteous; wise and learned, a logician and philosopher; a gentleman "singularly well spoken," and in no way lacking in aught that "was commendable in any man." He has even been called "the other eye of Florence in the time of Dante" (*alter oculus Florentiæ tempore Dantis*). Dante was not yet nineteen when the impress of this friend's positive character was first made upon him; and their close intimacy in friendship was continued for seventeen years. Longfellow notes the remarkable likeness of one of the poems of Guido Cavalcanti to the treatment of the same subject in Dante's master-piece, and says: "From the similarity between this poem and the lines of Dante one might infer that the two friends had discussed the matter in conversation, and afterwards that each had written out their common thought." Who can doubt that such a friendship had its shaping power on such a mind as Dante's? Nor is it strange that Dante makes recognition of his indebtedness to this early guide of his mind, when he pictures the father of Guido as inquiring of him, in his journey through Hell:

> "If through this blind
> Prison thou goest by loftiness of genius,
> Where is my son? and why is he not with thee?"

Not to dwell on other impressing friendships of Dante, like those of Giotto the painter, and Ulberti the poet, it is to be noted that another Guido—Guido Novello da Polenta—had a peculiar influence over his later life-course. This "splendid protector of learning, himself a poet, and the kinsman of that unfortunate Francesca whose story had been told by Dante with such unrivaled pathos," was a devoted friend of Dante, who made his home with him in Ravenna. Dante loved this princely friend, and was glad to exert his best abilities in proof of his friendship. Having failed to obtain an audience from the powers at Venice while on an embassy from his friend and patron, "Dante returned to Ravenna so overwhelmed with disappointment and grief, that he was seized by an illness which terminated fatally;" and so it was that the masterful life of the great poet was begun and continued and ended under the inspiration of friendship.

Petrarch also owed much to friendship apart from the inspiration of his regard for Laura. While yet but a school-boy he formed a close friendship with Guido Settimo, a Genoese youth of about his own age, whose parents, like those of Petrarch, were political exiles at

Avignon. That friendship continued unbroken for more than fifty years, until the death of Guido as archbishop of Genoa; and the constant influence of Guido over Petrarch was in the nature of both stimulus and sympathy. Another friendship that had much to do with shaping the career of Petrarch was formed, when he was just twenty-one years old, with James Colonna, of the illustrious Italian family. This friend became also his patron, and when appointed bishop of Lombes took him into his episcopal residence; and afterwards the two friends traveled and studied together. By means of this friendship Petrarch was brought into intimate relations with Cardinal Colonna, the brother of his friend, and thereby his opportunities for the study of life and of literature were promoted. So close was the friendship between Petrarch and James Colonna that, when the latter died in Lombes, the former, being at Parma, was consciously impressed with a sense of his friend's death at the very time of its occurrence.

Other friendships of importance were formed by Petrarch, all the way along in his career; for he could not live except by loving. His latest friendship was with Boccaccio. It was not long after Laura's death that the two poets met at Florence. "Their friendship," says Hueffer, "seems to have been instantaneous; a friendship at first sight, as warm and unselfish as was ever contracted by freshmen at college. Like school-boys, also, they at once begin telling each other their secrets; and their correspondence, commenced soon after their meeting and continued almost to the last day of their lives, is not surpassed in literature, as regards the variety of topics touched upon, and the familiarity and perfect mutual confidence evinced in every turn of expression." Boccaccio also had found inspiration to poetry in his recognition of a high womanly ideal in one to whom he could be only a friend, and his praises of "Fiammetta" are an indication of his measurable appreciation of the better spirit of Petrarch in this direction. Boccaccio's later years were impressed more profoundly than Petrarch's by this delightful friendship; and it would seem that its uplifting influence led Boccaccio to an entire change of life and character. But the chief value of its record is in its illustration of the truth that only he can be a poet who knows how to be a friend.

English poetry had its true beginning in Chaucer, whom Tennyson characterizes as

> ". . . The morning star of song, who made
>   His music heard below;
> Dan Chaucer, the first warbler, whose sweet breath
>   Preluded those melodious bursts that fill
> The spacious times of great Elizabeth
>   With sounds that echo still."

And the inspiration of Chaucer as a poet was that sentiment of unselfish friendship, or chivalrous love, which made poets of Dante and Petrarch. "The secret of the richness and enduring character of Chaucer's work," says Professor Minto, "is that he had a fruitful idea ready to his hand, an idea which had been flowering and bearing fruit in the minds of two centuries. . . . Chivalrous love had been the presiding genius, the inspiring spirit, of several generations of poets and critics when Chaucer began to write. Open any of his works, from the "Court of Love" down to the "Canterbury Tales," and you find that the central idea of it is to expound this chivalrous sentiment, either directly by tracing its operation or formulating its laws, or indirectly by setting it off against its counterpart, the sentiment of the villain or the churl." The love which had Chaucer's admiration was a love that was in itself purity and reverence, without any admixture of selfish craving; it was a love that took a man away from himself toward that which was more noble and more virtuous and more exalted than aught he had known before. It was the love that friendship is at its truest and best. It is of such a love, as over against a love that craves, that Chaucer's pure-hearted Delight speaks in praise, while contending with Lust, who would put all loves on one plane.

> "'Nay,' quod Delite, 'love is a vertue clere,
> And from the soule his progresse holdeth he:
> Blynd appityte of lust doth often stirre,
> And that is synne: for reason lakketh there.
>
> .   .   .   .   .
>
> For God, and saint, they love right verely
> Voide of al synne and vise: this know I wele,
> Affecion of flesh is synne truly;
> But verray[1] love is vertue, as I fele,
> For verray love may thy freyle desire akkele[2]
> For verray love is love withouten synne.'"

We do not know enough of the early life of Chaucer to be sure who it was that first inspired his highest friendship; but in view of the truth that chivalrous love was, in Chaucer's day, understood to be directed only toward a woman who was excluded from the possibility of his

[1] True.   [2] Cool.

possession, in order that its unselfishness might be the more evident, it is quite probable that his friendship for the Duchess of Lancaster, the first wife of John of Gaunt, was his earliest inspiration as a poet. It has been said that "Chaucer's A B C," an alphabetical prayer to the Virgin Mary, was composed "at the request of Blanche, Duchess of Lancaster, as a prayer for her private use, [she] being a woman in her religion very devout." It is certainly true that one of the earliest of Chaucer's poems is "The Dethe of Blaunche the Duchesse,"—this woman to whom he was a friend while she was the wife of his friend. James Russell Lowell has called this tribute of friendship "one of the most beautiful portraits of a woman that ever was drawn;" and such a portrait could have been made only by one who appreciated at the fullest its original, and therefore could attest his portrait with the assurance:

> "She was as good, so have I reste,
> As ever was Penelopee of Grece,
> Or as the noble wife Lucrece,
> That was the best,—he telleth thus
> The Romayne, Tytus Lyvyus,—
> She was as good, and no thynge lyke,
> Thogh hir stories be autentyke;
> Algate[1] she was as trewe as she."

"We have here," says Henry Morley, "the individual portrait of a gentlewoman who had been the poet's friend, and in whom he had seen a pattern of pure womanly grace and wifely worth;" and it is in an unselfish recognition of, and joy over, such an ideal, that a friend might find the inspiration of a poet.

[1] However.

A very early friendship of Chaucer, and a lasting one, was with John Gower, his senior in years and in the practice of the poetic art, although greatly his inferior in genius. Gower's spirit as a poet took him out of himself in love toward others and toward God. Chaucer called him "the moral Gower," and Gower's morality was based on self-abnegating love. The honor, the affection, and the sympathy given by Gower to Chaucer could not have been without their influence in a nature of such sensitiveness and grace and gentleness as Chaucer's. Each of these poets had words of affectionate praise for the other in his works, and to the last their intercourse was worthy of their place in history. The friendship of John of Gaunt had an important part in the life-shaping of Chaucer. He was both friend and patron to the poet; and it was through his friendship that Chaucer was sent to Italy, where he was brought under the inspirations of the work of Dante and Petrarch and Boccaccio; and the courtly training of Chaucer, which shows itself in every strain of his best verse, was an incidental result of John of Gaunt's affection. Some of Chaucer's choicest poems were written at the request of this princely friend. It would, indeed, seem hardly open to question that Chaucer was the poet he was through his conception of the sentiment of friendship at its highest and best, quickened by the illustrations of that sentiment in the life he lived.

It was a full century and a half after Chaucer, "the morning star of song," had preluded the brilliant day of literature in the Elizabethan age, that the first streaks of that day's dawn showed themselves, in the poetry of

Wyatt and Surrey; and it was unselfish love which made these poets co-workers in their goodly service to the world, and which inspired their highest poetic strains. It was as friends that they were poets, and they were poets of friendship. As to their place in literature, they have been called "the two chief lanternes of light to all others that have since employed their pennes upon English Poesies." The same sentiment of chivalrous love for a pure and noble woman, apart from any hope of her ever belonging to him who was her loyal friend, which was the inspiration of Dante, of Petrarch, and of Chaucer, was the inspiration alike of Wyatt and of Surrey; as, indeed, in their day there was no possibility of any sentiment being comparable with this as a means of uplifting and ennobling a man who had high poetic capabilities.

In the case of Wyatt, it would seem to have been Queen Anne Boleyn who thus drew him out of himself toward that which was loveliest and best. In the case of Surrey, it was "Geraldine," who is supposed to have been Elizabeth, a daughter of Gerald Fitz Gerald, ninth Earl of Kildare, a lovely girl of seven years at the time of Surrey's marriage, and who was married at fifteen to a man of sixty. The customs of the time justified the free expression of such a sentiment as this, and its cultivation was in the direction of the purest and highest manhood—in the triumph of self-abnegating affection over selfish desire. Purity of thought and of phrase in the treatment of the sentiment of love, and the separation of love from lust, are characteristics of the poetry of both Wyatt and Surrey beyond aught that was before known in English literature.

Of the gain to the lover, in a pure and unrequited affection, Wyatt makes Love reply to his unwise complaint of its cost and pains:

> "In his young age, I took him from that art,
> That selleth words, and make a clattering knight,
> And of my wealth I gave him the delight.
> Now shames he not on me for to complain,
> That held him evermore in pleasant game,
> From his desire, that might have been his pain:
> Yet thereby alone I brought him to some frame;
> Which now as wretchedness, he doth so blame;
> And toward honor quickened I his wit,
> Where as a dastard else he might have sit.
> He knoweth how great Atrides, that made Troy fret;
> And Hannibal to Rome so troublous;
> Whom Homer honored, Achilles that great;
> And African Scipion the famous;
> And many other, by much honor glorious;
> Whose fame and acts did lift them up above;
> I did let fall in base dishonest love.
> And unto him, though he unworthy were,
> I chose the best of many a million;
> That under sun yet never was her peer
> Of wisdom, womanhood, and of discretion;
> And of my grace I gave her such a fashion,
> And eke such way I taught her for to teach,
> That never base thought his heart so high might reach.
> Evermore thus to content his mistress,
> That was his only frame of honesty,
> I stirred him still toward gentleness;
> And caused him to regard fidelity;
> Patience I taught him in adversity:
> Such virtues learned he in my great soul;
> Whereof repenteth now the ignorant fool.
>   .   .   .   .   .
> But one thing yet there is, above all other:

> I gave him wings, wherewith he might upfly
> To honor and fame; and if he would to higher
> Than mortal things, above the starry sky:
> Considering the pleasure that an eye
> Might give in earth, by reason of the love;
> What should that be that lasteth still above?"

The gain of an unselfish love, despite its uttermost cost, is the glad theme of Surrey's rejoicing, even more than of Wyatt's. Recalling the outlay of blood and treasure in Troy's long siege, because of men's love for Helen, Surrey says:

> "Then think I thus: 'Sith such repair,
> So long time war of valiant men,
> Was all to win a lady fair,
> Shall I not learn to suffer then?
> And think my life well spent to be,
> Serving a worthier wight than she?'"

In assurance that his unswerving loyalty to this object of his affection is because of what she is in herself, and not for what she is to him, he declares:

> "Set me in high, or yet in low degree;
> In longest night, or in the shortest day;
> In clearest sky, or where clouds thickest be;
> In lusty youth, or when my hairs are gray:
> Set me in heaven, in earth, or else in hell,
> In hill, or dale, or in the foaming flood;
> Thrall, or at large, alive whereso I dwell,
> Sick, or in health, in evil fame or good,
>   Hers will I be; and only with this thought
>   Content myself, although my chance be nought."

As to the profit of such loving as this, he can say:

> "But chiefly this I know,
> That lovers must transform into the thing beloved,
> And live, (alas! who could believe?) with sprite from life removed."

That Surrey's love for Geraldine is a sincere friendship is shown in his appeal to her to show him favor as her ever-loyal friend:

> "The golden gift that Nature did thee give,
> To fasten friends and feed them at thy will,
> With form and favor, taught me to believe,
> How thou art made to show her greatest skill.
>
> . . . . .
>
> Now certes Garret,[1] since all this is true,
> That from above thy gifts are thus elect,
> Do not deface them then with fancies new;
> Nor change of minds, let not the mind infect:
> But mercy him thy friend that doth thee serve;
> Who seeks alway thine honor to preserve."

Like all true friendship, this love of Surrey's, being without a selfish end, is endless; in all changes it is changeless. Therefore he says of his purpose in it:

> "And so determine I to serve until my breath;
> Yea, rather die a thousand times, than once to false my faith.
> And if my feeble corpse, through weight of woful smart
> Do fail, or faint, my will it is that still she keep my heart.
> And when this carcass here to earth shall be refared,
> I do bequeath my wearied ghost to serve her afterward."

Thus it was that a new beginning was made in English poetry by two poet-friends, each of whom was inspired to his highest flight in poetry by the ideal of a pure and unselfish love for that which was most admirable, and

---

[1] The family name of the Fitz Geralds.

nearest to divine, in a true woman whose best personality commanded his unswerving friendship. The character and work of these friends have put an impress on all English poetry to the present day, as they in turn reflected the character and work of the great Italian poets who were inspired by the same lofty sentiment. Strange, indeed, it is that the critics have so often questioned the reality of the unselfish and inspiring love of Dante for Beatrice, of Petrarch for Laura, of Chaucer for the Duchess Blanche, of Wyatt for Queen Anne Boleyn, and of Surrey for Geraldine. As well might it be supposed that a vivid picture of a gorgeous sunset were painted by an ever-blind artist, as that these truthful portrayals of pure and reverent friendship, as a master-passion of the poet, were the creations of fancy in minds that never experienced the surpassing power of such a sentiment.

The uplifting of woman by chivalry and poetic thought, as worthy of man's reverent homage in a life-long friendship, proved to be her uplifting in man's esteem as wife and mother and sister and daughter. When it was realized that woman's highest value was in what she was, rather than in what she was to him who loved her, it was but a step to the recognition of a true woman's right to be thus esteemed by the man to whom she gave herself in the closest of family relations. Spenser, "the poet's poet," was first among poets to render the homage of friendship to his wife. Before this it had been deemed proper for a poet to give highest praise, in verse, only to some woman who could never be aught to him but his friend. But Spenser sounded the praises of his wife both for what she was in mere womanly attractiveness, and for what she was in higher womanly worth. And as Spenser had specifically affirmed his recognition of friendship's love as transcending conjugal love and kinship love, his unstinted praise of his wife's truest self was in the nature of a tribute of friendship.

> " Loe! where she comes along with portly pace,
> Lyke Phœbe, from her chamber of the East,
> Arysing forth to run her mighty race,
> Clad all in white, that seems a virgin best.
> So well it her beseemes, that ye would weene
> Some angell she had beene.
> Her long loose yellow locks lyke golden wyre,
> Sprinckled with perle, and perling flowres atweene,
> Doe lyke a golden mantle her attyre,
> And, being crownèd with a girland greene,
> Seem lyke some mayden queene.
> Her modest eyes, abashèd to behold
> So many gazers as on her do stare,
> Upon the lowly ground affixèd are,
> Ne dare lift up her countenance too bold,
> But blush to heare her prayses sung so loud,—
> So farre from being proud.
> Naithless, doe ye still loud her prayses sing,
> That all the woods may answer, and your eccho ring.
>   .   .   .   .   .
> But if ye saw that which no eyes can see,
> The inward beauty of her lively spright,
> Garnisht with heavenly guifts of high degree,
> Much more then would ye wonder at that sight,
> And stand astonisht lyke to those which red [1]
> Medusaes mazeful hed.
> There dwells sweet Love, and constant Chastity,
> Unspotted Fayth, and comely Womanhood,
> Regard of Honour, and mild Modesty;

[1] Saw.

> There Vertue raynes as queene in royal throne,
> And giveth lawes alone,
> The which the base affections doe obay,
> And yeeld theyr services unto her will;
> Ne thought of things uncomely ever may
> Thereto approch to tempt her mind to ill.
> Had ye once seene these her celestial threasures,
> And unrevealed pleasures,
> Then would ye wonder, and her prayses sing,
> That all the woods should answer, and your eccho ring."

It is because of this poet's uplifting an unselfish love above that craving love which

> "Doth not merit
> The name of love, but of disloyall lust,"

that Melissa says to him approvingly:

> "To thee are all true lovers greatly bound,
> That doest their cause so mightly defend:
> But most all wemen are they debtors found,
> That doest their bounty still so much commend."

From his early youth to his full maturity Spenser owed much to the inspiration and aid of friendship, and he was never unmindful of his indebtedness. While a student at Cambridge, an intimacy of the closest and most affectionate kind was formed between him and two fellow-students, Gabriel Harvey and Edward Kirke, the one older and the other younger than himself. It was Kirke, the younger of these friends, who presented to the public Spenser's first work, the "Shepherd's Calendar," without the poet's name; editing it, and giving an explanation of its meaning, in an introductory epistle addressed to Harvey. There is other evidence that Kirke "was deeply in Spenser's confidence as a literary coadjutor, and possibly in other ways." And Harvey, as a student of English verse, and as a man of warm heart and clear perceptions, was of real service to Spenser at a time when no one else could give him sympathetic aid. Dean Church is sure that Harvey "was a man who had influence on Spenser's ideas and purposes, and on the direction of his efforts;" and that, although he was somewhat vain and pedantic, "there is no want of hard-headed shrewdness in his remarks;" moreover, that "in his rules for the adaptation of English words and accents to classical meters, he shows clearness and good sense in apprehending the conditions of the problem, while Sidney and Spenser still appear confused and uncertain." Professor Minto thinks "it is clear that Spenser, who had sense enough not to be led astray by his eccentricities, received active and generous help from him, and probably not a little literary stimulus." It has been said, on the one hand, that Harvey did not at first appreciate the beauties, of the "Faerie Queene," and told Spenser plainly his objections to it. On the other hand, it has been suggested that we do not know the shape in which the earlier portions of this work were laid before Harvey; and that perhaps the criticism it then received at the hand of this true friend had a part in making it what it was when finally it appeared in print a dozen years later. At all events it is evident that Spenser looked upon this poet-critic as his "singular good friend," to whom he could pledge himself as a "devoted friend during life." Spenser, in his pastorals, designated himself as "Colin Clout" and Harvey as "Hobbinol."

Another friend from whom Spenser received inspiration

was Sir Philip Sidney. "That Sidney took to him, discussed poetry with him, introduced him at court, put him in the way of preferment,—are ascertained facts in his personal history," says Minto. It was no small matter to any man to be under the direct influence of that truest knight, that rarest embodiment of grace and courtesy, that wise statesman, that attractive poet, that lovable and fascinating personality; and to a nature like Spenser's the favor and approval of such a paragon of human excellence must have proved a trumpet-call to a higher, nobler life. No wonder that Spenser could refer to Sidney with grateful appreciation as:

"The hevens pride, the glory of our daies,
. . . . .
Who first my Muse did lift out of the flore,
To sing his sweet delights in lowlie laies."

And when it is remembered that Spenser declares it to be the "generall end" of his greatest poem "to fashion a gentleman or noble person in vertuous and gentle discipline," who can doubt that the ideal before his mind was this friend Sidney, who had then no equal in this sphere in all the earth?

Finally, it was Sir Walter Raleigh who proved a friend indeed to Spenser. Finding the poet in Ireland, with only a small portion of the "Faerie Queene," completed, after years of work upon it, Raleigh perceived the surpassing worth of that poem, and set himself to secure the return of its author to England in order to its publishing. After nine years' absence from England, Spenser returned with his friend Raleigh, and made ready to give to the world his master-piece. He recognizes his indebtedness to the friendship of Raleigh, in the introductory letter commending to him the "Faerie Queene;" as also in the story of his return to England, under the title of "Colin Clouts Come Home Again," which he presents to Raleigh as in "part of paiment of the infinite debt" in which he acknowledges himself bounden.

> "'One day,' quoth he, 'I sat, as was my trade,
> Under the foote of Mole, that mountaine hore,
> Keeping my sheepe amongst the cooly shade
> Of the greene alders by the Mullaes shore.
> There a straunge shepherd chaunst to find me out.
> . . . . .
> He, sitting me beside in that same shade,
> Provokèd me to plaie some pleasant fit;[1]
> And when he heard the musicke which I made,
> He found himselfe full greatly pleased at it.
> . . . . .
> He gan to cast great lyking to my lore,
> And great dislyking to my lucklesse lot,
> That banisht had my selfe, like wight forlore,
> Into that waste, where I was quite forgot.
> The which to leave thenceforth he counseld mee.
> . . . . .
> So what with hope of good and hate of ill,
> He me perswaded forth with him to fare.
> . . . . .
> So to the sea we came.'"

High above the highest poets towers Shakespeare, "the thousand-souled Shakespeare," "the most august of human intellects," "the greatest of all poetic geniuses that ever has been or ever will be." If any poet might have inspiration without the aid of friendship, it would

[1] Strain.

seem to be this pre-eminent and unique personality; and if friendship shows its mastery in a mind like Shakespeare's, no lesser mind could claim superiority to its sway.

It has been said that no poet ever made so small disclosure of himself in his poetry as this "first among all poets," for the very reason that "no man ever came near him in the creative powers of the mind." Hence it is that when Wordsworth suggests that the Sonnets of the great poet are autobiographical, and that

> "With this same key
> Shakespeare unlocked his heart,"

Browning resents the implied reflection on the poet's creative faculty, and responds:

> Did Shakespeare? If so, the less Shakespeare he!"

And a score of eminent Shakespearean critics have insisted that whatever of love or friendship is apparent in the Sonnets is the exhibit of an ideal sentiment, rather than an actual one. But, wholly apart from any question of Shakespearean interpretation, it is a psychological truth beyond dispute that no man can understand his fellows who lives wholly within himself; and that only as a man has experienced in some degree the power of any given sentiment or passion can he have ability to portray that sentiment or passion in face or words to others. He who never loved nor hated cannot express love or hate in exceptional vividness in his acting or in his writing. He whose soul was never stirred to its depths by a sense of loyalty to God or man, has no power to put in measured numbers the measureless power of true loyalty over all the powers of the human mind. If, therefore, we find in Shakespeare's poems an exhibit of friendship's sentiment at its highest, its extremest, and its best, we may be sure that Shakespeare had felt the fullest force of that sentiment, even though we be without a clue to those facts in his personal history that would identify the friend who drew him out of himself in that transcendent affection. We may, indeed, perceive that truth is presented by the poet in the guise of fiction, but it is none the less a truth for that. Judging by this test, while we have no proof that Shakespeare ever felt the inspiration of profound religious convictions or of intense spiritual aspirations, inasmuch as no character portrayed by him is under the sway of such feelings,—we have abundant evidence that in his thought and experience friendship transcends all love.

"Two souls in one body" are pictured in "A Midsummer Night's Dream," in Helena's reminder to Hermia of the growth and power of their "school-days' friendship:"

> "We, Hermia, like two artificial gods,
> Have with our needles created both one flower,
> Both on one sampler, sitting on one cushion,
> Both warbling of one song, both in one key,
> As if our hands, our sides, voices, and minds,
> Had been incorporate. So we grew together,
> Like to a double cherry, seeming parted,
> But yet an union in partition;
> Two lovely berries moulded on one stem;
> So with two seeming bodies, but one heart;
> Two of the first like coats in heraldry,
> Due but to one, and crownèd with one crest."

Seeing through another's eyes as through one's own, is

suggested as a test of unselfish love, in Queen Katharine's appeal to Henry VIII.:

> "Or which of your friends
> Have I not strove to love, although I knew
> He were mine enemy? What friend of mine
> That had to him derived your anger, did I
> Continue in my liking?"

And Cassius holds before Brutus a mirror of true friendship:

> "*Cassius.*   A friend should bear his friend's infirmities,
>   But Brutus makes mine greater than they are.
>
>   .   .
>   You love me not.
> *Brutus.*   I do not like your faults.
> *Cassius.*   A friendly eye could never see such faults."

"The Two Gentlemen of Verona" is throughout an exhibit of love and friendship in their relations and conflicts. Proteus is false in friendship, and therefore is false in love. Valentine being true in friendship is worthier than Proteus in all things to the end. With Proteus love is always selfish, and whether he seem true or false his main thought is ever of self. When he questions whether he shall be true to Julia and Valentine, or be false to both for love of Silvia, he argues:

> "To leave my Julia, shall I be forsworn;
> To love fair Silvia, shall I be forsworn;
> To wrong my friend, I shall be much forsworn;
> And even that power which gave me first my oath
> Provokes me to this threefold perjury;
> Love bade me swear and Love bids me forswear.
>
> .   .   .   .
>
> I cannot leave to love, and yet I do;
> But there I leave to love where I should love.

> Julia I lose and Valentine I lose:
> If I keep them, I needs must lose myself;
> If I lose them, thus find I by their loss
> For Valentine myself, for Julia Silvia.
> I to myself am dearer than a friend,
> For love is still most precious in itself;
> And Silvia—witness Heaven that made her fair!—
> Shows Julia but a swarthy Ethiope.
> I will forget that Julia is alive,
> Remembering that my love to her is dead;
> And Valentine I'll hold an enemy,
> Aiming at Silvia as a sweeter friend.
> I cannot now prove constant to myself,
> Without some treachery used to Valentine."

How different the noble-souled Valentine! When Proteus has betrayed him, and the disclosure of the false friend's shame has brought the craven traitor to his knees crying for pardon, Valentine has no thought of self, nor yet of personal resentment, but only of the claims of his own pledged friendship; and his answer to Proteus's plea of penitence, for seeking to win the love of Silvia by treachery, is:

> "Then I am paid;
> And once again I do receive thee honest.
> Who by repentance is not satisfied
> Is nor of heaven nor earth, for these are pleased.
> By penitence the Eternal's wrath's appeased:
> And that my love may appear plain and free,
> All that was mine in Silvia I give thee."

This triumph of generous friendship over selfish love proves a blessing to lovers as well as to friends, and all have reason to rejoice that Valentine was capable of such magnanimity through friendship.

Thus the plays of Shakespeare give incidental illustration of friendship's beauty and power; but it is in his matchless series of Sonnets that we have the specific proof of his inspiration as a poet through the force of this master-passion of his race. That these Sonnets are the expression of Shakespeare's personal feelings has, indeed, been questioned, as has been many another self-evident truth; but this is only an added wonder to their wonderfulness. "Were it not for the fact," says Furnivall, "that many critics really deserving the name of Shakespeare students, and not Shakespeare fools, have held the Sonnets to be merely dramatic, I could not have conceived that poems so intensely and evidently autobiographical and self-revealing, poems so one with the spirit and inner meaning of Shakespeare's growth and life, could ever have been conceived to be other than what they are, the records of his own loves and fears."

The real question for the critic is not whether Shakespeare felt the power of such a friendship, but whether the critic himself has had any experience of it. He who has felt all that which Shakespeare voices in his Sonnets, will not for a moment doubt that Shakespeare felt it. Minto recognizes this as the pith of the case when he says: "Friendship is not quite dead even in these degenerate days; there are still people alive to whom the warmth of the warmest of Shakespeare's Sonnets would not appear an exaggeration." And Dowden has a similar view, when he says of the naturalness of Shakespeare's friendship, as seen by one who is capable of such a sentiment: "That he should have given admiration and love without measure to a youth high born, brilliant, accomplished, who singled out the player for peculiar favor, will seem wonderful only to those who keep a constant guard upon their affections, and to those who have no need to keep a guard at all."

Who was the friend, "Mr. W. H.," to whom as their "onlie begetter" these Sonnets were dedicated by "T. T.," on their first publication, after the death of Shakespeare, is not positively known; yet there is good reason for supposing that he was William Herbert, Earl of Pembroke, a nephew of Sir Philip Sidney, to whom, in conjunction with his brother, as a well-known admirer and patron of the great poet, the First Folio of Shakespeare's Plays was dedicated. Fifty years ago Sir Henry Hallam said, in review of the claims for this identification: "This hypothesis is not strictly proved, but sufficiently so, in my opinion, to demand our assent;" and later investigation has brought out much material in its confirmation. "Though the initials have proved a sufficient blind to the eyes of posterity," says Professor Minto, "I doubt whether any blind was intended or effected by them when they first appeared. In all probability, the object of Shakespeare's Sonnets was perfectly well known to the first readers of them, and W. H. pointed to William Herbert as surely as T. T. pointed to Thomas Thorpe the bookseller." But, after all, this is a minor matter. The chief thing is, that Shakespeare was a friend to some one man, who drew him out of himself into such a love as only he could give; and that these Sonnets are the expression of that friendship, and the proof of its transcendent inspiration to their author. It is evident from the Sonnets themselves that Shakespeare loved his friend without measure, that his admiration of him was unbounded, that his power of loving grew with its exercise, that in time of absence and of his friend's estrangement his love never lessened nor swerved, that he suffered from his friend's lack and failures as only such a nature as his, and in such a friendship, would be capable of suffering; and that he fully realized his own indebtedness to this friendship for that uplifting of his nature which would surely give immortality to his writings.

No warmth of praise nor intensity of love to which he can give expression toward his friend seems to Shakespeare the equal of what the truth demands; albeit he knows that posterity will not realize that fact.

> "Who will believe my verse in time to come,
> If it were filled with your most high deserts?
> Though yet, heaven knows, it is but as a tomb
> Which hides your life and shows not half your parts.
> If I could write the beauty of your eyes
> And in fresh numbers number all your graces,
> The age to come would say, 'This poet lies;
> Such heavenly touches ne'er touched earthly faces.'"

> "A woman's face with Nature's own hand painted
> Hast thou, the master-mistress of my passion;
> A woman's gentle heart, but not acquainted
> With shifting change, as is false women's fashion;
> An eye more bright than theirs, less false in rolling,
> Gilding the object whereupon it gazeth;
> A man in hue, all 'hues' in his controlling,
> Which steals men's eyes and women's souls amazeth."

> "So are you to my thoughts as food to life,
> Or as sweet-seasoned showers are to the ground;
> And for the peace of you I hold such strife
> As 'twixt a miser and his wealth is found;

> Now proud as an enjoyer and anon
> Doubting the filching age will steal his treasure,
> Now counting best to be with you alone,
> Then bettered that the world may see my pleasure;
> Sometime all full with feasting on your sight
> And by and by clean starvèd for a look;
> Possessing or pursuing no delight,
> Save what is had or must from you be took."

> "Who is it that says most? which can say more
> Than this rich praise, that you alone are you?"

> "Let not my love be called idolatry,
> Nor my belovèd as an idol show,
> Since all alike my songs and praises be
> To one, of one, still such, and ever so."

This wonderful love seems fullest at its start; yet it grows with the passing years, and its power is greater and greater; so that the poet-friend can say to his friend:

> "Those lines that I before have writ do lie,
> Even those that said I could not love you dearer;
> Yet then my judgment knew no reason why
> My most full flame should afterwards burn clearer.
> But reckoning time, whose millioned accidents
> Creep in 'twixt vows and change decrees of kings,
> Tan sacred beauty, blunt the sharp'st intents,
> Divert strong minds to the course of altering things;
> Alas, why, fearing of time's tyranny,
> Might I not then say, 'Now I love you best,'
> When I was certain o'er incertainty,
> Crowning the present, doubting of the rest?
>   Love is a babe; then might I not say so,
>   To give full growth to that which still doth grow?"

But progress is the only change in this changeless love, despite absence and disappointment and evil-doing. He

who has given himself in friendship has given himself
for always. Even when deceived and wronged he can
not only forgive but love on as before.

> "I do forgive thy robbery, gentle thief,
> Although thou steal thee all my poverty;
> And yet, love knows, it is a greater grief
> To bear love's wrong than hate's known injury."

> "That god forbid that made me first your slave,
> I should in thought control your times of pleasure,
> Or at your hand the account of hours to crave,
> Being your vassal, bound to stay your leisure!
> .   .   .   .   .
> Be where you list, your charter is so strong
> That you yourself may privilege your time
> To what you will; to you it doth belong
> Yourself to pardon of self-doing crime.
>> I am to wait, though waiting so be hell;
>> Not blame your pleasure, be it ill or well."

> "When thou shalt be disposed to set me light
> And place my merit in the eye of scorn,
> Upon thy side against myself I'll fight,
> And prove thee virtuous, though thou art forsworn.
>   .   .   .   .   .
>> Such is my love, to thee I so belong,
>> That for thy right myself will bear all wrong."

> "Some say thy fault is youth; some wantonness;
> Some say thy grace is youth and gentle sport;
> Both grace and faults are loved of more and less;
> Thou mak'st faults graces that to thee resort."

> "O, never say that I was false of heart,
> Though absence seemed my flame to qualify.
> As easy might I from myself depart
> As from my soul, which in thy breast doth lie."

> "Love is not love
> Which alters when it alteration finds,
> Or bends with the remover to remove.
>
> .   .   .   .
>
> Love alters not with his brief hours and weeks,
> But bears it out even to the edge of doom.
> > If this be error and upon me proved,
> > I never writ, nor no man ever loved."

Such fidelity in love costs heart-blood; and the truer the friend in time of trial, the keener his suffering as a friend. Yet friendship like this is precious beyond its uttermost cost. Gleams of this truth are here and there in these soul-disclosing Sonnets.

> "If thou wilt leave me, do not leave me last,
> When other petty griefs have done their spite,
> But in the onset come; so shall I taste
> At first the very worst of fortune's might,
> > And other strains of woe, which now seem woe,
> > Compared with loss of thee will not seem so."

> "But do thy worst to steal thyself away,
> For term of life thou art assurèd mine,
> And life no longer than thy love will stay,
> For it depends upon that love of thine.
> Then need I not to fear the worst of wrongs,
> When in the least of them my life hath end."

> "How like a winter hath my absence been
> From thee, the pleasure of the fleeting year!
> What freezings have I felt, what dark days seen!
> What old December's bareness everywhere!"

> "What potions have I drunk of Siren tears,
> Distilled from limbecks foul as hell within,
> Applying fears to hopes, and hopes to fears,
> Still losing when I saw myself to win!

> What wretched errors hath my heart committed,
> Whilst it hath thought itself so blessed never!
> How have mine eyes out of their spheres been fitted
> In the distraction of this madding fever!
> O benefit of ill! now I find true
> That better is by evil still made better;
> And ruined love, when it is built anew,
> Grows fairer than at first, more strong, far greater.
>> So I return rebuked to my content,
>> And gain by ill thrice more than I have spent."

> "For if you were by my unkindness shaken
> As I by yours, you've passed a hell of time,
> And I, a tyrant, have no leisure taken
> To weigh how once I suffered in your crime."

There is inspiration to a great soul in a soul-expanding and soul-expending sentiment like this; and the master-poet acknowledges his indebtedness to the uplifting power of this master-passion.

> "How can my Muse want subject to invent,
>   While thou dost breathe, that pour'st into my verse
> Thine own sweet argument, too excellent
>   For every vulgar paper to rehearse?
> O, give thyself the thanks, if aught in me
>   Worthy perusal stand against thy sight;
> For who's so dumb that cannot write to thee,
>   When thou thyself dost give invention light?
> Be thou the tenth Muse, ten times more in worth
>   Than those old nine which rhymers invocate;
> And he that calls on thee, let him bring forth
>   Eternal numbers to outlive long date.
>>   If my slight Muse do please these curious days,
>>   The pain be mine, but thine shall be the praise."

> "Yet be most proud of that which I compile,
>   Whose influence is thine and born of thee:

> In others' works thou dost but mend the style,
> And arts with thy sweet graces gracèd be;
> > But thou art all my art, and dost advance
> > As high as learning my rude ignorance."

> "Your monument shall be my gentle verse,
> Which eyes not yet created shall o'er-read,
> And tongues to be your being shall rehearse
> When all the breathers of this world are dead;
> > You still shall live—such virtue hath my pen—
> > Where breath most breathes, even in the mouths of men."

> "Where art thou, Muse, that thou forget'st so long
> To speak of that which gives thee all thy might?
> Spend'st thou thy fury on some worthless song,
> Darkening thy power to lend base subjects light?
> Return, forgetful Muse, and straight redeem
> In gentle numbers time so idly spent;
> Sing to the ear that doth thy lays esteem
> And gives thy pen both skill and argument."

Without the outgoing and uplifting force of such a friendship, not even such a poet as Shakespeare could have been the poet he was; for only as the best that was in him was bettered could he attain to the better that was ever before him. There are signs in the very Sonnets themselves of the retarding influence of the social and moral standards of the day, and of the evil elements at work in the great poet's nature; but in all, and through all, the outworking and upworking of this self-controlling friendship tend to the purifying and transfiguring of the nature thus alloyed. It is not that the friend or his friendship is without spot or stain; but it is that the friend is by friendship ever bettering his best. And all that we can see of the progress of Shakespeare's power as a poet corresponds with what the Sonnets disclose of his growth through his friendship. "Sad as it may be to us," says Furnivall, "to be forced to conclude that shame has to be cast on the noble name we reverence, yet let us remember that it is but for a temporary stain on his career, and that through the knowledge of the human heart he gained by his own trials we get the intensest and most valuable records of his genius. It is only those who have been through the mill themselves, that know how hard God's stones and the devil's grind."

It was after the date of the earlier of his Sonnets, and after the beginning of his acquaintance with Pembroke, that Shakespeare wrote his master-pieces of creative genius, including the tragedies of Hamlet, Macbeth, Othello, and Lear. Reviewing the productions of this later period of the great poet's labors, Professor Baynes says appreciatively: "The typical plays of this period . . . embody Shakespeare's ripest experience of the great issues of life. In the four grand tragedies the central problem is a profoundly moral one. It is the supreme internal conflict of good and evil amongst the central forces and higher elements of human nature, as appealed to and developed by sudden and powerful temptation, smitten by accumulated wrongs, or plunged in overwhelming calamities. As the result, we learn that there is something infinitely more precious in life than social ease or worldly success—nobleness of soul, fidelity to truth and honor, human love and loyalty, strength and tenderness, and trust to the very end." And as recognizing the bearing of Shakespeare's experiences of good and ill in friendship, on this obvious progress of his in knowledge and power, Furnivall says: "I always ask that the Sonnets should be read between the second and third periods [of Shakespeare's dramatic work]; for the 'hell of time' of which they speak is the best preparation for the temper of that third period, and enables us to understand it." It was through the gainful cost of friendship, with its deepest and fullest involvings, that Shakespeare, being the man he was, became the poet he was.

In proving a general truth to be applicable in the more important spheres, there is carried the obvious inference that that truth is prevalent in the spheres of minor importance. Hence, when it is shown that the greatest poets of the ages have gained peculiar inspiration from friendship, it is fair to take it for granted that other poets have, in varying measure, been inspired through the same potent sentiment. It is, therefore, quite unnecessary to take up the later English poets, one by one, in order to show that their history illustrates the power of the master-passion of humanity; yet it would be easy to gain additional evidence in this line from the life-story of any one of them, or of them all.

Saintly George Herbert, whose books are made up, according to Richard Baxter, of "heart-work and heaven-work," was a living center of friendship in his day. Foremost among the friends who influenced him was Dr. John Donne, called by Dryden "the greatest wit, though not the greatest poet, of our [English] nation." Donne was the attached friend of Herbert's widowed mother. It was of her that he wrote:

> "No spring nor summer's beauty hath such grace
> As I have seen in one autumnal face.
>
> .   .   .   .   .
>
> If 'twere a shame to love, here 'twere no shame:
> Affeċtions here take reverence's name."

For the mother's sake Donne loved her son, and for her sake, and her son's, he sought to be an inspiration to him. Another inspiring friend of Herbert was Lord Bacon. They two were much together. Herbert translated some of Bacon's works into Latin, and Bacon in turn dedicated his poetic renderings of the Psalms of David to Herbert. Bishop Lancelot Andrewes and Sir Henry Wotton did their part, also, as friends, in making Herbert what he was.

Katherine Philips won a place as a poet by her appreciation and illustration of friendship. It was to her that Jeremy Taylor addressed his celebrated "Discourse on the Nature, Offices, and Measure of Friendship." Her extended correspondence with Sir Charles Cotterel was published, after her death, as "an admirable pattern for the pleasing correspondence of a virtuous friendship," and as showing "how an intercourse of writing between persons of different sexes ought to be managed with delight and innocence." In her closest friendships, with Mrs. Annie Owen and Mrs. Mary Awbrey, Mrs. Philips was known, after the fashion of the time, as "Orinda," and they, respeċtively, as "Lucasia" and "Rosania." Praised for her worth and her talent by Dryden, the Earl of Orrery and the Earl of Roscommon, and others known to fame, she was widely honored as the "Matchless Orinda." Abraham Cowley, whom Addison called "a mighty genius," and who had great repute in his day, gave her an exalted place as a poet, and as the poet of friendship, in an ode on her death.

> "To be a princess or a queen
> Is great, but 'tis a greatness always seen;
> The world did never but two women know
> Who, one by fraud, the other by wit, did rise
> To the two tops of spiritual dignities;
> One female pope of old, one female poet now.
>
> .   .   .   .
>
> The certain proofs of our Orinda's wit
> In her own lasting characters are writ,
> And they will long my praise of them survive.
>
> .   .   .   .   .
>
> The fame of Friendship, which so long had told
> Of three or four illustrious names of old,
> Till hoarse and weary of the tale she grew,
> Rejoices now to have got a new,
> A new and more surprising story,
> Of fair Lucasia and Orinda's glory."

Dyce, and Cibber, and more recently Rowton, assign a place to Mrs. Philips as "one of the best of our female poets," and as a poet "celebrated for her friendship." She was married when only sixteen, and she was quite a model as wife and mother, while showing such exceptional earnestness and devotion as a friend.

It would seem that a discourse on friendship, by Mr. Francis Finch, whom she addresses as "the excellent Palæmon," aroused Mrs. Philips to a sense of this masterpassion, and inspired her to its exercise and praise.

> "'Twas he that rescued gasping Friendship, when
> The bell tolled for her funeral with men:

> 'Twas he that made friends more than lovers burn,
> And then made love to sacred friendship turn.
>
> . . . .
>
> He's our original, by whom we see
> How much we fail, and what we ought to be."

Her love for her husband, called by her "Antenor," then rose to friendship. In a temporary parting with him she wrote:

> "Thou shalt in me survey
> Thyself reflected while thou art away.
> For what some forward arts do undertake,
> The images of absent friends to make,
> And represent their actions in a glass,
> Friendship itself can only bring to pass—
> That magic which both fate and time beguiles,
> And in a moment runs a thousand miles.
> So in my breast thy picture drawn shall be,
> My Guide, Life, Object, Friend, and Destiny:
> And none shall know, though they employ their wit,
> Which is the right Antenor, thou or it."

To her earliest woman-friend, "Rosania," she wrote:

> "Soul of my soul, my Joy, my Crown, my Friend—
> A name which all the rest doth comprehend;
> How happy are we now, whose souls are grown
> By an incomparable mixture, one:
> Whose well-acquainted minds are now as near
> As love, or vows, or friendship can endear!
> I have no thought but what's to thee revealed,
> Nor thou desire that is from me concealed.
> Thy heart locks up my secrets richly set,
> And my breast is thy private cabinet.
> Thou shed'st no tear but what my moisture lent,
> And if I sigh, it is thy breath is spent.
> United thus, what horror can appear
> Worthy our sorrow, anger, or our fear?"

To "Lucasia," who proved her ideal friend, "Orinda" multiplied poetic praises; and, as the years passed on, her love for this friend gained and grew in quietness of strength.

> "Come, my Lucasia, since we see
>   That miracles men's faith do move,
> By wonder and by prodigy,—
>   To the dull angry world let's prove
>   There's a religion in our love.
>
>   . . . .
>
> "Our hearts are mutual victims laid,
>   While they (such power in friendship lies)
> Are altars, priests, and offerings made:
>   And each heart which thus kindly dies,
>   Grows deathless by the sacrifice."
>
> "No bridegroom's nor crown-conqueror's mirth
>   To mine compared can be:
> They have but pieces of this earth,
>   I've all the world in thee."

In parting for a season from Lucasia, Orinda rose to the supremest height of self-abnegating love, in her wish to be discarded or forgotten rather than be a cause of discomfort to her friend:

> "And should I thy clear fortunes interline
> With the incessant miseries of mine?
> No, no, I never loved at such a rate
> To tie thee to the rigors of my fate.
> As from my obligations thou art free,
> Sure thou shalt be so from my injury.
> Though every other worthiness I miss,
> Yet I'll at least be generous in this.
> I'd rather perish without sigh or groan,
> Than thou shouldst be condemned to give me one;

>   Nay, in my soul I rather could allow
>   Friendship should be a sufferer, than thou.
>   Go then, since my sad heart has set thee free,
>   Let all the loads and chains remain on me."

Rarely has a poet owed more as a poet to the inspiration of friendship than Katherine Philips; and rarely has a poet shown a more hearty and discriminating appreciation of friendship than she in its poetic praises. Extolling love as "creation's soul," she saw in friendship the highest reach of love:

> "Friendship's an abstract of this noble flame,
>   'Tis love refined, and purged from all its dross,
> The next to angels' love, if not the same,
>   As strong as passion is, though not so gross:
> It antedates a glad eternity,
> And is a heaven in epitome.
>
> "Nobler than kindred, or than marriage-band,
>   Because more free; wedlock-felicity
> Itself doth only by this union stand,
>   And turns to friendship, or to misery.
> Force or design matches to pass may bring,
> But friendship doth from love and honor spring.
>
>   .   .   .   .   .
>
> "Thick waters show no images of things;
>   Friends are each other's mirrors, and should be
> Clearer than crystal or the mountain springs,
>   And free from clouds, design, or flattery.
> For vulgar souls no part of friendship share:
> Poets and friends are born to what they are.
>
>   .   .   .   .   .
>
> "Absence doth not from friendship's right excuse.
>   Them who preserve each other's heart and fame,
> Parting can ne'er divide, it may diffuse;
>   As a far stretched out river's still the same.

> Though presence helped them at the first to greet,
> Their souls now know without those aids to meet.

> "Constant and solid, whom no storms can shake,
>   Nor death unfix, a right friend ought to be;
> And if condemnèd to survive, doth make
>   No second choice, but grief and memory.
> But friendship's best fate is, when it can spend
> A life, a fortune, all to serve a friend."

Although Milton's

> "Soul was like a star, and dwelt apart,"

he could not be removed beyond the sway of personal friendship. From his school-days until he was returning from Italy, with the plans of his immortal poem already matured, he was in close intimacy with Charles Diodati, and the correspondence of these bosom-friends is proof of the important aid which this friendship was to Milton in his preparation for his life-work. It was in return for verses of Diodati that Milton wrote:

> "Art thou desirous to be told how well
> I love thee, and in verse? verse cannot tell.
> For verse has bounds, and must in measure move:
> But neither bounds nor measure knows my love."

His pastoral elegy on Diodati, *Epitaphium Damonis*, has been called "one of the noblest things that Milton has left us," and but for its Latin form it would have been more generally recognized as such. Andrew Marvel was, moreover, an inspiring poet-friend to this greater poet. Henry Lawes, a celebrated musical composer, was an attached friend of Milton; and he it was who induced the poet to write the words of Comus for the music of a Mask, to be performed at Ludlow Castle. If Milton had never written aught beyond this work, which he undertook at the call of friendship, he would have been entitled to immortality. And finally Milton's "Lycidas" was a tribute to the memory of his friend and college-mate, Edward King. Although King had no such hold as Diodati on Milton's heart, the beauty of this tribute is a proof of the transcending power of friendship over the poet's intellectual nature. "This piece," says Mark Pattison, "unmatched in the whole range of English poetry, and never again equaled by Milton himself, leaves all criticism behind."

It can hardly be doubted that Dryden had felt the sway of friendship when he put into the mouth of one of his characters the words:

> "I had a friend that loved me;
> I was his soul; he lived not but in me:
> We were so closed within each other's breasts,
> The rivets were not found that joined us first,
> That do not reach us yet. We were so mixed
> As meeting streams, but to ourselves were lost.
> We were one mass; we could not give or take
> But from the same; for he was I, I he."

We know that Dryden greatly prized the friendship of Sir Robert Howard in his young manhood, and of William Congreve in his later years, and that he felt the intellectual impulse of both these friendships. "To his friend John Hoddeson," Dryden, while yet less than twenty years old, wrote:

> "Thou hast inspired me with thy soul, and I
> Who ne'er before could ken of poetry,
> Am grown so good proficient, I can lend
> A line in commendation of my friend.

> Yet 'tis but of the second hand; if aught
> There be in this, 'tis from thy fancy brought.

What would Addison have been without Steele? "It was the firm hand of his friend Steele," says Henry Morley, "that helped Addison up to the place in literature which became him. It was Steele who caused the nice critical taste, which Addison might have spent only in accordance with the fleeting fashions of his time, to be inspired with all Addison's religious earnestness. . . . It was Steele who drew his friend toward the days to come, and made his gifts the wealth of a whole people." Steele is cited as declaring, after his friend's death, "that there was never a more strict friendship than between himself and Addison, nor had they ever any difference but what proceeded from their different way of pursuing the same thing;" and it is suggested that Addison had Steele in his mind, when his song of praise to God was:

> "Thy bounteous hand with worldly bliss
> Has made my cup run o'er,
> And in a kind and faithful friend
> Has doubled all my store."

But for his praises of friendship Young would not have the place that is his in popular esteem to-day. And he could never have sounded these praises without experiencing the sway of the sentiment they extol.

> "Can gold gain friendship? Impudence of hope!
> As well mere man an angel might beget.
> Love, and love only, is the loan for love.
> Lorenzo! pride repress; nor hope to find
> A friend, but what has found a friend in thee.

> All like the purchase; few the price will pay;
> And this makes friends such miracles below.
>
> . . . . .
>
> A friend is worth all hazards we can run.
> 'Poor is the friendless master of a world:
> A world in purchase for a friend is gain.'"

Pope was a man of friends. When about seventeen years old he formed an intimate friendship with Sir William Trumbull, a man of sixty; and this intimacy continued until the statesman's death. Trumbull introduced young Pope to Wycherly, the poet, then nearly seventy years of age; and in this way Pope came into relations of peculiar friendship with Wycherly. The old poet sought the counsel of his new friend in the correction and revision of his poems, and this mission had its value to the young poet if not to the old one. It was by Trumbull's earnest counsel that Pope undertook his translation of the Iliad, and the aid of Pope's friend Parnell was of importance in the prosecution of this work. Among other helpful friends of Pope were the unfortunate Atterbury, Bishop of Rochester, Spence of Oxford, Gay, Arbuthnot, and Swift. Pope, writing to Swift of the possibilities of the future life, said earnestly: "We are to believe we shall have something better than even a friend there, but certainly here we have nothing so good." And in the closing moments of his life, after he had received the last sacrament from a priest, Pope said: "There is nothing that is meritorious but virtue and friendship; and indeed friendship itself is only a part of virtue."

Friendship certainly had its part in inspiring and shaping the poet Thomson. Mr. Riccaulton, a friend of his father, first saw possibilities in young Thomson and sought to develop them. He undertook the teaching of the lad, and he interested him in poetic writing. "We have the poet's own acknowledgment," says Minto, "that the first hint of the Seasons came from a striking dramatic poem by Riccaulton, entitled A Winter's Day." A more intimate friend of Thomson was a classmate at the University of Edinburgh, David Mallet. Together these two friends studied and wrote, inspiring each other and rejoicing in each other. It was in the "Mask of Alfred," written conjointly by the two friends, that the song "Rule, Britannia," first appeared; and the authorship of that song has unfairly been claimed for Mallet. A life-long friend of Thomson was Dr. Cranston, whose counsel and cheer were a constant stimulus to the poet, as the extensive correspondence between them evidences.

The life-story of Gray is the story of his friendships. Four young Etonians, Gray, Walpole, West, and Asheton, were so closely bound as friends that they were known to their schoolfellows as the Quadruple Alliance. But West was nearest and dearest to Gray. They wrote verses together, and they entered into each other's lives in sympathy and mutual inspiration. "I singled you out for a friend," said West to Gray, "and I would have you know me to be yours, if you deem me worthy." While West lived he was dear to Gray; and when he was dead he was still a living force in the mind of his friend. It was while under the shadow of the death of West, that Gray composed his "Elegy in a Country Churchyard."

Akenside ascribed his best inspirings to his friendship for Dyson. Writing to this friend from Leyden, Akenside

said: "Believe me, my dear, my honored friend, I look upon my connection with you as the most fortunate circumstance of my life. I never think of it without being happier and better for the reflection. I enjoy, by means of it, a more animated, a more perfect relish of every social, of every natural pleasure. My own character, by means of it, is become an object of veneration and applause to myself. My sense of the perfection and beauty of the Supreme Being is nobler and more affecting. . . . It has the force of an additional conscience, of a new principle of religion; nor do I remember one instance of moral good or evil offered to my choice of late, in which the idea of your mind and manners did not come in along with the essential beauty of virtue and the sanction of the divine laws, to guide and determine me. It has enlarged my knowledge of human nature, and ascertained my ideas of the economy of the universe. In whatever light I consider, with whatever principle or sensation I compare it, it still continues to receive strength from the best and highest, and in return confirm and enlarge them,
> Like the sweet South
> That breathes upon a bank of violets,
> Giving and stealing odors."

It was doubtless because of this experience of the transcendent power of the master-passion, that the poet asked, in his searching of the Pleasures of Imagination:

> "Is aught so fair,
> In all the dewy landscapes of the Spring,
> In the bright eye of Hesper, or the morn,
> In Nature's fairest forms, is aught so fair
> As virtuous friendship?"

Cowper lived by friendship, and the friendships which did most for him were with noble-minded and tender-hearted women. Mrs. Unwin, the "Mary" of the poet's song, was a constant inspiration to him. He lived in her house more than thirty years, until death's stroke came to her, not long before it came to him. She was a few years older than himself, and his reverent friendship for her was almost as a grown son's for a mother-friend. "The lady in whose house I live," he wrote, "is so excellent a person, and regards me with a friendship so truly Christian, that I could almost fancy my own mother restored to life again to compensate me for all the friends I have lost and all my connections broken." And, loving the mother, he loved her young son. "Blessed be the God of our salvation," he added, "for such companions, and for such a life; above all, for a heart to like it." Cowper was nearly fifty years old when he began to write poetry, and he owed his promptings in this direction to friendship. "It was chiefly at the request of Mrs. Unwin," says his biographer, "that Cowper was induced to undertake a poetical piece of any extent. Affection is lynx-eyed in discovering whatever is beneficial to its object, and in pressing upon her friend an occupation for which nature had peculiarly adapted him she displayed considerable judgment." She suggested to him the Progress of Error as a theme, and so again various other subjects of his writing. Still later Cowper formed a friendship with Lady Austen, and "to her the world is mainly indebted for 'The Task,' 'John Gilpin,' and for the translation of Homer." No wonder that Cowper could say of the sentiment that had such power with him:

> "True friendship has, in short, a grace
> More than terrestrial in its face,
>   That proves it heaven-descended:
> Man's love of woman not so pure,
> Nor, when sincerest, so secure
>   To last till life is ended."

And it was fitting that the memorial of Mary Unwin, in East Dereham Church, should bear this tribute to the power of her friendship:

> "Trusting in God with all her heart and mind,
> This woman proved magnanimously kind:
> Endured affliction's desolating hail,
> And watched a Poet through misfortune's vale.
> Her spotless dust angelic guards defend!
> It is the dust of Unwin, Cowper's friend!
> That single title in itself is fame,
> For all who read his verse revere her name."

Burns showed the good and the evil of friendship in his thinking and doing. He confessed that a friendship formed by him with a reckless sailor-lad at Irvine, when he was a little more than twenty years old, did him serious mischief through that friend's treatment "of lawless love with levity." This companion, with his wild life and loose and irregular habits, had a wonderful fascination for Burns, who admired him for what he thought his independence and magnanimity; and the shadow of his pernicious influence was on much of the life and poetry of Burns. Again, it was his friendship for Gavin Hamilton, "a country lawyer who had fallen under church censure for neglect of church ordinances," that incited Burns to the writing of his bitterest satires against the ministers and elders of his day, including "The Holy

Fair" and "Holy Willie's Prayer;" while at the same time he was moved to show his appreciation of the truest and best religious life in " The Cotter's Saturday Night." It was Gavin Hamilton who prompted to the publication of the first volume of Burns's poems, which awakened a new demand on the poet's powers; and it was to this friend that Burns wrote heartily:

> "To phrase you, and praise you,
>   Ye ken your Laureate scorns:
> The prayer still, you share still,
>   Of grateful Minstrel Burns."

Mrs. Dunlop of Dunlop was a warm and helpful friend of Burns from the time that he made her acquaintance in Ayrshire, when he was twenty-seven years old, until the close of his life. The extensive correspondence between these friends was concluded with a letter written by Burns a few days before his death. A gleam of Burns's estimate of friendship is found in words like these, to one of his friends:

> "For me, I swear by sun and moon,
> And every star that blinks aboon,
> Ye've cost me twenty pair o' shoon
>   Just gaun to see you;
> And every other pair that's done,
>   Mair ta'en I'm wi' you."

And of all the songs that Burns has given to the world, none has had such a hold as his song of friendship, "Auld Lang Syne."

Scott was a man of too much tenderness and impressibility to be uninfluenced by his friendships. Foremost among his college friends, and " probably the one

who most stimulated his imagination in his youth " was
William Clerk. While it is true, as a biographer of Scott
suggests, that "Clerk never actually gained any other
distinction so great as his friendship with Scott conferred
upon him," it is also true that Clerk deserves the distinction of winning Scott's admiration and of arousing Scott's
purpose of being at his best. In his later years Scott
said of Clerk: "I never met a man of greater powers,
of more complete information on all desirable subjects."
The record of Scott's life gives evidence that Clerk was
a constant spur to the poet, as truly as another intimate
friend, William Erskine, was always a comfort and cheer
to him. Erskine loved Scott with warmth and tenderness, and he had a high ideal for his friend, toward which
he was always pointing him. "He was," says R. H.
Hutton, "Scott's confidant in all literary matters, and his
advice was oftener followed on all questions of style and
form, and of literary enterprise, than that of any other
of Scott's friends." It was to Erskine that Scott wrote,
in defense of his minstrelsy, as better for him than the
more classic themes suggested for him by his friend:

> "Nay, my friend, nay,—since oft thy praise
> Hath given fresh vigor to my lays;
> Since oft thy judgment could refine
> My flattened thought or cumbrous line,
> Still kind, as is thy wont, attend,
> And in the minstrel spare the friend!"

And then there was that rude genius, John Leyden, full
of poetic taste and of antiquarian zeal, "who once walked
between forty and fifty miles and back for the sole purpose of visiting an old person who possessed a copy of

a border ballad that was wanting" for the "Border Minstrelsy" that Scott was compiling. He was a devoted and inspiring friend of the poet. James Hogg and William Laidlow and George Ellis were other friends of Scott who did their part as friends in making him what he was.

Byron was too passionate, too jealous, and too intensely absorbed in self-gratification, to be under the permanent sway of an unselfish friendship; although a personality like his must have a keen sensitiveness to the impressions of this master-passion. In Byron's school-days "his friendships were passions," and his passions were the inspirings of his poetry. He was only fourteen when he poured out his heart in strains of love toward a young plebeian friend, whom he honored while living and mourned when dead.

> "Let Folly smile, to view the names
>   Of thee and me in friendship twined;
> Yet Virtue will have greater claims
>   To love than rank with vice combined."

> "O Friend! for ever loved, for ever dear!
> What fruitless tears have bathed thy honored bier!
> What sighs re-echoed to thy parting breath,
> Whilst thou wast struggling in the pangs of death!
>   .   .   .   .   .
> What though thy sire lament his failing line,
> A father's sorrow cannot equal mine!
> Though none like thee his dying hour will cheer,
> Yet other offspring soothe his anguish here:
> But who with me shall hold thy former place?
> Thine image, what new friendship can efface?
> Ah, none!—a father's tears will cease to flow,
> Time will assuage an infant brother's woe;

> To all save one is consolation known,
> While solitary friendship sighs alone."

At Harrow, Byron formed a friendship with young Fitzgibbon, the second Earl of Clare, which had its hold upon him for long years afterward. "To him his confidences were most freely given, and his most affectionate verses addressed." Nearly twenty years later Byron wrote: "I never hear the word 'Clare' without a beating of the heart even *now;*" and again, "I have always loved him better than any *male* thing in the world." It was at Harrow that Byron illustrated the spirit of friendship, when he went, in tearful helplessness and "blushing with rage," to ask a large-framed bully to allow him to "take half" of the undeserved torture that was being inflicted on his young friend Robert Peel. There were other early friendships that had their part in giving nobler impulses to Byron, and if he had yielded himself more trustfully to their swayings his poetry would have had a permanency of life that now it lacks.

Shelley and Byron, with all their differences, had much in common, including undeveloped possibilities of high friendship. They helped each other as poet-friends. Byron's best work—including the third and fourth cantos of "Childe Harold"—was done while under the impulse of Shelley's friendship; and no poems of Shelley's are superior to those which he wrote at this time, including his "Ode to the Skylark," with its recognition of an unselfish affection transcendently above "love's sad satiety." Even as a boy Shelley was powerfully swayed by his intense friendship for a young schoolfellow, and again by the friendship of the venerable Dr. Lind, a tutor at

Eton, whom the poet immortalized under the guise of Zonoras in his self-disclosing "Prince Athanase:"

> "Prince Athanase had one beloved friend,
> An old, old man, with hair of silver white,
> And lips where heavenly smiles would hang and blend
>
> "With his wise words; and eyes whose arrowy light
> Shone like the reflex of a thousand minds.
>   .   .   .   .   .
>
> "And sweet and subtle talk now evermore
> The pupil and the master shared; until,
> Sharing that undiminishable store,
>
> "The youth, as shadows on a grassy hill
> Outrun the winds that chase them, soon outran
> His teacher, and did teach with native skill
>
> "Strange truths and new to that experienced man.
> Still they were friends, as few have ever been
> Who mark the extremes of life's discordant plan."

Moreover, the friendships of Shelley with his college mate and subsequent companion Hogg, and yet later with Mr. and Mrs. Williams at Pisa, had an important influence on his life and writings.

To think of Wordsworth and Coleridge is to think of their friendship, and none would question that the world owes much to what they owed to each other. First of all, however, Wordsworth was indebted to the inspiration of his sister Dorothy's friendship; for her love for him was the love of a friend rather than of a sister. She lived for him, and she showed him what to live for. " It was she who called forth the shyer sensibilities of his nature, and taught an originally harsh and austere imagination to surround itself with fancy and feeling, as the rock fringes itself with ferns." Her service to her brother-friend justified his tribute of praise to her:

> "She gave me eyes, she gave me ears,
> And humble cares, and delicate fears;
> A heart, the fountain of sweet tears,
> And love, and faith, and joy."

Then there came Coleridge, as the friend of both Wordsworth and his sister, at a time when Wordsworth needed more than his sister's service could supply to him. "Under his sister's genial influence," says Minto, "he was groping his way doubtfully out of the labyrinth of poetic conventions, beginning to see a new pathos and sublimity in human life, but not yet convinced except by fits and starts of the rightness of his own vision. Stubborn and independent as Wordsworth was, he needed some friendly voice from the outer world to give him confidence in himself. Coleridge rendered him this indispensable service." Soon Coleridge was an inmate of Wordsworth's home, a real friend of the two friends already there; and that home of friendship contained "three bodies and one soul," as Wordsworth was wont to say. The poets thought and wrote together, and they inspired each other. Southey, who was already the intimate friend of Coleridge, also came within the sweep of this friendship-inspired circle of the Lake Poets; and the best work of all these poets was an outcome of the surpassing friendship that bound while it freed them, in their highest natures.

It were needless to multiply these illustrations along the course of modern English poetry. It will suffice, in this field, to point to the two greatest poets of the passing generation, in explicit witness to this unmistakable truth of the ages.

Robert Browning's life and thought find expression in the truth of his impassioned ejaculation,

"What a thing friendship is, world without end!"

Mrs. Sutherland Orr, telling enthusiastically of Browning's "constancy to all degrees of friendship and love," says: "What he loved once he loved always, from the dearest man or woman to whom his allegiance had been given to the humblest piece of furniture which had served him." And it is provable that the love which swayed Browning most powerfully was always that unselfish and out-going love which friendship is. Browning was not yet twenty when he became the attached friend of Alfred Dommett, whom he never ceased to love, and whose love was ever an inspiration to him. Dommett was the "Alfred, dear friend," of Browning's "Guardian Angel," and the "Waring" to whom, in his absence, a poem was addressed under that name in "Dramatic Romances."

> " Meantime, how much I loved him,
> I find out now I've lost him.
> I who cared not if I moved him,
> Who could so carelessly accost him,
> Henceforth never shall get free
> Of his ghostly company.
> . . . .
> Nay, my very wrist grows warm
> With his dragging weight of arm.
> . . . . .
> Oh! could I have him back once more,
> This Waring, but one half-day more."

It was at the very time when Dommett and Browning

became friends, that Browning became the friend of Miss Lizzie Flower, who had an important part, as his friend, in bringing to bear in his behalf influences which aided in deciding his life-work; and whose name he could never mention in his latest years without giving evidence of his loyal friendship. One of the warmest friendships of Browning's life was formed with Count de Ripert-Monclair, who first suggested to the poet the life of Paracelsus as a possible subject for a poem; and hence it was that Browning's "Paracelsus" was "dedicated, in fulfilment of a promise to the friend to whom its inspiration had been due." The writing of "Strafford" was an outcome of Browning's friendship with Macready the actor, as was probably also "A Blot in the 'Scutcheon." John Forster's friendship had its influence on Browning's thinking and writing; and so had more than one other friendship. But what were all these in comparison with Browning's friendship for Elizabeth Barrett!

It was no selfish love, but it was a love that was friendship from first to last, that Robert Browning gave to Elizabeth Barrett. When he first heard of her, he heard that she was a hopeless invalid. Injured through a fall from her horse when about fourteen years old, she had been practically shut into her room, and much of the time confined to her bed, for twenty-three years, when he was introduced to her, by his friend and hers, John Kenyon,—"Kenyon the Magnificent," Browning called him. As soon as he saw her, Browning was her friend; and the thought of his life from that time onward was, not what she could be to him, but what he could be to her. And when he asked that she would be his wife, he merely sought freer opportunities of serving her, without any prospect of joy or gain to himself beyond this privilege of service. Pointing out his nobleness of soul in this action, Mrs. Sutherland Orr says: "No sane man in Mr. Browning's position could have been ignorant of the responsibilities he was incurring. He had, it is true, no experience of illness. Of its nature, its treatment, its symptoms direct and indirect, he remained pathetically ignorant to his dying day. He did not know what disqualifications for active existence might reside in the fragile, recumbent form, nor in the long years lived without change of air or scene beyond the passage, not always even allowed, from bed-room to sitting-room, from sofa to bed again. But he did know that Miss Barrett received him lying down, and that his very ignorance of her condition left him without security for her ever being able to stand. A strong sense of sympathy and pity could alone justify or explain the act,—a strong desire to bring sunshine into that darkened life. We might be sure that these motives had been present with him if we had no direct authority for believing it; and we have this authority in his own comparatively recent words: 'She had so much need of care and protection. There was so much pity in what I felt for her!'"

At the first proposal of Mr. Browning to call upon her, Miss Barrett had expressed her unwillingness to see or to be seen by a stranger, saying with a touching sense of her desolateness: "There is nothing to see in me, nothing to hear in me. I am a weed fit for the ground and darkness." But the light that shines out of friendship's heaven will not be kept back from the ground and darkness toward which it shines. It was not long before these two friends were made one, in spite of the unwillingness of relatives and the seeming unreasonableness of their purpose. And how much the world owes to the inspirations of that union! No wonder that her heart went out in thankfulness for the discernment of his unselfish love, that saw her as she was, and that was devoted to her because she was what she was.

> "Because thou hast the power, and own'st the grace,
> To look through and behind this mask of me,
> (Against which years have beat thus blanchingly
> With their rains) and behold my soul's true face,
> The dim and weary witness of life's race,—
> Because thou hast the faith and love to see,
> Through that same soul's distracting lethargy,
> The patient angel waiting for a place
> In the new heavens,—because nor sin nor woe,
> Nor God's infliction, nor death's neighborhood,
> Nor all which others, viewing, turn to go, . . .
> Nor all which makes me tired of all, self-viewed, . . .
> Nothing repels thee, . . . dearest, teach me so
> To pour out gratitude as thou dost good."

In all history there is no fitter illustration of the inspiring power of friendship to a poet than that furnished in the life of our still living Laureate. Tennyson's "In Memoriam" is in itself a refutation of the charge that friendship has no such potency in the Christian heart of to-day as it had in the heart of the classic Greek. Alfred Tennyson was still a young man when his bosom-friend Arthur Hallam, whom he "held as half-divine," was parted from him by death; and for seventeen years the friendship-inspired poet and his inspiring poem of friendship made progress alike, until both were perfected. And all the world now knows how much the poet and the world owe to the poet's friendship.

> "My Arthur, whom I shall not see
>   Till all my widowed race be run;
>   Dear as the mother to the son,
> More than my brothers are to me.
>
> .   .   .   .
>
> "The path by which we twain did go,
>   Which led by tracts that pleased us well,
>   Through four sweet years arose and fell,
> From flower to flower, from snow to snow.
>
> .   .   .   .   .
>
> "When each by turns was guide to each,
>   And Fancy light from Fancy caught,
>   And Thought leapt out to wed with Thought
> Ere Thought could wed itself with speech.
>
> .   .   .   .   .
>
> "But thou art turned to something strange,
>   And I have lost the links that bound
>   Thy changes; here upon the ground,
> No more partaker of thy change.
>
> .   .   .   .
>
> "Thy spirit ere our fatal loss
>   Did ever rise from high to higher;
>   As mounts the heavenward altar-fire,
> As flies the lighter through the gross.
>
> .   .   .   .
>
> "Dear friend, far off, my lost desire,
>   So far, so near in woe and weal;
>   Oh, loved the most, when most I feel
> There is a lower and a higher;

"Known and unknown; human, divine;
　　Sweet human hand and lips and eye;
　　Dear heavenly friend that canst not die,
　Mine, mine, for ever, ever mine;

"Strange friend, past, present, and to be;
　　Loved deeplier, darklier understood;
　　Behold, I dream a dream of good,
　And mingle all the world with thee.

"Thy voice is on the rolling air;
　　I hear thee where the waters run;
　　Thou standest in the rising sun,
　And in the setting thou art fair.

"What art thou then? I cannot guess;
　　But though I seem in star and flower
　　To feel thee some diffusive power
　I do not therefore love thee less.

"My love involves the love before;
　　My love is vaster passion now;
　　Though mixed with God and Nature thou,
　I seem to love thee more and more.

"Far off thou art, but ever nigh;
　　I have thee still, and I rejoice;
　　I prosper, circled with thy voice;
　I shall not lose thee though I die."

In France, as in Italy and in England, friendship was an inspiration to the poets, who were the inspiration of the nation. A few illustrations of this truth will prove as effective as many.

French modern poetry began with Pierre Corneille, the "Grand Corneille," as his nation calls him. Corneille made a new beginning for the French language, and for French genius. A French critic assigning him his place in history says: "When the Academy was endeavoring to correct the language which Pascal was destined to fix and Racine to polish, Corneille formed and created it by giving it force and precision in reasoning, energy and profoundness in discourse, elevation and sublimity in sentiment, dignity and majesty in the utterances of kings and heroes." And George Saintsbury says of Corneille that " his rank among the greatest of dramatic poets is not a matter of question; for a poet is to be judged by his best things, and the best things of Corneille are second to none." It was because of an unexpected rivalry with a friend that Corneille was turned from law to poetry as a life pursuit, and was prompted to the writing of *Mélite*, his first dramatic piece. It was after this, but while he was yet but a beginner in his poetic writing, that Corneille formed the acquaintance and won the friendship of M. de Chalon, a former secretary of Marie de Medicis. This friend perceived Corneille's higher possibilities, and set himself at developing them. "The kind of comedy that you have hitherto written," he said, "can only procure for you temporary credit. You will find in the Spanish dramatists some subjects which, if they are treated after our [French] fashion and by hands as competent as yours, would produce a great effect. You should learn their language. It is not difficult. I will teach you what I know of it; and until you can read by yourself I will translate you some passages out of Guillen de Castro." Thus incited and guided, Corneille "began his study of the Spanish masters, and rewarded his good-natured friend by writing 'The Cid,'" a drama which has been characterized as "perhaps the most 'epoch-making' play in all literature," and which won undying fame for its author. Another friend of Pierre Corneille who influenced his writing was his younger brother Thomas, of whose ability Voltaire says: "He was a man of great merit and of vast learning; and, if we except Racine, he was the only French author of his time worthy to be ranked next to his brother." Pierre and Thomas Corneille were bosom-friends as well as brothers. They married sisters, and they lived in adjoining houses. Guizot quotes in description of them these lines of Ducis:

> "Their houses twain were made in one;
> With keys and purse the same was done;
> Their wives can never have been two.
> Their wishes tallied at all times;
> No games distinct their children knew;
> The fathers lent each other rhymes;
> Same wine for both the drawers drew."

And Guizot adds: "It is said that when Peter Corneille was puzzled to end a verse he would undo a trap that opened into his brother's room, shouting: "*Sans-souci*, a rhyme!"

Closely following the great Corneille, in the beginnings of French poetic triumphs, came La Fontaine, Molière, Boileau, and Racine; and these four poets were friends together, and were fellow-helpers in poetry and friendship. On this latter point La Fontaine is explicit in the introduction to his "Psyche." These "four friends," he says, "who had learned to know each other on Parnassus, formed a kind of society, which I would have called an Academy if it had had more members." Racine he calls "Acanthus;" Boileau, "Aristus;" Molière, "Gelaste;" himself, "Polyphilus." He tells of their passing their time together lovingly, inspiring and helping one another in their literary work, and he freely acknowledges his own indebtedness to these friends; as the world has reason to acknowledge its indebtedness to their friendship. "A rare friendship united the [four] poets," says Lothheissen, a German biographer of Molière; yet such a friendship between such men is not so rare as many would suppose. Classifying these four poets in their place in the history of literature, Hallam finds that La Fontaine is "most popular" among French poets who are known to posterity, having left more "verses which, in the phrase of his country, have 'made their fortune,' and been like ready money always at hand for prompt quotation." "Molière is, perhaps, of all French writers the one whom his country has most uniformly admired, and in whom her critics are most unwilling to acknowledge faults. . . . "Of Shakespeare we may justly say that he had the greater genius, but perhaps of Molière that he has written the best comedies." "Boileau is the analogue of Pope in French literature." His was the earliest French poetry "where the style was always pure and elegant, where the ear was uniformly gratified." He improved the style of his own nation, and his influence was felt abroad. Racine is counted "second only to Virgil among all the poets," and is "next to Shakespeare among all the moderns." Each of these four poet-friends had other inspiring friendships besides the one that was common to them all; but this one by itself is of sufficient prominence to indicate the transcendency of the master-passion in poetry, in France as elsewhere.

For a final illustration of the inspiring power of friendship to a poet, it will suffice to point to Goethe, who was not only the greatest poet of Germany, but one of the greatest of the world's poets. Emerson calls Goethe "the head and body of the German nation." Hutton more discriminatingly says that "next to Luther he was the greatest of the Germans." Professor Seeley is sure that "scarcely any man has been to any nation all that Goethe has been to Germany;" moreover, that "he is . . . a great mover of modern thought, one of the principal makers of modern opinion." Carlyle indicated the position which is claimed for Goethe by his enthusiastic admirers when he wrote: "Goethe is by many of his countrymen ranked at the side of Homer and Shakespeare as one of the only three men of genius that have ever lived." And since Carlyle's day it has been a favorite comparison to name Homer, Dante, Shakespeare, and Goethe as the four representative poets of the ages. Oscar Browning sums up the more favorable estimates of the genius and work of Goethe in the statement: "As Homer concentrated in himself the spirit of antiquity, Dante of the middle ages, and Shakespeare of the renaissance, so Goethe is the representative of the modern spirit, the prophet of mankind under new circumstances and new conditions." Yet many who admit the greatness of Goethe as a thinker and a poet, are unable to see in him any traces of that self-abnegating nature which is essential to the truest friendship, and they would be unready to perceive in him a friendship-inspired poet.

Goethe, like Napoleon, had two very different sides to his nature, and his exceptional genius intensified the force of the opposing characteristics in his personality. Goethe could never be held up as an example of unswerving devotion in friendship; for his loves would not remain changeless through all changes. But Goethe's loves were always out-going rather than craving affections; and so far he was free from selfishness in his loves and friendships. His loving was like the sun's shining, always outward and toward the planet immediately before it; but, as a change in the planet brings the sun's beams of light and warmth to bear on a new focal center, so the removal of any one object of Goethe's most unselfish affections would result in those affections going out toward a new object newly brought within their range. His love was not like the magnetic needle, which has but one object of attraction, and which will turn persistently toward that object in spite of all changes of position. He gave out his love unselfishly, instead of selfishly craving the love of another, and thus far he had the gain and inspiration of friendship's loving. But to whom his unselfish love should go out depended entirely on his position and circumstances for the hour; therefore he was without the inspiration of a fixed center of life-absorbing friendship.

Goethe could never have shown such unchanging devotion to one object of affection, through absence and death, as Dante felt toward Beatrice, or Petrarch toward Laura; yet his life-story justifies his sincerity when he says of his life's ideal: "To be unselfish in everything, especially in love and friendship, was my highest pleasure, my maxim, my discipline." Hutton, whose opinion of Goethe is that "the conception of really *living* for another probably never occurred to him," yet recognizes the fact that "Goethe never became a *selfish* man in the coarse sense of the term;" and to Hutton's mind "it is curious to note how all Goethe's finest lyrics cluster round his attachments. Few things else seem ever to waken in him the same tones of unconscious airy melody. His other poetry, often exquisitely fine, has the polish of high art upon it,—but his lyrics seem to escape as unconsciously from the essence of the earth and air as the scent from the violet or the music from a bird." It was the friendship side of Goethe's affections that gave to them their inspiring poetic power. It was the fickleness of Goethe's sincerest affections in every change of surroundings that prevented his being as true a man as he was great a genius. At the best and at the worst, with Goethe as he was, he was profoundly indebted, as a man and as a poet, to the inspirations of his friendships, and to the inspiring influences of his friends.

Goethe's first friendship was with his sister Cornelia, who was a little younger than himself. She was more than a sister to him, and "there were few things in the world so precious to him as her love and sympathy." In his boyhood "no one had half so much control over his restless and fiery spirit" as she; and until her death at twenty-seven she remained "her brother's most intimate friend." It was by her persistent endeavors that Goethe was induced to complete his first great drama, *Götz von Berlichingen*, when he had already long delayed it. And she "was consulted at every stage of the work." Goethe was not yet ten when he became the attached friend of Count de Thorane, an officer of the

French army quartered at his father's house during the Seven Years' War. This friendship had its impress upon his tastes and opinions throughout his life. Another friendship of his boyhood that was a factor in his life's being was with the Fraulein von Klettenberg, a Moravian sister of saintly character, who was his mother's friend as well as his own. Her influence over him was very positive, and for a time pervading. It was never wholly lost to him. Her lovely character is pictured by Goethe in the Confessions of a Beautiful Soul, in "Wilhelm Meister." Fraulein von Klettenberg was a poet as well as a saint, and she inspired Goethe to poetry as well as to religious aspirations. "Moved by her influence, he wrote a series of Religious Odes, after the fashion of that day," and through her friendship he was led to earnest thought on the profoundest questions of human life and destiny. Then there came Goethe's peculiar attachment to Gretchen, a lovely girl several years his senior,—he being not yet fifteen. It has been said of Goethe's feeling toward Gretchen, that "he worshiped her as Dante worshiped Beatrice;" yet when Goethe found that he was viewed by Gretchen as a good little boy instead of as a reverent worshiper he ceased his devotions, as Dante would have been incapable of doing. The inspirations of this pure friendship were, however, always in the heart of Goethe; and her name and memory are embalmed in his greatest poem.

Goethe's university life at Leipsic pivoted on his friendships. Among his earlier friends there were Schlosser and Behrisch. Schlosser was ten years older than Goethe, but they became warm friends, and Schlosser afterwards married Goethe's sister. He introduced Goethe into a new world of German, French, English, and Italian poetry, and had his part in the shaping of Goethe's habits of poetic thought. Behrisch was tutor to the young Count Lindenau. He also was much older than Goethe, to whom he became warmly attached. Behrisch had such interest in the poems of Goethe that he always copied them out for him in a neat and careful hand. " He probably had a considerable effect in producing the simplicity and naturalness of Goethe's earlier style." For the time being, certainly, Goethe was unselfishly the devoted friend of Behrisch; and when the latter must leave Germany, in consequence of personal troubles, his poet-friend was inspired to the expression of the most self-forgetful reach of friendship:

> " Death 'tis to part;
> 'Tis threefold death
> To part, not hoping
> Ever to meet again.
>
> " Thou wouldst rejoice to leave
> This hated land behind,
> Wert thou not chained to me
> With friendship's flowery chains.
>
> " Burst them, I'll not repine.
> No noble friend
> Would stay his fellow-captive,
> If means of flight appear.
>
> " The remembrance
> Of his dear friend's freedom
> Gives *him* freedom
> In his dungeon."[1]

[1] E. A. Bowring's translation.

For more than forty years Goethe and Behrisch kept up a close and affectionate correspondence, however far separated; and they were friends until parted by death.

It was while studying law at Strasburg, after his course at Leipsic, that Goethe entered into a friendship with Herder, that was of great importance to his intellectual career. Herder brought Goethe to a new understanding of Shakespeare, and introduced him to the more enthusiastic study of both Greek and English poetry, the results of which were afterwards manifest in some of the choicest work of Goethe. "Thanks to the influences under which he was brought by Herder, Goethe," says James Sime, "during his residence at Strasburg, experienced a great intellectual awakening. . . . He had met Herder at the very moment when he needed and was capable of responding to the stimulus of an original mind at a stage of development more advanced than his own." Oscar Browning thinks that it was through the influence of his friend Herder that "Goethe's spirit was liberated from its trammels, and 'Götz' and 'Wilhelm Meister' became possible to his mind." The friendship thus begun continued unbroken for more than twenty years. It originated in Goethe's unselfish attention to Herder when the latter was suffering from an affection of the eyes, and it was finally clouded by the selfish moroseness of Herder in the later years of his life. On his return to Frankfort from Strasburg, Goethe gained another friend in Merck, an army paymaster, then just entering on the editorship of a new literary review. This friendship also was fruitful in results to Goethe. It has been said that while "Goethe had dominated over all his other friends,

Merck dominated over him." Goethe attached himself to Merck's review, and freely consulted Merck as to his own writings outside of this. Merck printed Goethe's first drama, after giving it his approval. The friendly criticisms of Merck were of real service to Goethe, and his fidelity never wavered. It was certain qualities of Merck that suggested the character of Mephistopheles to Goethe; but Goethe realized the better characteristics of his friend. Because of Merck's being cynical rather than enthusiastic, peculiar value attaches to his praise of Goethe, when, after six years of their intimate friendship, he wrote, during a visit to his friend at Weimar: "Goethe directs everything, and every one is pleased with him, for he serves many and hurts none. Who can resist the unselfishness of the man?" At every turn in his life Goethe formed a new friendship, or it might be said that every friendship formed by Goethe made a new turn in his life. He was yet but twenty-five when he won the friendship of young Karl August, the reigning Duke of Saxe-Weimar, then just seventeen—a friendship that continued without wavering for more than fifty years, and that potentially shaped Goethe's life destiny.

Karl August invited Goethe to make his home with him at Weimar, and the acceptance of that invitation gave immortality to what had before been an insignificant duchy. To Goethe, says Longfellow, this was "a circumstance that fixed his career and destiny." Friendship was Goethe's life at Weimar, and Goethe's life at Weimar was the life that the world knows best, and that enabled him to do most for the world. "From the moment of his arrival he became the inseparable

Inspiring Poetry. 377

and indispensable companion of the grand-duke. . . . Goethe and the duke dined together and bathed together; the duke addressed his friend by the familiar *thou*. Goethe slept in his chamber and attended him when ill." In order to bind Goethe more closely to Weimar, Karl August gave him a seat and voice in the privy council. Announcing this appointment to the poet's father, Karl August added: "Goethe can have but one position—that of my friend; all others are beneath him." The poets Wieland and Herder, already friends of Goethe, were with him at Weimar. The opportunities and incitements given to Goethe by the life at Weimar, as a result of the grand-duke's friendship, found their issue in much of his best intellectual work. It was there, also, that he formed his life-shaping friendship with Charlotte von Stein, wife of the master of the horse. She was then thirty-three years old, some six years older than Goethe. She had been married eleven years, and was the mother of seven children. At once she won the admiration and confidence of Goethe, and from first to last she drew out his best impulses and aspirations. They became the best of friends. With her husband also Goethe was on excellent terms. "He was a sensible, practical person, who did not interfere with his wife's friendships; and the idea that there was any reason why he should be jealous of Goethe seems never to have entered his mind." The influence of this friendship on the character and tastes of Goethe was most important.

Wilhelm Scherer, in his "History of German Literature," says on this point: "Goethe's relation to Frau von Stein developed the tenderest side of his nature. She was open and sincere, not passionate, not enthusiastic, but full of intellectual ardor; a gentle seriousness dignified her demeanor; a pure sound judgment, united with a noble thirst for knowledge, rendered her capable of sharing all Goethe's poetic, scientific, and human interests. . . . The moral and religious forces of his nature were strengthened and elevated by Frau von Stein. Purity is the name he has for that nobler inward life which she awakened in him, and in which he seemed to rise more and more to the passionless wisdom of Spinoza. . . . His poetry, too, became at this time a mirror of purity." This friendship of Goethe with Frau von Stein was so close for ten years that "he made her acquainted with every action, every thought of his mind, all the working of his brain;" and although it was interrupted, and its tenor somewhat changed, by his absence in Italy, the two were friends for fifty years, and she is said to have had more than a thousand letters from him. Lewes characterizes this friendship of Goethe's as "a silver thread woven among the many-colored threads which formed the tapestry of his life;" and he calls attention to the fact that Goethe, under the impulse of this affection for Frau von Stein, finds himself aroused to an "ambition to do something which will make him worthy of her." Goethe's friendship with the mother showed itself in his friendship for her son Fritz, who by her consent lived with him for a time, and accompanied him in travel. "It was a constant delight to him to have the boy's companionship, to direct his education, and to watch the gradual unfolding of his mind and character."

These friendships, among others, were shaping factors in the life of Goethe while his mind and character were developing to maturity. He was about forty-five years old when he formed the friendship with Schiller that was so potent a force in the more prolific years of his intellectual activity. Schiller was ten years younger than Goethe. Although they had met on several occasions before, it was not until Schiller visited Goethe and passed a fortnight with him, in the autumn of 1794, that they were drawn together in sympathy and friendship. Then, however, "each gave his heart to the other without reserve, and to the end of Schiller's life nothing was permitted to stand in the way of their mutual love and confidence."

"The history of literature," says Lewes, "presents nothing comparable to the friendship of Goethe and Schiller. The friendship of Montaigne and Etienne de la Boëtie was, perhaps, more passionate and entire; but it was the union of two kindred natures, which from the first moment discovered their affinity, not the union of two rivals incessantly contrasted by partisans, and originally disposed to hold aloof from each other. Rivals Goethe and Schiller were and are; natures in many respects directly antagonistic; chiefs of opposing camps, and brought into brotherly union only by what was highest in their natures and aims. . . . Goethe had much to give, which Schiller gratefully accepted; and if he could not in return influence the developed mind of his great friend, nor add to the vast stores of its knowledge and experience, he could give him that which was even more valuable, *sympathy* and *impulse*. He excited Goethe to work. He withdrew him from the engrossing pursuit of science, and restored him once more to poetry. He urged him to finish what was already commenced, and not to leave his works all fragments. They worked together with the same purpose and the same earnestness, and their union is the most glorious episode in the lives of both, and remains as an external exemplar of a noble friendship."

The completion of "Wilhelm Meister" by Goethe was the first fruit of Schiller's friendship. Then there came "Hermann and Dorothea." After this there were Ballads written by the two friends, each in his own way as influenced by the other; and their *Xenien*, a series of sharply pointed epigrams, whose keen criticism of current art and literature had large influence for good, were written and published by them conjointly. And there was new work done by Goethe on the long-planned "Faust." Meanwhile Schiller was growing through the inspirations of this friendship, and his best poems were written. The co-work of the two friends was continued for ten years, until the death of Schiller. After this Goethe worked on, to the close of his life, under the impellings which he had received from friendship. "Since that time Schiller and Goethe have been inseparable in the minds of their countrymen, and have reigned as twin stars in the literary firmament." Their statues stand together on one pedestal, their hands clasped in friendship, on the public square of Weimar. And so Goethe, as one of the world's greatest poets, is an illustration of what the poets, all the world over, have owed as poets to the inspirations of friendship.

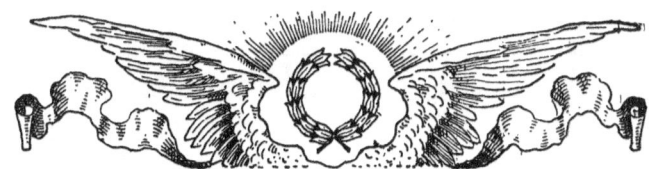

TRANSFIGURING ALL LIFE.

SINCE the world began, unselfish love has been the highest outreach of the human heart and the heart's richest blessing. To be loved unselfishly, to be loved for one's own sake, and to be sure of such a love in spite of all lack or failure on one's own part, is a cause of unfailing joy to the gladdest soul or to the saddest. A consciousness of such a love has uplifted the lowliest peasant to a height that no throne of earth could secure to its possessor; and it has been more to the occupant of the loftiest throne than all his royal treasures and prerogatives. It has nerved the cowardly to acts of heroism, and has given added grace to the heroic daring of the bravest. It has won the evil-minded to a life of goodness, and has brought the purest-hearted to a holier consecration of himself and all his powers to God. It has enabled the sufferer to endure, and the hopeless to hope. It has brought light into the gloom of the despairing, and has given to the sorrowing a foretaste of heavenly joys. This transfiguring power of a sense of being loved unselfishly it is that Elizabeth Barrett bore testimony to, while she still felt that it was her duty to refuse as a lover him of whom she would be always sure as a friend:

> "Go from me. Yet I feel that I shall stand
> Henceforward in thy shadow. Nevermore
> Alone upon the threshold of my door
> Of individual life, I shall command
> The uses of my soul, nor lift my hand
> Serenely in the sunshine as before,
> Without the sense of that which I forbore,—
> Thy touch upon the palm. The widest land
> Doom takes to part us leaves thy heart in mine
> With pulses that beat double. What I do
> And what I dream include thee, as the wine
> Must taste of its own grapes. And when I sue
> God for myself, he hears that name of thine,
> And sees within my eyes the tears of two.
>
> "The face of all the world is changed, I think,
> Since first I heard the footsteps of thy soul
> Move still, oh, still, beside me, as they stole
> Betwixt me and the dreadful outer brink
> Of obvious death, where I, who thought to sink,
> Was caught up into love, and taught the whole
> Of life in a new rhythm. The cup of dole
> God gave for baptism, I am fain to drink,
> And praise its sweetness, sweet, with thee anear.
> The names of country, heaven, are changed away
> For where thou art or shalt be, there or here;
> And this . . . this lute and song . . . loved yesterday,
> (The singing angels know) are only dear
> Because thy name moves right in what they say."

It is good to have a friend, but it is better to be a friend. The gain of being unselfishly loved and sympathized with and helped and cheered is not to be compared with the gain of unselfishly loving and sympathizing with and helping and cheering another. No glad incoming to one's heart from without can uplift and enlarge it like the expansive force of a generous and self-forgetting love outworking from within. Not only is it more glorious to be a central sun than to absorb a measure of the sun's light and warmth, but the soul, which is more than a sun, is made newly glorious in an inspired endeavor to reach with its out-sent beams an object that has called forth a reverent purpose of praise and homage and service unknown to it before. He who has a pure and unselfish love for any one being in the universe, has thereby a new life, new powers, new possibilities, and new perceptions of all; and the very universe itself is a new universe to him, as viewed from his new center of love and light. Thus it was that Dante experienced the transfiguring power of his unselfish love at every fresh sight of her to whom he was a true friend, when he bore witness to the marvelous effects of such a vision: " There no longer remained to me an enemy; nay, a flame of charity possessed me which made me pardon every one who had done me wrong; and had any one at that time questioned me of anything, my only answer would have been 'Love,' and my face would have been clothed with humility." And Emerson gives like assurance of his gain through friendship, in its transfiguring light over all that he sees, and over himself as the seer :

> "O friend, my bosom said,
>   Through thee alone the sky is arched,
>   Through thee the rose is red;

> All things through thee take nobler form,
> And look beyond the earth;
> The mill-round of our fate appears
> A sun-path in thy worth.
> Me too thy nobleness has taught
> To master my despair;
> The fountains of my hidden life
> Are through thy friendship fair."

To be loved unselfishly is a blessing. To love unselfishly is a greater blessing. A union in a love that is reciprocally unselfish is the greatest blessing of all. When he who loves unselfishly is unselfishly loved by the object of his affection, so that each of the two loses himself, and finds more than himself, in the other, life seems to be all that life can be here, and to have promise of more than all that can here be gained. So far from such an unselfish union of souls making either soul selfish in its satisfaction with itself or with the other, its inspirations are sure to cause ceaseless and unsatisfied, though ever hopeful, aspirations after that which it newly opens to view, and toward which it impels. Thus Michael Angelo, with all his extraordinary power of perceiving truth and beauty, confesses to new visions of loveliness in the realms of mind and matter, in the added light from the eyes of his young friend, Tommaso de' Cavalieri:

> "Through thee I catch a gleam of tender glow,
> Which with mine own eyes I had failed to see;
> And walking upward, step by step with thee,
> The once oppressive burdens lighter grow.
> With thee my groveling thoughts I heavenward raise
> Borne upward by thy bold aspiring wing;
> I follow where thou wilt,—a helpless thing,

> Cold in the sun and warm in winter days.
> My will, my friend, rests only upon thine;
> Thy heart must every thought of mine supply;
> My mind expression finds in thee alone,
> Thus like the moonlight's silver ray I shine.
> We only see her beams on the far sky,
> When the sun's fiery rays are o'er her thrown."[1]

And it is of this transforming influence of a merging of soul with soul in unselfish and aspiring love, that Schiller tells in his address to his friend Körner as "Raphael:"

> "Did not the same strong mainspring urge and guide
> Our hearts to meet in love's eternal bond?
> Linked to thine arm, O Raphael, by thy side
> Might I aspire to reach to souls beyond
> Our earth, and bid the bright ambition go
> To that perfection which the angels know!
>
> "Happy, oh, happy—I have found thee; I
> Have out of millions found thee, and embraced;
> Thou, out of millions, mine!—Let earth and sky
> Return to darkness and the antique waste;
> To chaos shocked, let warring atoms be,—
> Still shall each heart unto the other flee.
>
> "Do I not find within thy radiant eyes
> Fairer reflections of all joys most fair?
> In thee I marvel at myself. The dyes
> Of lovely earth seem lovelier painted there,
> And in the bright looks of the friend is given
> A heavenlier mirror even of the Heaven!"[2]

Friendship-love, as a love that is unselfish, uncraving, ever out-going, and ever on-going, is in its very nature divine love. It is such a love as God gives, and as man

[1] J. A. Symonds's translation.   [2] Bulwer's translation.

ought to give to God. It is such a love as man should give to his fellow-man for God's sake. "If ye love them that love you, what thank have ye?" asks our Lord; "for even sinners love those that love them." A love or a friendship that is conditioned on an equivalent return is not friendship-love, except in name. That love which is represented to us in the Bible as of God, and from God, and due toward God and toward those who are God's, is friendship-love—the purest and best of loves.

It is *agapē*, a "love without desire" or craving, not *philia*, a love which goes out "longingly" for the possession of its object, that seems to be recognized in Bible usage as friendship-love, and that would be better thus translated.[1] "Friendship-love is of God; and every one that [thus] loveth is begotten of God and knoweth God." "God is friendship-love; and he that abideth in friendship-love abideth in God, and God abideth in him."

The closest attainable union of man with God is a union in friendship-love,—such a union as God proffered to his loved friend Abraham, and as is a possibility, through the Friend of friends, to every one who by faith is a child of faithful Abraham. The divinest exhibit of God-likeness in man is in this friendship-love, of which the Apostle Paul sounds the praises so glowingly: "If I speak with the tongues of men and of angels, but have not friendship-love, I am become sounding brass or a clanging cymbal. And if I have the gift of prophecy, and know all mysteries and all knowledge; and if I have all faith, so as to remove mountains, but have not friendship-love, I am nothing. And if I bestow

[1] See Excursus, p. 389 f.

all my goods to feed the poor, and if I give my body to be burned, but have not friendship-love, it profiteth me nothing. Friendship-love suffereth long, and is kind; friendship-love envieth not; friendship-love vaunteth not itself, is not puffed up, doth not behave itself unseemly; seeketh not its own, is not provoked, taketh not account of evil; rejoiceth not in unrighteousness, but rejoiceth with the truth; beareth all things, believeth all things, hopeth all things, endureth all things. Friendship-love never faileth: but whether there be prophecies, they shall be done away; whether there be tongues, they shall cease; whether there be knowledge, it shall be done away. . . . But now abideth faith, hope, friendship-love, these three; and the greatest of these is friendship-love."

EXCURSUS

ON THE NEW TESTAMENT WORDS FOR "LOVE" AND "FRIENDSHIP-LOVE."

Failing to perceive clearly the distinction between a love that instinctively grows out of a relationship, or that is based upon a natural desire for possession, and a voluntary and distinguishing love that goes out unselfishly and admiringly toward its chosen object, New Testament critics and commentators generally have been confused in their minds, while seeking to account for the apparent difference between the two words—*philia* and *agapē*—employed in the sacred text for the designation of "love." It is practically admitted by all that *philia* was a word in common use, in New Testament times, as expressive of the love between parents and children, and brothers and sisters, and also of craving love between the sexes. It is also admitted that the word *agapē* comes into a new prominence in New Testament use, as applicable to man's love to God and to love that is otherwise peculiarly pure and sacred. But these two words seem at times to be employed interchangeably; and many an eminent scholar has confessed his inability to see the real difference between the words in their using, as accounting for the often indicated superiority of *agapē*, in spite of the greater warmth and intensity of *philia*.

Cremer, in his "Biblico-Theological Lexicon of New Testament Greek," covers the important facts in the case when he says: "We find *agapē* used to designate a love unknown to writers outside of the New Testament,—*love in its fullest conceivable form;* love as it is the distinguishing attribute, not of humanity, but, in the strictest sense, of Divinity." Trench, in seeking to differentiate the meaning of the two words *agapē* and *philia*, says: "The first expresses a more reasoning attachment, of choice and selection (*diligere = deligere*), from seeing in the object upon whom it is bestowed that which is worthy of regard; ... while the second, without being necessarily an unreasoning attachment, does yet oftentimes give less account of itself to itself; is more instinctive, is more of the feelings, implies more passion." Woolsey, after an exhaustive study of the history of the two terms, says of Trench's definition: "We believe that this is a true statement of the difference between the two words and notions." And all this is in confirmation of the claim made in this volume that *philia* represents a love that grows out of relationship or craving, while *agapē* represents a love that goes out voluntarily without any intermingling of selfishness,—the one being ordinary love, and the other the higher form of friendship-love.

As has been already stated (page 17, *ante*), the Sanskrit makes a similar distinction to this, in its use of *lubh* = "covetousness" or "greed" for "love," as over against *pri* = "unselfish love" for "friendship." And there are other reasons for believing that there were many outreachings of the human heart, all the world over, in the direction of an unselfish friendship-love, as nobler and purer than a love that craves, before the truth concerning it was brought out in explicitness in New Testament revelations.

Men are said to love, or crave (*philein*), "the chief place at feasts" (Matt. 23 : 6), and "salutations in the marketplaces" (Luke 20 : 46), and to have this self-interested love (*philein*), as growing out of relationship, for "father or mother," or for "son or daughter" (Matt. 10 : 37). On the other hand, the Roman centurion is said by the Jews to have had an unselfish friendship-love (*agapān*) for their nation, as evidenced by his building for them a synagogue (Luke 7 : 5). God's children are commanded to have friendship-love (*agapān*) for their "neighbors" (Matt. 5 : 43; Gal. 5 : 14), and for their "enemies" (Matt. 5 : 44), because love does not go out in those directions instinctively, but must be given unselfishly, and of deliberate choice. Yet the saints are enjoined to have a feeling of family love (*philein*) for their Lord (1 Cor. 16 : 22) and for one another in the household of faith (Titus 3 : 15). "The world" is said to give a selfish, interested love (*philein*) to "its own," because of the mutual relation between the two (John 15 : 19). But Jesus is said to give a pure and unselfish friendship-love (*agapān*) to Mary and Martha and their brother Lazarus, in the home so dear to him at Bethany (John 11 : 5). God is said to be moved by unselfish friendship-love (*agapān*) toward the world, in the gift of his Son (John 3 : 16). But Jesus says that the Father loves as with a feeling of family-love (*philein*) those who have come into his inner family circle through love for his Son (John 16 : 27). And many another passage seems to recognize and accentuate these distinctions in the force of the two words severally.

A striking illustration of the significant uses of the two words in the same conversation is found in the narrative of the interview of Jesus with Peter, on the shore of the Sea of Galilee, after the Resurrection (John 21 : 15-19). Jesus asks Peter if he gives him friendship-love (*agapān*) more truly than the other disciples, as Peter had asserted that he was ready to do. Peter, remembering his denial of his Lord, replies that Jesus knows that he gives him longing love (*philein*). The second time Jesus asks Peter if he can claim to give him *any* measure of friendship-love (*agapān*) apart from all comparison with others. Again Peter affirms that the Lord knows that he gives him a longing love (*philein*). Then Jesus changes his form of question, and asks Peter if he is sure that he gives him even a longing love (*philein*). At this Peter is "grieved" (not because the question is repeated the third time, but because in its third putting it seems to imply a doubt whether Peter has any love for his Lord even on the lower plane); and his earnest answer is, "Lord, thou knowest all things; thou knowest that I love thee"—with a longing love (*philein*); and Jesus quietly goes on to say that he would have Peter bear himself towards his dear ones just as he would if he were his devoted friend above all the other disciples. Thus the way is opened for Jesus to tell Peter plainly of what is in store for him in his faithful service.

Trench just misses the meaning of this narrative, through not perceiving the transcendency of friendship-love in comparison with longing-love, or relationship-love. Luthardt comes nearer to the meaning, but without recognizing the true distinction between the two kinds of love. Meyer, again, falls short of an apprehension of the reason for the change in the forms of question and answer in this conversation. Only in the light of the distinction here pointed out is the full force of Divine love to be comprehended in the teachings of the New Testament.

INDEX.

INDEX.

ABBÉ, Browning's, instanced, 97.
Aboo Bekr and Muhammad, 106, 184-189.
Abraham, the friend of God, 29, 48 f., 175.
Absence no bar to friendship, 60 f., 346 f.
Abydos, inscription at, 123.
Academy, the, at Athens: its origin, 255.
Achates and Æneas, 156, 161.
Achilles and Patroclus, 156 f., 285.
Actium, naval battle at, 130.
Adams, C. F.: cited, 240 f.
Adams, John: his action concerning Hamilton, 247.
Addison, Joseph: a friend of Berkeley, 276; cited, 342 f.; as poet and friend, 349.
Aeger, Henry, and Gerhard Groot, 199.
Æneas and Achates, 156, 161.
Africa, South: its folk-lore tales of friendship, 84.
Africanus: his friendship for Lælius, 21.
Agamemnon and Achilles, estranged through lust, 284.
Agapē, the Bible word for friendship-love, 17, 386, 389 f.
Agrippa and Augustus Cæsar, 128-131.
Ahithophel, a friend of David, 125.
Akbar Muhammad and Shaykh Solayman, 153 f.
À Kempis, Thomas: his friendships, 199-202.
Akenside, Mark, as friend and poet, 351 f.
Akim and Alyósha, 164.
Alcæus: cited, 233.
Alcuin and Charlemagne, 132 f.
Alden, John, as a friend, 56.

Alexander and Hephæstion, 106, 126-128.
Alexander, Bishop, and Origen, 177 f.
Alexander the Great: his trust of a friend, 42; his friendships, 126-128, 257.
"Alfred, Mask of," a product of friendship, 351.
Alger, W. R.: his translation from Jâmee, 22; his "Friendships of Women," 110.
Alison, Sir Archibald: cited, 146.
"All for Love," Dryden's, 95.
Alliance, The Quadruple, at Eton, 351.
Alyósha Popovich and Akím Ivánovich, 164.
Alypius and Augustine, 183 f.
Ambrose, St., and Monica, 108.
Ambrose of Alexandria, and Origen, 179.
American Board of Commissioners for Foreign Missions: its origin, 227 ff.
American Independence, promoted by friendship, 239-247.
American Indians, friendship among, 71 f.
Ames, Fisher: cited, 240.
Amitsi, wife of Merira Pepi, 124.
Ammon, message from oracle of, 127.
Amo: Latin for "love," 17.
Amys and Amylion, 167 f.
Andrewes, Lancelot: a friend of Bacon, 263; a friend of Herbert, 342.
Angelo, Michael, and Vittoria Colonna, 109.
Anglo-Catholic movement, affected by friendships, 229 f.
Anglo-Saxon term for "friend," 14.
Anne, Queen, and the Duchess of Marlborough, 106.
Anniceris, a friend of Plato, 255.
Anselm and his friends, 191-194.

Antipho: his answer to Dionysius, 232 f.
Apocrypha, the, friendship in, 75, 100 f.
Apollo and Diana, 110.
Apostles, the, sent out in pairs, 175 f.
Appeals to God in vows of friendship, 71 f.
Aquinas, Thomas, and Bonaventura, 106, 196-199.
Arabia, friendship in, 108.
Arabia, a king of, influenced by friendship, 131.
"Arabian Nights:" cited, 152.
Arabic folk-lore: its lessons of friendship, 82 f.
Arbuthnot, John, a friend of Pope, 350.
Archbishop of Mentz, a friend of Leibnitz, 279.
Aretheus, a Corinthian, 30, 31.
Aristogiton and Harmodius, 231-233.
Aristotle: cited, 20, 31, 35, 59 f., 64, 73, 94, 97 f., 119, 155 f.; his indebtedness to friendship, 256 f.; his friendship for his wife, 257.
Arjuna and Krishna, 286 f.
Arnauld, a friend of Leibnitz, 279.
Arnold, Matthew: cited, 202.
Arnold of Schoonhaven and Thomas à Kempis, 200 f.
Arnold, Thomas, and his friends, 230.
Artemesia and Mausolus, 112.
Asheton, a friend of Gray, 351.
Ashley, Lord, (Earl Shaftesbury,) and John Locke, 268-270.
"Athanase, Prince," Shelley's: its meaning, 359.
Athenian liberties advanced by friendship, 231-233.
Atterbury, Bishop, a friend of Pope, 350.
Augustan Age, the: friendship its glory, 131.
Augustine, St.: cited, 94; his relations with his mother, 110; his friendships, 181-184.
Augustus Cæsar and his friend Agrippa, 128-131.
"Auld Lang Syne," a song of friendship, 355.
Austen, Lady, a friend of Cowper, 353.
"Autocrat of the Breakfast Table," quotation from, 91.

Awbrey, Mrs. Mary, a friend of Katherine Philips, 342.

BABYLONIA: its early records, 122.
Bacon, Lord: cited, 13, 52, 63, 87, 121, 263 f.; his relations with Essex, 259-262; his indebtedness to friendship, 259-264; a friend of George Herbert, 342.
"Banquet," Plato's: cited, 155.
Barnabas and St. Paul, 176 f.
Barrett, Elizabeth, as friend and wife, 112, 363 f.; inspired by Browning's unselfish love, 364; her testimony to the power of friendship, 382.
Bartoli, a biographer of Loyola, 219 f.
Bassus, Cæsius, a friend of Persius, 296.
Bastile, the: its storming, 248 f.
Baxter, Richard: cited, 237; his estimate of Herbert, 341.
Baynes, T. S.: cited, 340.
Beaconsfield, Lord and Lady, 112.
Beatrice and Dante, 300-304.
Behrisch, a friend of Goethe, 374 f.
Bele and Thorstein, 163.
Believing better than seeing, 41 f.
Benedict, St., and St. Scholastica, 111.
Benson, Bishop, a friend of Berkeley, 276.
Bentinck, William, and King William III., 106, 135-139.
Berkeley, Bishop: his philosophy and his friendships, 273-276.
Bhagavad Gîtâ: its nature and origin, 287.
Bias, false theory of, 45.
Bible, the: its view of friendship, 25, 47-51, 386-393.
"Biblico-Theological Lexicon of New Testament Greek," Cremer's: cited, 390.
Bion and Mosehus, poet-friends, 290 f.
Bishop Jeremy Taylor: cited, 13, 57 f., 88, 95; as a friend, 342.
Bishop Lancelot Andrewes: a friend of Lord Bacon, 263; of George Herbert, 342.
Blanche, Duchess of Lancaster, 316.
Blood, transfusion of, in friendship, 70 f.
"Blot in the 'Scutcheon, A:" an outcome of friendship, 362.

Bohemond and Tancred, 170 f.
Boileau and his friends, 368.
Boineburg, Baron von, a friend of Leibnitz, 279.
Bonaventura and Thomas Aquinas, 106, 196-199.
Booddhism: its estimate of friendship, 78 f., 90.
Bowring, E. A.: his translation from Goethe, 374.
Boyle, Robert: a friend of the Countess of Ranelagh, 111; of John Locke, 270.
Broad Church, the, movement and friendships, 229 f.
Bronté, Charlotte, Anne, and Emily, 111.
Brooke, Lord, and Sir Philip Sidney, 106.
Brothers of the Common Life, friendships among, 199-202.
Brougham, Lord: cited, 239, 249.
Browne, Mrs., and Mrs. Hemans, 110.
Browne, Sir Thomas: cited, 31, 52 f., 119.
Browning, Elizabeth B.: cited, 60.
Browning, Robert: cited, 23, 33, 34, 56, 86, 97, 328; as poet and as friend, 361-364; as friend, lover, and husband, 112, 362-364.
Bruce, King Robert, and Sir James Douglas, 171.
Brunhild and Kriemhild, rivalry of, 287.
Brutus and Collatinus, 234 f.
Bryant, W. C.: quotation from his translation of the Iliad, 285.
Budgel: cited, 156.
Bunsen, Baron: his friendships, 112, 230.
Burnet, Bishop: cited, 111.
Burns, Robert, as friend and poet, 354 f.
Burr, Aaron, and Theodosia, 110.
Butler, Lady Eleanor, and Miss Sarah Ponsonby, 106.
Byron, Lord, as friend and poet, 357 f.

CÆSAR, Julius: cited, 162.
Calderon de la Barca: cited, 81.
Calvin, John: his relations with John Knox, 213, 215-218; with Nicholas Cop and Louis du Tillot, 218.

Cardinal Colonna, a friend of Petrarch, 313.
Cardinal de Berulle, a friend of Descartes, 265.
Carlyle, Thomas: cited, 370.
Carter, Elizabeth, and Catharine Talbot, 106.
Carton, Sydney, and Lucie Manette, 173 f.
Castor and Pollux, 109 f., 289, 297.
Catherine, Countess of Ranelagh, and Robert Boyle, 111.
Catullus and Veranius, 292.
Caulaincourt: cited, 148.
Cavalieri, Tommaso de', a friend of Michael Angelo, 384 f.
Chalon, M. de, a friend of Pierre Corneille, 367 f.
Chanut, Pierre, a friend of Descartes, 266.
Charixenus, a Sicyonian, 30, 31.
Charlemagne and Alcuin, friendship of, 132 f.
Charles the Great, or Charlemagne, 132 f
Charles V. and his young friend, 133 f.
Charlotte, Queen Sophia, of Prussia, a friend of Leibnitz, 279 f.
Chaucer, Geoffrey: cited, 44; his poetry and his friendships, 314-317.
Chesterfield, Lord: his friendship for Thomas Prior, 275.
"Childe Harold:" its impress of friendship, 358.
China, friendship in ancient, 125 f.
Chinese classics, lessons of friendship in, 76.
Chinese maxim, 97.
Chivalry and friendship, 166-169, 297-300.
Chivalry: its work for woman, 297-300.
Choo He: cited, 51.
"Christabel," quotation from, 68.
Christianity more favorable than paganism to friendship, 202.
Christina, Queen of Sweden, a friend of Descartes, 266 f.
Chrysostom, St., and Olympias, 108.
Church, Dean: cited, 192, 259-262, 325.
Cicero: cited, 13, 21, 32, 45, 52, 60, 61, 67, 73, 87, 97, 119, 258, 291.
Cicero and Tullia, 110.

"Cid, The," Corneille's, an outcome of friendship, 367 f.
Clare, Earl, a friend of Byron, 358.
Clare, St., and St. Francis, 109, 194-196.
Clarendon: cited, 236 f.
Clarke, Edward, a friend of John Locke, 270.
Clarke, Mary, and Julius Mohl, 112.
Clayton, John, and the Wesleys, 225.
Clerk, William, a friend of Scott, 356.
Clerselier, Claude, a friend of Descartes, 266.
Codex Amoris, 298.
Coleridge, Sir John T.: cited, 36.
Coleridge, Samuel T.: cited, 55, 67 f.
Coleridge and Wordsworth: their friendships, 229, 359 f.
Coleridge, Sara, mother and daughter, 110.
Colet, John, and Erasmus, 106, 202-207.
"Colin Clouts Come Home Again," Spenser's, quotation from, 327.
Collatinus and Brutus, 234 f.
Collins, Anthony, a friend of John Locke, 272.
Colonna, James, a friend of Petrarch, 313.
Colonna, Vittoria, and Michael Angelo, 109.
Comic poetry of Terence, 292.
"Commentaries," Cæsar's, quotation from, 162.
"Commonplaces of Theology," Melanchthon's: its origin and influence, 213 f.
"Comus," Milton's: its prompting in friendship, 347 f.
Confidence, a feature of friendship, 66.
Confucius: a disciple of, cited, 43, 51; his estimate of friendship, 76, 87, 250 f.
Congreve, William, a friend of Dryden, 348.
Contarini, Thomas, a friend of George Berkeley, 275.
Cooke, John Esten: cited, 63.
Coolidge, Susan: cited, 91.
Cop, Nicholas, and John Calvin, 218.
Corneille, Pierre: as friend and poet, 366-368; his place in French literature, 366 f.

Corneille, Thomas, brother and friend of Pierre, 368.
Cornelia, sister and friend of Goethe, 372.
Corpus Christi, origin of liturgy for, 198.
Correspondence of friends, 61.
Cotterel, Sir Charles, a friend of Katherine Philips, 242.
Count de Ripert-Monclair, a friend of Browning, 362.
Count de Thorane, a friend of Goethe, 372 f.
Court of Love: its code of laws, 298 f.
Cowley, Abraham, cited, 342.
Cowper, William, as poet and friend, 109, 353.
Cranch, C. P.: his translations of Virgil, 161 f.
Cranston, Dr., a friend of Thomson, 351.
Craterus, a friend of Alexander, 127 f.
Cremer: cited, 390.
Critias, a Greek artist, 232.
Crito, a friend of Socrates, 254.
Cross-brotherhood in Russia, 163 f.
Crotus Rubianus and Martin Luther, 208.
Crusades, the, friendship in, 169 f.
Cudworth, Damaris, a friend of John Locke, 272 f.
Cur Deus Homo, Anselm's: friendship its prompting, 194.
Curtius, Quintius: cited, 127.
Cyrnus and Theognis, 290.

DACRE: translator of Petrarch, 309.
D'Aubigné, J. H. Merle: cited, 209 f., 213 f.
Damon and Pythias, 106; influence of their friendship, 131; disciples of Pythagoras, 252.
Dante and Beatrice, 300-304.
Dante: his place as a poet, 300, 310 f.; his friendship for Cavalcanti and Guido Novello da Polenta, 311 f.; cited, 383.
Danton, Georges Jacques, and Camille Desmoulins, 248-250.
David: his estimate of friendship, 48; his friendship for Jonathan, 27 f., 37, 38, 63, 106; for Saul, 56 f.: his friends Ahithophel and Hushai, 125.

De Amicitia, Cicero's, 64, 292.
De Balzac, Guez, a friend of Descartes, 266.
De Berulle, Cardinal, a friend of Descartes, 265.
De Bobadilla, a friend of Loyola, 221.
Definition of "friendship," 12-18.
Degrees of friendship, 93-104.
Démasis, a friend of Napoleon, 144 f.
Denman, Ann, and John Flaxman, 112.
De Quincey: cited, 202.
Descartes: his place as a philosopher, 264 f.; his indebtedness to friendship, 264-267.
Desmoulins, Camille, and Georges Jacques Danton, 248-250.
"Dethe of Blaunche the Duchesse, The," Chaucer's, 316.
Dhammapada: its estimate of love, 78.
Diana and Apollo, 110.
Dickens, Charles: cited, 173 f.
Diede, Charlotte: a friend of Wilhelm von Humboldt, 61, 109.
Dietrich, Sir, a hero in the Nibelungenlied, 289.
Diligere: Latin for "love," 17, 390.
Dimitriev: cited, 81.
Diodati, Charles, a friend of Milton, 347 f.
Diodorus: cited, 160.
Diogenes Laertius: cited, 98, 258.
Diomedes and Glaucus, 285.
Diomedes and Ulysses, 158, 285.
Dion, a friend of Plato, 255.
Dionysius, of Syracuse: influence of friendship on, 131; his oppression of Plato, 255.
Distrust, excluded from friendship, 35-46.
Divina Commedia, Dante's, 303 f.
Divine friendship, 26, 385 f.
Dobrýnya and Dúnaï, 164.
Dominicans and Franciscans, 194-198.
Dommett, Alfred, a friend of Browning, 362 f.
Donne, Dr. John, friend of George Herbert and his mother, 341 f.
Dorothy Wordsworth, her brother's friend, 359 f.
Douglas, Sir James, and King Robert Bruce, 171.
Dowden, Edward: cited, 332 f.

"Dramatic Romances," Browning's, quotation from, 361.
Draupadî, the wife of five brothers, 286.
Drummond, biographer of Erasmus, 204.
Dryden: cited, 60, 63, 95, 342; as poet and friend, 348.
Duane, James, Alexander Hamilton's letters to, 243 f.
Ducis: cited, 368.
Dúnaï Ivánovich and Dobrýnya Nikitich, 164.
Dunlop, Mrs., of Dunlop, a friend of Burns, 355.
Duroc, a friend of Napoleon, 146-149.
Duryodhana, leader of Kauravas, 286.
Du Tillot, Louis, and John Calvin, 218.
Dyson, Jeremiah, a friend of Akenside, 351 f.

EA, a god of the Babylonians, 122.
Eabani and Izdubar, 122 f.
Eadmer and Anselm, 193 f.
Ebers, Georg: cited, 41.
Edgeworth, Richard and Maria, 110.
"Education," Locke's treatise on: its origin, 270.
Egmont, Earl of, a friend of Berkeley, 275.
Egypt, friendship in ancient, 41, 123.
Electra and Orestes, 110.
"Elegy," Gray's: its prompting in friendship, 351.
Eliot, George: cited, 25, 46.
Eliot, Sir John, John Hampden, and John Pym, 236-239.
Elizabeth, Princess, a friend of Descartes, 266.
Elliott, Sir Gilbert, a friend of Hume, 278.
Ellis, George, a friend of Scott, 357.
Emerson, Ralph Waldo: cited, 23, 36, 38, 43, 53 f., 60 f., 82, 96, 256, 370, 383 f.
"Encyclopædia Britannica," quotation from, 243 f.
Endamidas, a Corinthian, 30, 31.
Engel: cited, 53.
English poetry, shaped by friendship, 321 f.
Enmity, costs less than friendship, 89.

Ennius: cited, 80; his estimate of friendship, 292.

"'Enoch, Book of," an Arabic classic, 82 f.

Envy, excluded from friendship, 35-46.

Epaminondas and Pelopidas, 106, 159 f.

Epic poems the world's first literature, 284.

Epicureans and Stoics, friendship among, 258.

Epicurus: cited, 24.

Epitaphium Damonis, Milton's: cited, 347.

"Epithalamion," Spenser's, quotation from, 323 f.

Epochs of history: their center in individuals, 117.

Erasmus, his friendship for John Colet, 106, 202-207; compared with Luther, 203; cited, 213.

Erdmann: cited, 255.

Erskine, William, a friend of Scott, 356.

Eskimo, folk-lore tales of, 85.

"Essay Concerning Human Understanding," Locke's: its origin and influence, 269.

Essex, Earl of, and Lord Bacon, 259-262.

Estrangement, a cause of suffering, 68.

Eton, Gray's friendships at, 351.

Euripides, cited, 52, 87; friendship in his poetry, 289 f.

Euryalus and Nisus, 161 f.

Eusebius and Pamphilus, 106, 179-181.

Evelyn, John: cited, 53.

Exchanges, symbolic, in friendship, 73 f.

Excursus on New Testament words for "love" and "friendship," 389 f.

FABER, Peter, and Ignatius Loyola, 218-221.

"Faerie Queene," Spenser's: its writing, 325-327.

Faithfulness, the hunger of a faithful heart, 46.

"Faust," Goethe's: friendship's influence on it, 376, 380.

Fear, out of place in love, 40.

Feather-on-the-Head, and Three Bears, 165 f.

Fell, Margaret, and George Fox, 221-223.

Fenelon and Mme. Guion, 109.

Fichte, J. G., and his friends, 281 f.

Fiction, friendship in, 173.

Finch, Francis, a writer on friendship, 343 f.

Flaxman, John, and Ann Denman, 112.

Flower, Miss Lizzie, a friend of Browning, 362.

Folk-lore: its lessons of friendship, 82-86.

Forster, John, a friend of Browning, 362.

Foster, John: his illustration of degrees of friendship, 96.

Fox, George, and Margaret Fell, 221-223.

Francis, St., of Assisi, and St. Clare, 109, 194-196.

Franciscan Order: friendship in its founding, 194-196.

Franklin, Benjamin, maxim of, 45.

Fraser, Professor A. C.: cited, 273.

Frau von Stein, Goethe's friendship for, 377 f.

French poetry: friendship an inspiration in, 366-369.

French Revolution, the: friendship's part in, 248-250.

Friend, a: of art, 16; of country, 16; of literature, 16; of science, 16; as one's own self, 47.

Friend, the one: a court title in ancient Egypt, 123.

Friendliness not friendship, 97-101.

Friends, the Society of: its early history, 221-223.

Friends, who can be? 105-114.

Friendship: conflicting estimates of, 13; as a sentiment, not as a relation, 14; meaning of the word, 14; misconceptions of its nature, 14; its etymology, 14; unselfishness of, 15-17,18; not incompatible with love,18, 105-114; consists in being a friend, 19; may be a mutual affection, 19; does not pivot on reciprocity, 19-26; is loving rather than being loved, 19-26; is loving another for his own sake, 20; may be coexistent with other loves, 20; what faults are seen in it, 20 f.; its disinterestedness, 21; is wholly unselfish, 27-34; its joy in serving, 33; includes readiness for all service, 34; excludes selfishness, 35; is its own excuse for being, 35; is without envy or distrust, 35-46; transcends all loves, 47-58; is a tie of the soul, 49-51; is more than conjugal or kinship love, 50-58, 69 f.; is changeless in changes, 59-68; legacies of, 63 f.; is of world-wide honor, 69-86; its permanency, 70 f.; its sacredness, 70 f.; is equality, 73; lightens burdens, 87; is gainfully expensive, 87-92; is gainful only to the unselfish, 88 f.; its limitations and imitations, 93-104; is "charity," 95; is soul-expanding, 101 f.; that might have been, 104; is possible between whom? 105-114; between man and man, 106 f.; between woman and woman, 106 f.; between man and woman, 107-109; preceding and accompanying wedded love, 112; following wedded love, 113; compatible with every relation of life, 114; its surpassing potency, 117-120; its power in all the ages, 118; its strongest hold is on the strongest, 118; is a possession of the great-hearted, 119; influencing royalty, 121-154; promoting heroism, 155-174; in ancient chivalry, 162-169; impelling religious movements, 175-230; advancing civil liberty, 231-250; affecting philosophic thought, 251-282; its uplifting power, 352; inspiring poetry, 283 380; among the Greeks, 296 f.; in classic days and in Christian, 296-300; for one's wife, 322-324; is an element of virtue, 350; is earth's best gift to man, 350; its power for good or ill, 354; amongst French poets, 368 f.; what it has done for the world, 381; transfiguring all life, 381-387.

Friendship-dance, 71 f.

Friendship-love: such love as God gives, 385-387; its prominence in the New Testament, 389-393.

"Friendships of Women," Alger's work on, 110.

Fritz, the son of Frau von Stein, 378.

Froude, Hurrell, and his friends, 230.

Froude, J. A.: cited, 203.

Furnivall, F. J.: cited, 332, 340.

GAIN: of having a friend, 382; of being a friend, 382 f.; of union in friendship, 384 f.

Gambold, John, and the Wesleys, 225 f.

Gardner, Samuel Rawson: cited, 237.

Gaunt, John of, a friend of Chaucer, 316 f.

Gay, John: cited, 55; a friend of Pope, 350.

Gemini, the, a sign of the zodiac, 122.

Geraldine (Elizabeth Fitz Gerald), Surrey a friend of, 318, 322.

German: proverb from, 53; root-term for friendship in, 74.

Gesta Romanorum, 84.

"Gilpin, John," Cowper's, inspired by friendship, 353.

Gladstone, William Ewart, and Catherine Glynne, 112; cited, 240.

Glaucus and Diomedes, 285.

Gnomic poems of Theognis, 290.

Godfrey and Tancred, 106, 170 f.

Goethe, cited, 32, 33, 57; his place in literature, 370; his characteristics as a friend, 370-372; his friendship for Schiller, 106, 379 f.; for Count de Thorane, 372; for his sister, 372; for Gretchen, 373; for Fraulein von Klettenberg, 373; for Schlosser and Behrisch, 373 f.; for Herder, 375; for Merck, 375 f.; for Karl August, 376 f.; for Frau von Stein, 377 f.

"Golden Words" of Pythagoras, 252.

Götz von Berlichingen, Goethe's: its prompting, 372.

Gower, John, a friend of Chaucer, 317.

Gracchi, the, 110.

Gray, Thomas, as friend and poet, 351.

Greek, "love" and "friendship" in, 17, 74, 389 ff.

Green, a friend of Kant, 281.

Green, J. R.: cited, 203 f., 215-217, 237 f.

Gretchen, Goethe's friendship for, 373.

Grignan, Mme. de, and Mme. de Sévigné, 110.

Grimm, the Brothers: cited, 83 f.

Groot, Gerhard, and Henry Aeger, 199.

Grote, George: cited, 232, 255.
"Guardian Angel," Browning's: a tribute of friendship, 361.
Guillaume, Francois Pierre, and Mme. Guizot, 110.
Guion, Mme., and Fenelon, 109.
Guizot, M.: cited, 240, 244, 249, 368.
Guizot, Mme., and Francois Pierre Guillaume, 110.
Gunnar and Njal, 84 f.
Gunther and Siegfried, 287.

HADRIAN, and Theodore of Tarsus, 189-191.
Hafiz: cited, 81.
Hagen: his friendships and his treachery, 287-289.
Halfdan and Viking, 162.
Hall, Gordon, and Samuel J. Mills, 227-229.
Hallam, Arthur, the friend of Tennyson, 38, 106, 364 f.
Hallam, Sir Henry: cited, 236, 264, 269, 310, 333, 369.
Hamilton, Alexander, and George Washington, 239-247.
Hamilton, Gavin, a friend of Burns, 354 f.
Hamilton, Sir William, and Lady, 112.
Hampden, John, and his friends, 106, 236-239.
Hare, J. C., and his friends, 230.
Harmodius and Aristogiton, 231-233.
Haroon-ar-Rasheed and Jaafer, 152 f.
Harrow, Byron's friendships at, 358.
Harvey, Gabriel, a friend of Spenser, 324 f.
Hassan, the poet: cited, 185 f.
Hatstein, Marquard von: cited, 204.
"Hava-mal," quotation from, 79 f.
Heart, a bleeding, a symbol of friendship, 171.
Hebrew word for "friend," 48; words for "love" and "friendship," 99 f.
Hector and Andromache, 297.
Hegel and his friends, 281 f.
Helen of Sparta, a cause of discord, 284.
Hemans, Mrs., and Mrs. Browne, 110.
"Henry VIII.," Shakespeare's, quotation from, 330.

Hephæstion, the friend of Alexander, 106, 126-128.
Herbert, George: cited, 23; his mother's friendship, 110; his friendship for Lord Bacon, 263; as poet and as friend, 341 f.
Herbert, William, Earl of Pembroke, 333, 340 f.
Hercules and Iolaüs, 156 f.
Herder, J. G.: his friendship for his wife, 112; for Goethe, 375.
"Hermann and Dorothea," Goethe's: a fruit of friendship, 380.
Hermias, of Atarneus, a friend of Aristotle, 257.
Heroism promoted by friendship, 155-174.
Herschel, William and Caroline, 111.
Hervey, James, and the Wesleys, 225.
"Hexapla," Origen's: its character, 177 f.
Hildreth, Richard: cited, 241.
Hindoos, sacred books of, 43, 51, 76.
Hipparchus and Hippias, sons of Pisistratus, 231 f.
Hiram of Tyre, a friend of David and Solomon, 63.
"History of German Literature," Scherer's, quotation from, 377 f.
History, the world's, as history of individuals, 117.
Hoddeson, John, a friend of Dryden, 348 f.
Hoff, a friend of Shelley, 359.
Hogg, James, a friend of Scott, 357.
Holland, F. M.: cited, 305.
Holmes, Dr. O. W.: cited, 91.
"Holy Fair, The," Burns's: its prompting, 354 f.
"Holy Willie's Prayer," Burns's: its prompting, 355.
Homâyoon and Koornivati, 164 f.
Homer: cited, 63, 73, 156, 160.
Horace: his friendship for Virgil, 106; for Mæcenas, 293-295.
Hortalus, brother-friend of Catullus, 292.
Houghton, Lord: cited, 68.
Howard, Sir Robert, a friend of Dryden, 348.
Howitt, William and Mary: cited, 79 f.
Hugh de Sade, husband of Petrarch's "Laura," 306.

Humboldt, Wilhelm von: cited, 61 f.; his friendship for Charlotte Siede, 109; for Caroline von Dacheröden, 112.

Hume, David: his philosophy and his friendships, 273, 276-278.

Hunt, Helen: cited, 25.

Hushai, a friend of David, 125.

Hutchinson, John, and Lucy, 112.

Hutton, R. H.: cited, 356, 370 f.

ICELANDIC folk-lore tales, illustrations from, 84 f.

Icelandic sagas: illustrations from, 41, 42; their lessons of friendship, 79 f.; quotation from, 162 f.

Ideal: seen in or for a friend, 36, 37, 39.

Iliad, the, friendship and love in, 284-286.

"Imitation of Christ:" its origin in friendships, 199-202.

Imitations and limitations of friendship 93-104.

"In Memoriam:" quotations from, 39, 55, 90, 96, 365 f.; its place as a lyric of friendship, 364-366.

India, friendship in, 107 f., 164 f.

Indians, North American, friendship among, 165 f.

Ingham, Benjamin, and the Wesleys, 225.

Intimacies of friendship separable from friendship, 65.

Iolaüs and Hercules, 156 f.

Irving, Washington: cited, 244.

Izdubar and Eabani, 122 f.

JAAFER and Haroon-ar-Rasheed, 152 f.

Jackmann, a friend of Kant, 281.

Jâmee, translation from, 22.

James, St.: his reference to Abraham, 48 f.

Jefferson, Thomas: his relations with Hamilton, 246.

Jehan, Shah, and Nour Jehan, 112.

Jelal-ed-Deen and Shaykh Solayman, 153 f.

Jerome, St., and Paula, 108.

Jesuitism: its origin and influence, 218-221.

Jesus Christ: his standard of loving, 26; his estimate of friendship, 49 f., 75; his friendship unchanging, 66; his lessons on friendship, 88 f.; he chooses John as a friend, 175; his conversation with Peter, 392.

Jewish standard of friendship, 66.

John, St.: the friend of Jesus, 175; of St. Paul, 176.

John the Baptist, as a friend, 38.

Johnson, Dr., and Mrs. Thrale, 109.

Jonathan and David: their friendship, 27, 28, 37, 38, 62, 106.

Joseph, the one friend of Pharaoh, 124.

Josephine, the truest friend of Napoleon, 149-152.

Josephus: cited, 66.

"Julius Cæsar," Shakespeare's, quotation from, 33.

KANT, Immanuel: David Hume's influence on, 276; his philosophy and his friendships, 280 f.

Karl, August: his friendship for Goethe, 376 f.

Keble, John, and his friends, 230.

Kenyon, John, a friend of the Brownings, 362.

Ketel, John, and Thomas à Kempis, 201 f.

Khaleefs, Muhammadan, 152.

King, Edward, a friend of Milton, 348.

Kings: their longing to be loved, 121.

Kingsley, Charles: his story of two monk-friends, 31, 32; his friendship for Fanny Grenfell, 112; citation of, 119; his friendships, 230.

Kinship, friendship coexistent with, 109-111.

Kirke, Edward, a friend of Spenser, 324 f.

Kirkham, Robert, and the Wesleys, 225.

Klettenberg, Fraulein von: her influence on Goethe, 373.

Knight, Professor William: cited, 276.

Knox, General, a friend of Washington, 246 f.

Knox, John, and George Wishart, 218.

Koornivati and Homâyoon, 164 f.

Köstlin, Julius: cited, 209, 213.

Kriemhild, her love and vengeance, 287-290.
Krishna and Arjuna, friendship of, 286 f.

LA BRUYÈRE: cited, 22, 37, 119.
Lacordaire and Mme. Swetchine, 109.
Lælius and Scipio: their friendship, 21, 64, 292.
Lafayette: cited, 244.
La Fontaine and his friends, 368.
Laidlow, William, a friend of Scott, 357.
Lake Poets, the: their friendships, 360.
Lamb, Charles: cited, 55; his friendship for his sister, 111.
Lanfranc and Anselm, 192.
Lannes, General, at Arcole, 172.
La Rochefoucauld: cited, 24, 43.
Latin, root-term for friendship in, 73 f.
Laura and Petrarch, 305-310.
Laurens, Colonel John: cited, 243.
Lavater, John C.: cited, 61, 81; his friendship for Fichte, 282.
Lawes, Henry, a friend of Milton, 347 f.
Laynez, Diego, an associate of Loyola, 221.
Le Clerc, a friend of John Locke, 270.
Lefort, Franz, and Peter the Great, 139-142.
Legacies of friendship, 30, 31, 63 f.
Leibnitz, Baron: his philosophy and his friendships, 278-280.
Leoline, Sir, and Lord Roland, 68.
"Letters of Julius to Raphael," Schiller's, quotation from, 385.
Lewes, George H.: cited, 264, 378 f.
Leyden, John, a friend of Scott, 356 f.
Liberty, civil, advanced by friendship, 231-250.
Liddon, Canon: cited, 202.
"Life in a Love," Browning's, 23.
Life transfigured by friendship, 381-387.
Liking, or likening, in love, 74.
Limborch, Philippus van, a friend of John Locke, 270.
Limitations and imitations of friendship, 93-104.

Lind, Dr., a friend of Shelley, 358 f.
Locke, John: his friendship for Lady Masham, 109; his indebtedness to friendships, 267-273.
Lodge, Henry Cabot: cited, 243, 246.
Loft, C., a translator of Petrarch, 307.
Longfellow, Henry W.: cited, 56, 304, 311 f., 376.
Lothheissen: cited, 369.
Love: differentiated from friendship, 14-17, 389-393; selfish element in, 15-17; not incompatible with friendship, 18, 105-114; begets love, 19; cannot be wasted, 104; as an inspiration of poetry, 283 f.
Lover, a: differentiated from a friend, 14-17; a true friend is, 100; of art, 16; of country, 16; of literature, 16; of science, 16.
Loving, rather than being loved, 19-26.
Lowell, James Russell: cited, 316.
Loyola, Ignatius: his work and his friendships, 218-222.
Lubh: Sanskrit for "love," 17, 390.
"Lucasia," a friend of Katherine Philips, 342, 345.
Lucilius: his help from friendship, 292.
Lucretia, wife of Collatinus: her wrong and its avenging, 233 f.
Luke, St., and St. Paul, 177.
Luthardt: cited, 393.
Luther, Martin, and his friendships, 106, 208-215; compared with Erasmus, 203.
Lyric poetry of Pindar, 289 f.
"Lycidas," Milton's, a tribute of friendship, 348.
Lysis and Menexenus, 254.

MACAULAY, T. Babington: cited, 138 f., 141, 237 f., 261, 270.
Macgregor: a translator of Petrarch, 307, 310.
Macready, W. C., a friend of Browning, 362.
Mæcenas, a friend of poets, 292-295.
Magdalen, Lady, and George Herbert, 110.
Mahâbhârata, the, illustrations from, 51, 76, 284, 286 f.
Mahaffy, Professor J. P.: cited, 266.
Malebranche, a friend of Leibnitz, 279.

Index. 407

Mallet, David, a friend of Thomson, 351.
Mansfield, Lord, and Charles Wesley, 224.
"Mânu, Institutes of," lessons of friendship in, 76.
Manuel, a Castilian poet: cited, 43.
Mapletoft, John, a friend of John Locke, 270.
Maratti, Faustina, and Giambattista Zappi, 112.
Marbois, as a friend, 143 f.
Marlborough, the Duchess of, and Queen Anne, 106.
Marriage: a tie of the flesh, 49-51.
Martin, Sir Theodore: cited, 293 f.
Mary Queen of Scots and Mary Seton, 106.
Masham, Lady, a friend of John Locke, 109, 272 f.
Masham, Sir Francis, husband of Damaris Cudworth, 273.
Matthew, Toby, a friend of Lord Bacon, 263.
Maurice, F. D., and his friends, 230.
Mausolus and Artemesia, 112.
Melanchthon, Philip, and Martin Luther, 106, 210-215.
Mélite, Corneille's, an outcome of friendship, 367.
Menander: cited, 80; his friendship for Epicurus, 268.
Mencius: cited, 36, 125.
Mendelssohn, Felix and Fanny, 111.
Menelaus: his friendship for Telemachus, 63.
Menexenus and Lysis, 254.
Menshikof and Peter the Great, 142 f.
Mentz, Archbishop of, a friend of Leibnitz, 279.
Merck, J. H.: his influence over Goethe, 375 f.
Merira Pepi and Una, 123 f.
Mermet, Claude: his epigram, 101.
Mersenne, Marin, a friend of Descartes, 264-266.
Methodism: its origin in friendships, 223-226.
Meyer: cited, 393.
Michael Angelo: cited, 384 f.
Michaud, J. F.: cited, 170.
"Midsummer Night's Dream, A," Shakespeare's, quotation from, 329.

Mill, John Stuart: his friendship for Mrs. Taylor, 112; cited, 267 f.
Mills, Charles: cited, 167; his estimate of chivalry, 299.
Mills, Samuel J., and his friends, 227-229.
Milman, H. H., and his friends, 230.
Miltitz, von, a friend of Fichte, 282.
Milton, John, as poet and friend, 347 f.
Minto, Professor William: cited, 314 f., 325 f., 332 f., 351, 360.
Missions, Moravian: their origin, 226; from America, beginnings of, 227-229.
Mithra, the god of light to Parsees, 77.
Modern poetry: its beginning with Dante, 300.
Mohl, Julius, and Mary Clarke, 112.
Molière and his friends, 368.
Molyneaux, Samuel, a friend of George Berkeley, 275.
Molyneaux, William, a friend of John Locke, 270-272.
Monica, St., a friend of St. Ambrose, 108; mother of St. Augustine, 110.
Monks, Charles Kingsley's story of two, 31 f.
Monmouth, Lord, a friend of John Locke, 270.
Montagu, a biographer of Lord Bacon, 261 f.
Montaigne: his story of two friends, 29-31; cited, 35, 53, 94, 98.
Moravian missions: their origin in friendships, 226 f.
More, Hannah and Martha, 111.
Morgan, William, and the Wesleys, 225.
Morley, Henry: cited, 316, 349.
Morse, John T.: cited, 242, 247.
Moschus and Bion, poet-friends, 290 f.
Moses: his view of Divine love, 25; his estimate of friendship, 48 f.
Motley, J. L.: cited, 134 f.
Mountain-peaks of history noted, 120.
Muhammad: his view of friendship, 75; his friendship for Aboo Bekr, 106, 184-189.
Muhammadan: estimate of Abraham, 49; estimate of friendship, 75.
Muir, Sir William: cited, 186.
Mure, Baron William, of Caldwell, a friend of David Hume, 277 f.

Murray, Lady Sophy, and Lady Dorothea Sydney, 106.
Mygorge, Claude, a friend of Descartes, 265.

NAOMI and Ruth, 28, 29, 106.
Napoleon: cited, 13; friendships of, 143-152.
Necker, M., and Mme. de Staël, 110.
Newman, John Henry: cited, 62; his friendships, 230.
New Testament: words for "love" in, 17, 386-393; its view of friendship, 25, 75, 95.
Newton, Sir Isaac, a friend of John Locke, 270.
Nibelungenlied, the: friendship and love in, 284, 287-289.
Niebuhr, B. G.: cited, 240.
Nimrod, the Bible record of, 122.
Nisus and Euryalus, 161 f.
Njal and Gunner, 84 f.
Njorfe and Viking, 163.
Nooman III., influence of friendship on, 131.
Norseland Eddas: their lessons of friendship, 79 f.
Nour Jehan and Shah Jehan, 112.

OCTAVIANUS, Caius, afterwards Augustus Cæsar, 128-130.
"Ode to the Skylark," Shelley's: its suggestion of friendship, 358.
Old Testament: its view of friendship, 25, 47 f.
Oliphant, Mrs.: cited, 195 f.
Oliver and Roland, 106, 169.
Olympias and Chrysostom, 108.
Onesimus, a friend of Paul, 50.
"Order of the Grain of Mustard Seed," 226.
Orestes and Electra, 110, 297.
Orestes and Pylades, 106, 158 f., 289 f., 291.
Oriental view of friendship, 22.
Origen and Alexander and Ambrose, 177-179.
"Orinda," a designation of Katherine Philips, 342, 345.
Orpah and Naomi, 28, 29.
Orr, Mrs. Sutherland: cited, 361, 363.
Orrery, Earl of: cited, 342.
Osbern and Anselm, 193.

Osiris and Rā, union of, 73.
Oswald, James, of Dunnekier, a friend of Hume, 278.
Owen, Mrs. Annie, a friend of Katherine Philips, 107, 342.
Oxford movement, the, friendships in, 229 f.

PÆTUS, Thrasea, a friend of Persius, 296.
Palmer, Professor E. H.: cited, 152 f.
Pamphilus and Eusebius, 106, 180 f.
Pantheon, the, a memorial of friendship, 130.
"Paracelsus," Browning's, an outcome of friendship, 362.
Parnell, Thomas, a friend of Pope, 350.
Parsees, the, sacred books of, 77.
Patroclus and Achilles, 156 f., 285.
Pattison, Mark: cited, 348.
Paul St.: and Barnabas, 176 f.; and Luke, 177; and Silas, 177; and Timothy, 177; his views of marriage and friendship, 49 f.; his estimate of friendship-love, 386 f.
Paula and St. Jerome, 108.
Paulina and Seneca, 112.
Peel, Robert, a friend of Byron, 358.
Pelopidas and Epaminondas, 106, 159f.
Pembroke, Earl of, the friend of Shakespeare, 333, 340.
Pembroke, Lord, a friend of John Locke, 270.
Percival, Sir John, a friend of Berkeley, 275.
Persian poet, a: cited, 81.
Persius and Cornutus, 295 f.
Pestalozzi, a friend of Fichte, 282.
Peter: his friendship for John, 176; his conversation with Jesus, 392.
Peter the Great, friendships of, 139-143.
Peterborough, Lord, George Berkeley chaplain to, 276.
Petrarch: his friendship for Laura, 305-310; his other friends, 312-314.
Pharaoh Merira Pepi, story of, 123.
Phelps, Austin: cited, 36.
Philia: Greek word for love, 17, 386, 389-393.
Philip of Macedon: his appreciation of friendship, 160; a friend of Aristotle, 256.

Philippa, Queen, and Philippa Picard, 106.
Philips, Katherine: cited, 58; her friendship for Annie Owen, 107; as poet and friend, 342-347.
Philosophers and their friends, 251-282.
Philosophic thought affected by friendship, 251-282.
Picot, Abbé, a friend of Descartes, 265.
Pindar, friendship in the poetry of, 289 f.
"Pippa Passes," illustration from, 33, 34.
Pirithoüs and Theseus, 157.
Pirqe Aboth, maxim from, 24.
Pisistratides, the: their place in Athenian history, 231, 232.
Pisistratus, a friend of Solon, 233.
Plato: cited, 20, 59, 155; his idea of friendship, 108; his indebtedness to friendship, 253-256.
Plautus: cited, 57.
"Pleasures of Imagination:" its tribute to friendship, 352.
Pliny: cited, 110.
Plutarch: cited, 24, 42, 127, 157, 160.
Poetry: inspired by friendship, 283-380; preceding prose in the world's literature, 284; more than philosophy, 284; its sources of inspiration, 289.
Poets and their friendships, 290-380.
Ponsonby, Miss Sarah, and Lady Eleanor Butler, 106.
Pope, Alexander, as friend and poet, 350.
Prî: Sanskrit for "friendship," 17, 390.
Prior, Matt: cited, 82; his friendship for George Berkeley, 274 f.
Proverbs, Book of: quotations from, 99.
Proxenus of Atarneus, a friend of Aristotle, 256 f.
Psalms, the, quotations from, 100.
"Psyche," Corneille's: cited, 368.
Publius Rutilius and his brother, 110.
Publius Syrus: maxims of, 40; cited, 74.
Pusey, Dr. E. B., and his friends, 230.
Pylades and Orestes, 106, 158 f.
Pym, John, and his friends, 106, 236-239.

Pythagoras, the first philosopher, 251.
Pythagoreans: their estimate of friendship, 252.
Pythias and Damon, 106.

QUARLES, Francis: cited, 24, 45.
Queen Anne Boleyn, a friend of Sir Thomas Wyatt, 318, 322.
Queen Anne: her friendship with the Duchess of Marlborough, 106; George Berkeley at the court of, 275.
Queen Christina, of Sweden, a friend of Descartes, 266 f.
Queen of Scots, Mary, and Mary Seton, 106.
Queen Philippa and Philippa Picard, 106.
Queen Sophia Charlotte, of Prussia: a friend of Leibnitz, 279 f.
Quintius Curtius: cited, 127.
Qurán, the: friendship in, 75; its preparation and finishing, 189.

RÃ and Osiris, union of, 73.
Racine and his friends, 368.
Raleigh, Sir Walter, a friend of Spenser, 326 f.
Ramsay, Michael, a friend of David Hume, 277.
Rashnoo, the god of truth to the Parsees, 77.
Récamier, Mme., and Mme. de Staël, 106.
Religious movements impelled by friendship, 175-230.
Reverence, a factor in friendship, 36.
Riccaulton, a friend and tutor of Thomson, 350 f.
Richards, James, and Samuel J. Mills, 227-229.
Richter, Jean Paul: cited, 102, 119; a friend of Kant, 280 f.
Robespierre and Camille, 249 f.
Rodriguez, Simon, an associate of Loyola, 221.
Roland and Oliver, 106, 168 f.
Roland, Lord, and Sir Leoline, 67 f.
Roland, M. and Mme., 112.
Rollins, Alice Wellington: cited, 114.
"Rosania," a friend of Katherine Philips, 342, 344.
Roscommon, Earl of: cited, 342.
Rose, H. J., and his friends, 230.

Roux, Joseph: cited, 51.
Royalty influenced by friendship, 121-154.
Rüdiger von Bechlarn: his oath of friendship, 287-289.
"Rule, Britannia," a product of friendship, 351.
Rundle, Bishop, a friend of George Berkeley, 276.
Russell, Earl, on Washington, 239 f.
Russia, epic songs of, 163 f.
Russian poet: cited, 81.
Ruth: her friendship for Naomi, 28, 29, 106.

SACRAMENT, the holy, a bond of friendship, 167.
Sacred books of the ages, the, friendship in, 74-80.
"Sacred Band of Theban Friends," 160, 162.
Sacrifice, love's joy in, 24, 25.
Saint-Amand: cited, 149 f.
Saintsbury, George: cited, 867.
Salmeron, Alfonso, an associate of Loyola, 221.
"Sanatsugâtiva," the, lessons of friendship in, 76 f.
Sanskrit: "love" and "friendship" in, 17, 74, 390; translation from, 80.
Satires, Roman: of Lucilius, 292; of Persius, 296 f.
"Saul," Robert Browning's, 56.
Schaff, Philip: cited, 214.
Schelling, F. W. J., and his friends, 281 f.
Scherer, Wilhelm: cited, 377 f.
Schiller: cited, 81; his friendship for Goethe, 106, 379 f.; his testimony to the power of friendship, 385; his friendship for Körner, 385.
Schlegels, the, friends of Hegel, 282.
Schleiermacher, Ernest and Charlotte, 111.
Schlosser, a friend of Goethe, 373 f.
Scholastica, St., and St. Benedict, 111.
Schublî, Sheik: his idea of friendship, 22.
Schultz, a teacher and a friend of Kant, 280.
Schuyler, Eugene: cited, 140-142.
Schwegler: cited, 280.
Scipio: his friendship for Lælius, 21, 64.

Scipio Africanus and Ennius, 292.
Scipios, the two, 110.
Scotch proverb on friendship, 89.
Scott, Sir Walter, as friend and poet, 355-357.
"Seasons, The," Thomson's: their prompting by a friend, 351.
Secker, Archbishop, a friend of Berkeley, 276.
Seeley, Professor J. R.: cited, 370.
Self-interest: an element of love, 16; not an element of friendship, 16.
Seneca: cited, 45, 57; his friendship for Paulina, 112.
Sentiment, the potency of, in history, 117.
Septuagint, the, word for "love" in, 27.
"Serapis," Ebers's, illustration from, 41.
Seton, Mary, and Mary Queen of Scots, 106.
Seventy disciples, the, sent out in pairs, 176.
Sévigné, Mme. de, and Mme. de Grignan, 110.
Sex no barrier to friendship, 105-114.
Sextus, son of Tarquin, 234.
Shaftesbury, Earl: his friendship for John Locke, 268-270.
Shah Jehan and Nour Jehan, 112.
Shairp, Principal: cited, 289 f., 296 f.
Shakespeare: cited, 13, 33, 45, 60, 95, 234 f.; as poet and friend, 327-341; friendship in his plays, 329-331; friendship in his sonnets, 332-341; his indebtedness to friendship, 339-340 f.
Sharp, Matthew, of Hoddam, a friend of David Hume, 278.
Shea, J. D. G.: cited, 243 f.
Shelley, Percy Bysshe, as friend and poet, 358 f.
"Shepherd's Calendar," Spenser's: edited by a friend, 324.
"Shı King," lessons of friendship in, 76.
Shinar, Land of, in the Bible story, 122.
Shirley, James: cited, 54 f.
"Shoo King," lessons of friendship in, 76.
Shun and Yâo, friendship of, 125 f.

Index. 411

Sidney, Sir Philip: his friendship for Lord Brooke, 106; for his sister Mary, 111; for Edmund Spenser, 325 f.
Siegfried and Gunther, friendship of, 287.
Silas and St. Paul, 177.
Sime, James: cited, 375.
Simpson, Richard: cited, 300.
Sirach, Son of: cited, 75, 101 f.
Siva and Vishnoo, union of, 73.
Smith, Adam: a friend of David Hume, 278; cited, 278.
Socrates: his indebtedness to friendship, 253-256.
Solayman, Shaykh, and Akbar Muhammad, 153 f.
Soldurii, the, of Aquitania, 162.
Solomon: his estimate of friendship, 48, 74 f.; Zabud a friend of, 125.
Solon: his friendship for Pisistratus, 233.
Somers, Lord, a friend of John Locke, 270.
"Sonnets from the Portuguese," Mrs. Browning's, quotations from, 364, 382.
"Sonnets," Shakespeare's, quotations from, 334-339.
Sophocles: cited, 52.
Sordello: his conception of unselfish love, 304 f.
Sorrows, bearing a friend's, 32.
Southey, Robert, a friend of Coleridge and Wordsworth, 360.
Spalatin, George, and Martin Luther, 208.
Spanish proverb, 23.
Spedding, James, a biographer of Lord Bacon, 261 f.
Spence, Joseph, a friend of Pope, 350.
Spenser, Edmund: cited, 54; as friend and poet, 322-327.
Sprenger, A.: cited, 185.
St. Augustine, Petrarch's dialogue with, 309.
Staël, Mme. de: her friendship for Mme. Récamier, 106; for M. Necker, 110.
Standish, Miles: his appeal to John Alden, 56.
Stanley, Dean: cited, 177; his friendships, 230.

Staupitz, John von, and Martin Luther, 209 f.
Steele, Richard: a friend of George Berkeley, 276; a friend of Addison, 349.
Stein, Frau von: Goethe's friendship for, 377 f.
Stoics and Epicureans, friendship among, 258.
Story, Joseph: cited, 240.
"Strafford," Browning's, an outcome of friendship, 362.
Stuckenberg, J. H. W., a biographer of Kant, 281.
Suffering through friendship, 89-92.
Suicide, proposed as a proof of friendship, 112.
Sun and moon, friendship of, 77.
Surpassing potency of friendship, 117-120.
Surrey, Earl of, and Sir Thomas Wyatt, as friends and poets, 318-321.
Svyatogór and Ilya, 163 f.
Swetchine, Mme., and Lacordaire, 109.
Swift, Dean: a friend of Berkeley, 275 f.; of Pope, 350.
Sydenham, Thomas, a friend of John Locke, 270.
Sydney, Lady Dorothea, and Lady Sophy Murray, 106.
Syrus, Publius: cited, 57, 89.

TALBOT, Catharine, and Elizabeth Carter, 106.
"Tale of Two Cities," Dickens's, illustration from, 173 f.
Talleyrand, Prince: cited, 240.
Talmud, the, friendship in, 24, 75.
Tancred: his friendship for Godfrey, 106, 170 f.; for Bohemond, 170 f.
Tarquin the Arrogant: his overthrow, 234 f.
"Task, The," Cowper's, inspired by friendship, 353.
Taylor, Jeremy: cited, 13, 57 f., 88, 95; a friend of Katherine Philips, 342.
Taylor, W.: cited, 79 f.
Telemachus: welcomed by Menelaus, 63.

Index.

Tennyson, Alfred: cited, 38, 39, 55, 90, 96; as friend and poet, 106, 364-366.
Terence: his help from friendship, 292.
Theban Band of Friends, The, 160.
Theodore of Tarsus and Hadrian, 189-191.
Theognis and Cyrnus, 290.
Theseus and Pirithoüs, 157.
Thirlwall, Connop, and his friends, 230.
Thomson, James, as poet and friend, 350 f.
Thorpe, Thomas, the bookseller, 333.
Thorstein and Bele, 163.
Thrale, Mrs., and Dr. Johnson, 109.
Three-Bears, and Feather-on-the-Head, 165 f.
Timon of Athens: cited, 13.
Timothy, St., and St. Paul, 177.
"Toleration," Locke's essay on: its origin, 269.
Tragic poetry of Euripides, 289 f.
Transfiguring power of love, 381-387.
Trench: cited, 390, 392.
Troy, friendship at the siege of, 157 f.
Trumbull, Sir William, a friend of Pope, 350
Tullia and Cicero, 110.
Turpin, Archbishop, and his friends, 169.
Tyerman, L.: cited, 225 f.

"UARDA," quotation from, 41.
Ueberweg: cited, 255, 276 f.
Ulysses and Diomedes, 158, 285.
Una and Merira Pepi, 123 f.
Union in friendship, 72-74.
Union of friends sought in blended blood, 70 f.
Union of souls, a result of mutual friendship, 94.
Universality of friendship's sway, 69-86.
Unselfishness of friendship, 27-34.
Unwin, Mrs. Mary, the friend of Cowper, 109, 353 f.

"VERONA, Two Gentlemen of," Shakespeare's, quotations from, 330 f.
Viking and Halfdan and Njorfe, 162 f.

Virgil: cited, 73, 161 f.; his friendship for Gallus, 293; for Horace, 106, 292 f.; for Mæcenas, 293; for Pollio, 293; for Varius, 293.
Vishnoo and Sivâ, union of, 73.
Vita Nuova, Dante's, 300 f., 304.
Voltaire: cited, 81.

WALES, Prince of, John Locke presented to, 275.
Walpole, Horace, a friend of Gray, 351.
"Waring," Browning's, a tribute to Alfred Dommett, 361.
Washington, George, and Alexander Hamilton, 239-247.
Watteville, Baron von, and Count Zinzendorf, 226 f.
Webster, Daniel: cited, 245.
Weimar: its fame through Goethe's fame, 376 f.
Weisse, a friend of Fichte, 282.
Wesley, John and Charles: their friendships, 224-226.
Wesleyanism: its origin in friendships, 223-226.
West, Richard, a friend of Gray, 351.
What is friendship? 12-18.
Whately, Richard, and his friends, 230.
Whitefield and the Wesleys, 225.
Whittier, John G.: cited, 24, 60.
Who can be friends? 105-114.
Wife and friend in one, 49-51, 109-114, 322-324, 344.
"Wilhelm Meister," Goethe's, references to, 373, 375, 380.
William III. and William Bentinck, 106, 135-139.
William the Silent and Charles V., 133-135.
Williams, Mr. and Mrs., friends of Shelley, 359.
Wishart, George, and John Knox, 218.
Wollaston: cited, 308.
Woman as an object of friendship, 297-300.
Woman's place among the Greeks, 297 f.
Woolsey, Theodore: cited, 390.
Words: the more familiar the more vague, 14.
"Words of the Heart," Lavater's, quotation from, 81.

Index. 413

Wordsworth, William: his friendship for his sister, 111; for Coleridge, 229, 359 f.; cited, 328.

World-wide honor of friendship, 69-86.

Wotton, Sir Henry, a friend of George Herbert, 342.

Wrangham: a translator of Petrarch, 308.

Wright, W. Aldis: a biographer of Lord Bacon, 261 f.

Wyatt, Sir Thomas, and Earl of Surrey, as friends and poets, 318-321.

Wycherly, William, a friend of Pope, 350.

XAVIER, Francis, and Ignatius Loyola, 218-221.

Xenien: the joint work of Goethe and Schiller, 380.

Xerxes: his capture of statues of Athenian friends, 232.

YAHYA, grand vizier of Haroon-ar-Rasheed, 152.

Yâo and Shun, friendship of, 125 f.

Young, Edward: cited, 45, 89, 92; as friend and poet, 349 f.

ZABUD, a friend of Solomon, 125.

Zappi, Giambattista, and Faustina Maratti, 112.

Zayd, a friend of Muhammad, 75, 184.

Zend, root-term for friendship in, 74.

Zend-Avesta, the, lessons of friendship in, 77.

Zeno the Stoic: his view of friendship, 258.

Zinzendorf, Count, and Baron von Watteville, 226.

Zonoras and Prince Athanase, 359.

John Eadie Titles

Solid Ground is delighted to announce that we have republished several volumes by John Eadie, gifted Scottish minister. The following are in print:

Commentary on the Greek Text of Paul's Letter to the Galatians
Part of the classic five-volume set that brought world-wide renown to this humble man, Eadie expounds this letter with passion and precision. In the words of Spurgeon, "This is a most careful attempt to ascertain the meaning of the Apostle by painstaking analysis of his words."

Commentary on the Greek Text of Paul's Letter to the Ephesians
Spurgeon said, "This book is one of prodigious learning and research. The author seems to have read all, in every language, that has been written on the Epistle. It is also a work of independent criticism, and casts much new light upon many passages."

Commentary on the Greek Text of Paul's Letter to the Philippians
Robert Paul Martin wrote, "Everything that John Eadie wrote is pure gold. He was simply the best exegete of his generation. His commentaries on Paul's epistles are valued highly by careful expositors. Solid Ground Christian Books has done a great service by bringing Eadie's works back into print."

Commentary on the Greek Text of Paul's Letter to the Colossians
According to the New Schaff-Herzog Encyclopedia of Religious Knowledge, "These commentaries of John Eadie are marked by candor and clearness as well as by an evangelical unction not common in works of the kind." Spurgeon said, "Very full and reliable. A work of utmost value."

Commentary on the Greek Text of Paul's Letters to the Thessalonians
Published posthumously, this volume completes the series that has been highly acclaimed for more than a century. Invaluable.

Paul the Preacher: A Popular and Practical Exposition of His Discourses and Speeches as Recorded in the Acts of the Apostles
Very rare volume intended for a more popular audience, this volume begins with Saul's conversion and ends with Paul preaching the Gospel of the Kingdom in Rome. It perfectly fills in the gaps in the commentaries. Outstanding work!

DIVINE LOVE: A Series of Doctrinal, Practical and Experimental Discourses
Buried over a hundred years, this volume consists of a dozen complete sermons from Eadie's the pastoral ministry. "John Eadie, the respected nineteenth-century Scottish Secession minister-theologian, takes the reader on an edifying journey through this vital biblical theme." - Ligon Duncan

Lectures on the Bible to the Young for Their Instruction and Excitement
"Though written for the rising generation, these plain addresses are not meant for mere children. Simplicity has, indeed, been aimed at in their style and arrangement, in order to adapt them to a class of young readers whose minds have already enjoyed some previous training and discipline." – Author's Preface

SGCB Titles for the Young

Solid Ground Christian Books is honored to be able to offer a full dozen uncovered treasure for children and young people.

The Child's Book on the Fall by Thomas H. Gallaudet is a simple and practical exposition of the Fall of man into sin, and his only hope of salvation.

Repentance & Faith: *Explained and Illustrated for the Young* by Charles Walker, is a two in one book introducing children to the difference between true and false faith and repentance.

The Child at Home by John S.C. Abbott is the sequel to his popular book *The Mother at Home*. A must read for children and their parents.

My Brother's Keeper: *Letters to a Younger Brother* by J.W. Alexander contains the actual letters Alexander sent to his ten year old brother.

The Scripture Guide by J.W. Alexander is filled with page after page of information on getting the most from our Bibles. Invaluable!

Feed My Lambs: *Lectures to Children* by John Todd is drawn from actual sermons preached in Philadelphia, PA and Pittsfield, MA to the children of the church, one Sunday each month. A pure gold-mine of instruction.

Heroes of the Reformation by Richard Newton is a unique volume that introduces children and young people to the leading figures and incidents of the Reformation. Spurgeon called him, *"The Prince of preachers to the young."*

Heroes of the Early Church by Richard Newton is the sequel to the above-named volume. The very last book Newton wrote introduces all the leading figures of the early church with lessons to be learned from each figure.

The King's Highway: *Ten Commandments to the Young* by Richard Newton is a volume of Newton's sermons to children. Highly recommended!

The Life of Jesus Christ for the Young by Richard Newton is a double volume set that traces the Gospel from Genesis 3:15 to the Ascension of our Lord and the outpouring of His Spirit on the Day of Pentecost. Excellent!

The Young Lady's Guide by Harvey Newcomb will speak directly to the heart of the young women who desire to serve Christ with all their being.

The Chief End of Man by John Hall is an exposition and application of the first question of the Westminster Shorter Catechism. Full of rich illustrations.

Call us Toll Free at 1-877-666-9469
Send us an e-mail at sgcb@charter.net
Visit us on line at solid-ground-books.com